Expert Advice From the
National Association for Gifted Children

Success Strategies for
Parenting
Gifted Kids

NATIONAL ASSOCIATION FOR
Gifted Children

Edited by Kathleen Nilles, Jennifer L. Jolly, Ph.D.,
Tracy Ford Inman, Ed.D., and Joan Franklin Smutny

PRUFROCK PRESS INC.
WACO, TEXAS

Library of Congress Cataloging-in-Publication Data

Names: Nilles, Kathleen, 1961- editor. | Jolly, Jennifer L., 1972- editor.
  | Inman, Tracy F. (Tracy Ford), 1963- editor. | Smutny, Joan F., editor.
Title: Success strategies for parenting gifted kids : expert advice from
  the national association for gifted children / edited by Kathleen
  Nilles, Jennifer L. Jolly, Ph.D., Tracy Ford Inman, Ed.D., and Joan
  Franklin Smutny.
Description: Waco : Prufrock Press Inc., [2019] | Includes bibliographical references. | Summary: "When
  parents need guidance on raising gifted kids, they can turn to "Success Strategies for Parenting Gifted Kids:
  Expert Advice From the National Association for Gifted Children." This collection of practical, dynamic
  articles from NAGC's "Parenting for High Potential" magazine will allow parents to find the support and
  resources they need to help their children find success in school and beyond. Written by experts in the
  field, this book provides realistic, how-to advice for navigating complex issues such as underachievement,
  twice-exceptionality, acceleration, underrepresented populations, student advocacy, and more. Each article
  provides parents with an easy-to-understand overview of the topic based on research and best practices, as
  well as processes, step-by-step action plans, and realistic advice. Additionally, the book includes discussion
  and reflection questions that are perfect for parent support groups, conversations with families and
  children, and individual parent reflections"-- Provided by publisher.
Identifiers: LCCN 2019033297 (print) | LCCN 2019033298 (ebook) | ISBN
  9781618219039 (paperback) | ISBN 9781618219046 (ebook) | ISBN
  9781618219244 (epub)
Subjects: LCSH: Parents of gifted children. | Gifted children--Education.
Classification: LCC HQ773.5 .S83 2019 (print) | LCC HQ773.5 (ebook) | DDC
  649/.155--dc23
LC record available at https://lccn.loc.gov/2019033297
LC ebook record available at https://lccn.loc.gov/2019033298

Copyright ©2019, National Association for Gifted Children

Edited by Stephanie McCauley

Cover design by Micah Benson and layout design by Raquel Trevino

ISBN-13: 978-1-61821-903-9

Printed in the United States of America.

At the time of this book's publication, all facts and figures cited are the most current available. All telephone
numbers, addresses, and website URLs are accurate and active. All publications, organizations, websites,
and other resources exist as described in the book, and all have been verified. The author and Prufrock Press
Inc. make no warranty or guarantee concerning the information and materials given out by organizations
or content found at websites, and we are not responsible for any changes that occur after this book's
publication. If you find an error, please contact Prufrock Press Inc.

Prufrock Press Inc.
P.O. Box 8813
Waco, TX 76714-8813
Phone: (800) 998-2208
Fax: (800) 240-0333
http://www.prufrock.com

Success Strategies for
Parenting
Gifted Kids

TABLE OF CONTENTS

PART VIII

FOREWORD

Parenting a talented child is not for wimps. It can be confusing yet thrilling, frustrating yet energizing, humbling yet enlightening . . . quite the roller-coaster! This is especially true when a child's talents are different from his or her parents'. On top of the issues related to gifted children's considerable strengths, they also experience all of the craziness of normal development—the frustrations, the complexities of friendships, the self-doubts, the heartbreaks.

Add another layer on top of that: Much like the misconception that gifted students don't need special services because "they'll figure it out on their own," many people think parenting a talented child is a cake walk. They don't see the perfectionism, extreme boredom in school, or difficulties finding like-minded peers. In my experience, this attitude of "it's easy parenting a gifted student" prevents parents of talented children from seeking out the assistance they know they need.

For a long time, there wasn't nearly enough assistance to provide, given that the resources available to parents of high-potential students was thin. But thanks in large part to the efforts of the National Association for Gifted Children—from whose publication *Parenting for High Potential* this book's content is drawn—we are starting to create a wide and deep reservoir of helpful, research-based information and advice for parents.

This book is a comprehensive sampling of all of the knowledge that reservoir contains, and the editors—all highly respected experts and advocates—carefully crafted the volume to be as useful as possible to parents. This book is low on jargon and high on practical strategies, it covers a wide range of important topics but avoids being superficial, and it is research-based yet doesn't get bogged down in those details. The authors are all distinguished experts with impressive track records of working with parents of gifted students, and that experience jumps off every page.

I especially encourage readers to make use of the reflection questions provided with each reading. These questions can serve as a guide and source of support for the difficult questions parents often have (and need to have) with their children's teachers, administrators, psychologists, and counselors. Within my own family, we have found frank discussions on these issues to be eye-opening, especially when the kids are involved. Children always notice and think about more than we realize, and that is even more the case when those children are intellectually talented.

Of course, we have a long way to go before we are fully supporting parents of gifted students. Perhaps that's an unattainable goal, as the needed assistance will keep evolving as society and education change. But striving to provide that support is a laudable, necessary goal, and the book you are holding in your hands represents a major step forward in providing that support. Thanks for all that you do for your gifted child!

—Jonathan A. Plucker, Ph.D.,
NAGC President, 2019–2021

PART I

CHARACTERISTICS, IDENTIFICATION, AND TALENT DEVELOPMENT

This opening section includes chapters that discuss several issues that beguile parents in their journey of raising their gifted and twice-exceptional children. Parents or caretakers are often the first ones to observe their child's behavior, which provides an inkling that alternative and/or additional interventions, accelerated and/or challenging curriculum, or outside-of-school opportunities will be required. Each author combines research-informed approaches to offer best practices and strategies in regard to identification, characteristics, and talent development.

In Chapter 1, Matthews and Foster offer an overview of intelligence tests, their role in gifted identification and programming, and how to use IQ test results in obtaining appropriate services. In addition, the authors provide suggestions for translating results into meaningful ideas for children. The practical information presented can help parents navigate the use of IQ tests.

In Chapter 2, Hasan details how she balanced her daughter's advanced learning ability and challenging behavior. Drawing from her own experiences as a high school student at a specialized math and science high school, Hasan realized that some of her classmates had failed to thrive due to their rigid approach to challenging situations. She applied these lessons when parenting her own daughter, particularly when her daughter wanted to attempt activities that she was mentally ready for but perhaps did not have the fine motor skills for yet.

Chapter 3 and Chapter 4 address talent development. Welch delves into the demands and intricacies of those students who are both academically and musically talented. Her background as a music teacher, an accomplished musician, and gifted education professional provides a unique perspective to help guide parents, caretakers, and dually talented students on their developmental trajectory. Kiewra uses his extensive research on talented youth across a number of domains to present seven ways parents can support and develop their children's talent. These practical strategies provide a foundation for parents to begin a talent development journey with their child.

Taken alone or used as the introduction before reading the remaining chapters, this section offers a primer on characteristics, identification, and talent development with the opportunity for additional resources and readings.

—Jennifer L. Jolly

CHAPTER 1

INTELLIGENCE, IQ, TESTS, AND ASSESSMENTS: WHAT DO PARENTS NEED TO KNOW?

by Dona Matthews and Joanne Foster

What is intelligence? Do intelligence quotient (IQ) tests really measure intelligence? Are there better ways than measuring IQ to decide who needs gifted programming? What can parents request by way of results of any assessments and their interpretation? What should parents tell their kids about the results? These are some of the thorny questions that parents ask about testing, and rightly so, because their child's educational future can hang in the balance. Here are some fundamentals.

WHAT IS INTELLIGENCE?

There are hundreds of definitions, many from people with serious expertise in one field or another. Here's the perspective we advocate, based on evolving findings in neuroscience and cognitive psychology (Matthews & Foster, 2014):

> Intelligence is the ability to understand complex ideas, adapt effectively to the environment, overcome obstacles, engage meaningfully in various forms of reasoning, and learn from experience. It develops incrementally, and varies across time, situations, and domains. (pp. 24–25)

Considered like this, intelligence isn't as mysterious as it sometimes seems to be. Current research shows it to be far more dynamic, accessible, and vibrant than people once thought.

DO IQ TESTS MEASURE INTELLIGENCE?

There are many tests that describe themselves as IQ or intelligence tests, and provide the score in the form of an intelligence quotient. Some of these are solidly respectable, but many are questionable. Our recommendation is to steer clear of any but the most comprehensive, valid, and reliable tests—the current editions of the Wechsler and Stanford-Binet tests of intelligence. These are administered one-on-one by trained psychologists, not done on the Internet or administered by a classroom teacher. They assess vocabulary, general knowledge, different kinds of reasoning, and short-term memory, all of which contribute to academic learning.

Some of the less reliable tests can be interesting when done for personal information, and others can provide useful information in the hands of an expert, but too often these less reliable tests provide misleading scores, and add confusion to a topic that is already more confusing than it ought to be.

A very high score on one of the strong IQ tests (especially Wechsler and Stanford-Binet) can confirm a child's need for gifted education, but a lower score doesn't necessarily mean a child would not be well-placed in gifted programming. A score that is below a gifted cutoff can reflect a problem at the time of testing, such as illness, emotional concerns, hunger, a creative or contrarian attitude, test anxiety, a learning problem, or one of many other reasons that children don't demonstrate what they can do, as fully or as well as possible.

Another concern with IQ testing is the narrow range of skills assessed. Many important dimensions of real-world functioning are barely touched upon, including social and emotional abilities, creativity, motivation, drive, and persistence. According to what's known about how intelligence develops, and how assessment results might be used to inform programming, it makes better sense to say, "Her mathematical and scientific reasoning skills are highly advanced for her age," than, "She's highly intelligent."

Contrary to many people's belief, IQ is not stable. And for many reasons, the younger a child when assessed, the more likely the scores will change substantially over time. Alfred Binet, a pioneer in intelligence testing, recognized the changeable nature of intelligence long before today's findings on neural plasticity: "With practice, training, and above all, method, we manage to increase our attention, our memory, our judgment, and literally to become more intelligent than we were before" (as cited in Kaufman, 2013, p. 28).

Another important criticism concerns the persistent IQ differences across race, geography, and socioeconomic status. These differences reflect many factors that are unrelated to intelligence, including differences in test-taking ability and sophistication, attitudes toward testing, and opportunities to learn the kinds of things that are included in IQ testing.

Finally, IQ scores have little to do with current definitions of intelligence—how effectively children adapt to different environments, how well they learn from experience, whether they're likely to invest the hard work over time that's necessary for success, or how they deal with obstacles. Yes, an IQ score has something to do with how well a person understands complex ideas and is able to perform certain kinds of reasoning tasks on a given test on a given day, but it's not a great measure of a person's intelligence. Nor does it have very much to do with whether or not someone needs gifted-level academic programming, or whether his or her abilities have been assessed within the broader scope of talent development identification processes: "Although giftedness is typically associated with schooling, gifted individuals exist across academic and non-academic domains" (Worrell, Subotnik, Olszewski-Kubilius, & Dixson, 2019, p. 551).

ARE THERE BETTER WAYS THAN IQ TESTS TO DECIDE WHO NEEDS GIFTED PROGRAMMING?

Parents with concerns about whether their child's learning needs are being met sometimes ask for a gifted assessment. It can be more productive for the child, however, if parents ask the teacher these practical questions:

» What are my child's areas of strength, weakness, and interest?
» What does my child need right now in order to be both challenged and supported in learning?
» How can I help?

The best way of answering these questions is not with an IQ score, but by carefully considering academic achievement, reasoning, interest, and persistence, as each of these components applies to specific subject areas.

Generally speaking, IQ tests make sense only when a child experiences learning problems that interfere with the ability to do well on standard measures of academic achievement and reasoning. Children with learning or attentional problems usually have difficulty with these kinds of paper-and-pencil tests and do better with the one-on-one oral format of top-tier IQ tests. Parents should also be aware that large gaps in subscores (particularly in the areas of working memory or processing speed) may indicate a learning disability or twice-exceptionality.

WHAT CAN PARENTS REQUEST BY WAY OF RESULTS AND THEIR INTERPRETATION?

After an assessment, parents often ask, "Is my child gifted?" However, it's far more productive to ask, "Does my child have abilities that are advanced compared to others of the same age?" and then to inquire, "Now what? Are there areas needing special educational adaptations in order for my child to get suitable and meaningful learning challenges?" In order to answer these questions, parents can request:

1. **Results by academic subject areas.** Knowing the score breakdown by subject area helps parents ensure their child is being given the level of programming that matches ability and domain going forward.
2. **Degree of advancement.** Knowing that a child is "mathematically gifted" is a start. The next questions to ask are, "How far advanced? What level of programming would be best?" A third-grade child who scores at a grade 9 level mathematically needs different challenges than a third-grader who scores at a grade 5 level.
3. **Scores in percentiles.** Percentile scores are more user-friendly than raw scores or standard scores. A child who scores at the 60th percentile in language skills (that is, better than 60% of same-age others) and better than 99.9% of

others mathematically, will require mathematical advancement, but probably not verbal advancement. That sort of discrepancy is much easier to determine from percentile scores than any other kind of score.

WHAT SHOULD PARENTS TELL THEIR CHILD ABOUT THE TEST RESULTS?

When parents realize—and explain—that ability develops over time with opportunities to learn, and they position tests as useful tools for decision-making purposes, they can disclose test results without worrying about damaging or inflating their child's confidence. Some suggestions include the following:

1. **Be open and honest.** Give as much information as the child wants, sharing the numbers if asked.
2. **Translate results into practical implications.** A parent might say, "Your verbal reasoning scores were exceptionally high. I guess that's why you're so great at arguing with your sister. It also means you'll need more challenging work than most kids." Or, "Your science scores weren't so strong. Maybe that's because you haven't had a chance yet to learn what was on the test. What would you enjoy learning more about?"
3. **Remind your child that everyone has areas of strength and weakness.** No matter how well your child has done on a test, you can chat together about people who are exceptional achievers in one or more areas, but not necessarily in others. Discuss how some strengths show up in academic assessments, and some don't.
4. **Emphasize the hard work component of learning and achievement.** This applies both to your child's areas of strength and relative weakness.
5. **Steer away from the gifted label.** Keep the emphasis squarely on test scores as indications of learning strengths and challenges.

If your child meets the scoring criteria for gifted identification, this indicates some excellent reasoning and test-taking skills. But if your child misses the cut, nobody should conclude that he or she is not a gifted learner, or (if it was close) presume to use the term "almost gifted." Nobody is "almost gifted"; that is a nonsensical term suggesting a dichotomy between those who are gifted and those who are not. A child may have advanced learning needs in one or more areas, either now or in the future—abilities that just didn't show up in the particular assessment at that point in time.

No matter how your child scores, remember that intelligence develops step by step with the right kinds of supports and opportunities to learn. High-level abilities develop when children engage meaningfully in various forms of reasoning and a range of learning experiences, confronting challenges, overcoming obstacles, and developing resilience along the way. Parents can encourage their children's interests and nurture their creativity and critical thinking. Parents can also help kids build their children's skills by modeling patience, persistence, and hard work in their own pursuits.

REFLECTION QUESTIONS

1. What sort of additional challenges do you think your child might benefit from in one subject area or another?
2. What other learning opportunities might be best suited for your child (e.g., mentorships, extracurricular programs, acceleration)?
3. How does your child respond to testing situations? Which kinds of assessments do you think might provide the best information about your child's abilities and educational needs (e.g., one-on-one orally administered IQ tests or other forms of assessments, such as oral presentations and real-world problem-solving activities)?
4. How might you work with your child's teacher and school to help implement the adaptations your child needs?
5. In what ways can you advocate for gifted education, and perhaps collaborate with other parents in advocacy efforts?

REFERENCES

Kaufman, S. B. (2013). *Ungifted: Intelligence redefined.* New York, NY: Basic Books.

Matthews, D., & Foster, J. (2014). *Beyond intelligence: Secrets for raising happily productive kids.* Toronto, ON: House of Anansi Press.

Worrell, F. C., Subotnik, R. F., Olszewski-Kubilius, P., & Dixson, D. D. (2019). Gifted students. *Annual Review of Psychology, 70,* 551–576.

CHAPTER 2

BEND OR BREAK: YOUR IQ IS NOT YOUR IDENTITY

by Melissa R. Hasan

Conceptual physics saved my sanity. A seemingly unimportant metallurgical fact I learned in high school has made parenting possible on most days.

I graduated from a 2-year public high school for gifted students. Juniors and seniors from high schools all over the state are accepted each year to live in a dormitory on a university campus, far from home, and take classes following a typical college schedule. To say that I graduated from there is no small achievement, because in my years there, a little more than 25% of students left before graduation.

My high school experience prepared me for adult life, especially as a parent, in a much more real sense than my undergraduate or even graduate school experiences. It was during this time that I learned that I am really smart. My mind can think amazing thoughts about all of the stuff I am smart about (like dangling prepositions and dense sentences). But no matter what subject it is, someone is always smarter. I may have helped my friend deconstruct Faust, but someone else had to lead me with baby steps through analytical geometry. And U.S. history. And economics. But not *civitas*, because I rocked philosophy.

What was the most important thing I learned in high school? I learned from conceptual physics and interpersonal relationships that what is rigid—breaks. If it won't bend, and you keep applying pressure, it will break. Shatter. Explode. And that is what happened to some of my classmates, usually those who chose to return to their home schools. They were unable to cope with the idea that someone else in the room was smarter, was faster at solving a problem, or found a more elegant way to express the intangible.

In *Genius Denied*, Jan and Bob Davidson (2004) wrote that "the most common problem that gifted kids face is underachievement" (p. 82). They proposed that self-confidence is built by taking risks and pursuing challenging goals, which require all of one's effort to reach. They went on to suggest that many gifted individuals become perfectionists who are afraid to fail, simply because they have never experienced failure. These individuals cannot meet their true potential because they are terrified of taking the risks necessary for substantial intellectual growth. They avoid intellectual or academic challenges, perhaps believing that having to work hard will prove that they are not gifted after all.

I have since learned about incremental and entity theories, popularly called growth and fixed mindsets by Carol Dweck (2006), and have a new vocabulary for what I saw in high school. Students whose identity was wholly tied up in being *the smart one* could not face a reality that included so many gifted peers; believing that intelligence was "an unchangeable, fixed 'entity,'" their focus was on measuring or proving their intelligence level (Blackwell, Dweck, & Trzesniewski, 2007, p. 247). They could not handle the frustration of truly difficult academic work, feeling that hard work proved that they weren't so smart after all. Rigid students, with a fixed mindset, either broke and left or found a way to forge an entirely new identity to confront this new reality by changing their mindset. Flexible students, with a growth mindset, grew and blossomed—one adolescent drama after another. These were students who were excited to experiment, in class and in life, and who found a pool of wild new problems to solve on every front. They believed in their own power to change their intelligence level and looked at mistakes as opportunities to learn and improve.

In high school, I learned that sometimes you have to give a little or lose a lot. I learned how to take a deep breath and change my expectations. I learned that sometimes it's okay to change the rules in the middle of the game, if that's what it takes to keep the game going. Most of all, I learned how to learn from failure.

That is how conceptual physics saved my sanity as a mother: I must bend or I will break. That is true of any mother of any child. As the mother of a gifted child, however, I use this high school lesson every day in another important way. I know that I must constantly find something challenging for my daughter, because I must teach her how to be flexible. I must intervene early to teach high-level cognitive functions that will help her to regulate her emotional reactions. Dawson and Guare (2018) outlined several executive functions that help humans meet challenges and accomplish goals. Four of these, I believe, are crucial for gifted individuals to learn at a young age in order to cope with the anxiety and frustration that comes from being an intellectual outsider. Dawson and Guare defined them as follows:

1. **Sustained attention:** The capacity to attend to a situation or task in spite of distractibility, fatigue, or boredom.

2. **Flexibility:** The ability to revise plans in the face of obstacles, setbacks, new information, or mistakes; involving adaptability to changing conditions.

3. **Emotional control:** The ability to manage emotions in order to achieve goals, complete tasks, or control and direct behavior.

4. **Goal-directed persistence:** The capacity or drive to follow through to the completion of a goal and not be put off by other demands or competing interests. (p. 4)

I know that I must encourage my daughter to continue challenging activities that become frustrating and praise her for effort. I praise that she didn't give up, not that she was smart enough to figure it out. And if she didn't happen to figure it out this time, I can point out that some things are hard and take more time to learn. We will try again on another day.

For my daughter, this has meant guiding her to do gross and fine motor activities regularly, because without that encouragement her motor skills will fall years behind her intellectual interests. It has meant almost 5 years of gymnastics classes, even when she made little progress. It also meant finding a one-on-one coach when she switched to ice-skating, because sustained attention in the face of difficult skills is *hard*. It meant working puzzles labeled "age 3+" at age 20 months, and continuing to work that puzzle even when she got frustrated. The important part is what happens at the breaking point. I give her a hug, tell her that this is really hard work, and remind her it will get easier if she tries her best. When she was a toddler, I would say, "I'm so proud that you're a big girl who always tries and tries again." We would take a break by running through the house shouting "I did it" or something similar. Or, when she dissolved into a screaming, crying tantrum, we would take a break and try again later. We repeated this process for writing in kindergarten, cross-stitching in first grade, "cross-overs" in ice skating, and the list goes on and on.

Together we have found a few methods that help her cope with frustration and failure anxiety. When she was 2, we learned to "stop, breathe, and think," just the way Steve says in the *Blue's Clues* episode "Blue Is Frustrated" (Johnson, Kessler, & Santomero, 1998). I realized how fully she has internalized this script when she told an Angry Birds toy: "It's okay, Angry Bird. Take a deep breath. Do you need a hug, Angry Bird?" For more than an hour in the car that day, I watched my 2-year-old daughter demonstrate almost every coping mechanism we've tried, and it was a great opportunity to suggest several new ones, including alone time and a nap. At age 5, she spent several months in occupational therapy for emotional regulation and sensory integration, learning new techniques for calming down. Now that my daughter is almost 9 years old, she continues to need these coping mechanisms. Research shows that gifted children *feel* more intensely (Bainbridge, 2019); they need to be taught how to cope with their overexcitabilities, without diminishing how real their feelings are.

When my daughter decided, at 21 months, that she wanted to tie her shoes all by herself, we had a few rough mornings. We switched from tennis shoes to Velcro leather shoes. But when we woke up one rainy morning, I realized something had to change. Her need to be independent with her shoes wasn't going to change, so I changed the rules. I asked her to please help me put on the shoes, and then said, "Let's hurry. You tie this one and I'll tie the other one, and we'll be done so fast!" After one was tied (and double knotted with the sock folded down over the tie, of course), I said, "Oh man, you're doing such a good job! Tying shoes is really hard, though. It takes lots of practice before it gets easier. I've had years and years of practice. Can I help you with that one because we're trying to hurry?" And she said yes! Even better, the next day she told me that tying shoes is really hard, and that was the end of the shoe tantrums. She understood and accepted that she wasn't ready to tie her own shoes, once I validated her need for independence and found a way to include her in the shoes routine.

Obviously there are days when I don't bend enough, or she won't bend at all, and someone has a crying meltdown. Sometimes it's her, and sometimes it's me. I know now that the real lesson in life is how to deal with frustration without having a major tantrum and without quitting. I accept that part of my responsibility to my gifted daughter is to teach her this life skill and to support the development of her executive functions, especially of sustained attention, flexibility, emotional control, and goal-directed persistence. I realize now that this is the centerpiece of parenting, and will be for decades. My gifted daughter has not suddenly blossomed into a flexible, attentive learner with zen-like calm who can focus throughout the most boring work. And honestly, I wouldn't trade away her intense empathy or the joy of getting truly lost in a book. I just know that she needs the tools to be able to calm herself down as she spirals down the dark side of empathy: fear, hopelessness, anxiety.

I also know that I must convince her that true identity cannot be wholly consumed with IQ or EQ (emotional intelligence) or learning preference (Fleming & Mills, 1992; Goleman, 1995/2005). These factors are a part of each of us, but they are not core. Armed with these lessons, I hope that I can prepare her for the day that she walks into a classroom of geniuses who shake her confidence to its very core. And I hope that she will walk out of that room knowing that her deep inner value as a human being is untouched by rising or falling intellectual rank.

REFLECTION QUESTIONS

1. Gifted children are often called "melodramatic" when they are experiencing strong emotions, especially empathy. Think of a time when you felt overwhelmed by emotion. What was the cause? Imagine if you felt that strongly about many things in life.

2. For those who have a fixed mindset, any challenge is a threat to their intellectual standing. An antidote to this type of thinking is to remember a time when you struggled *and succeeded*. What is one time when you had to really put in 100% of your effort to succeed? What is something that your gifted child struggled to learn, but eventually succeeded?

3. This chapter references four executive functions: sustained attention, flexibility, emotional control, and goal-directed persistence. As an adult, which of these is difficult for you? Which is a strength? What techniques do you use to support these executive functions? Consider sharing your techniques with your child.

REFERENCES

Bainbridge, C. (2019). Dabrowski's overexcitabilities in gifted children. *Verywell Family*. Retrieved from https://www.verywell family.com/dabrowskis-overexcitabilities-in-gifted-children-144 9118

Blackwell, L. S., Dweck, C. S., & Trzesniewski K. H. (2007). Implicit theories of intelligence predict achievement across an adolescent transition: A longitudinal study and an intervention. *Child Development, 78,* 246–263.

Davidson, J., & Davidson, B. (2004). *Genius denied: How to stop wasting our brightest young minds.* New York, NY: Simon & Schuster.

Dawson, P., & Guare, R. (2018). *Executive skills in children and adolescents: A practical guide to assessment and intervention* (3rd ed.). New York, NY: Guilford Press.

Dweck, C. S. (2006). *Mindset: The new psychology of success.* New York, NY: Random House.

Fleming, N. D., & Mills, C. (1992). Not another inventory, rather a catalyst for reflection. *To Improve the Academy, 11,* 137–155.

Goleman, D. (2005). *Emotional intelligence: Why it can matter more than IQ.* New York, NY: Bantam. (Original work published 1995)

Johnson, T. P., Kessler, T., & Santomero, A. C. (Writers). (1998). Blue is frustrated [Television series episode]. In S. Chumsky (Producer), *Blues clues season 2.* New York, NY: Nickelodeon.

CHAPTER 3

THE ACADEMICALLY AND MUSICALLY GIFTED STUDENT: THE CHALLENGE OF MAINTAINING IDENTITY AND MAKING DIFFICULT CHOICES

by Alicia M. Welch

Students who are gifted in multiple areas have generated a fair amount of discussion—and for good reason. Often referred to as having multipotentiality, students who are academically gifted and also have exceptional musical talent embody human potential and the product of diligent practice. However, this abundance of promise can contribute to emotional stress as students transition out of high school. The decision to pursue a major in music in college can have greater emotional implications than what others may perceive, often resulting in the forfeit of a hard-earned portion of the student's identity. Students facing this unique set of choices are likely to need support to navigate the emotional hurdles that often accompany the transition into college and career planning.

WHO ARE THESE STUDENTS?

Academically and musically gifted students may be easily identified given their participation and accomplishments in school or community music programs and impressive academic record. However, identification may be more elusive if they play guitar or piano—instruments that are not typically included in structured school music programs. They may also be gifted composers with even fewer opportunities to showcase their abilities in a school setting. Although identification may not always be easy, these multipotentialed students tend to share the following characteristics:

- » **They are exceptionally dedicated.** In addition to schoolwork, highly successful student musicians dedicate hours every day, over many years, to ensemble rehearsals, individual practice, and private lessons. They compete in private or school-sponsored programs, some of which occur nearly every weekend. They prepare for local, regional, state, and national solo and ensemble competitions through private instruction with local professional musicians.

- » **They are motivated.** To excel musically requires not only innate ability, but also a great deal of motivation and self-regulation. For multipotentialed students, this motivation may also be used to maintain or improve academic endeavors. One may consider Bloom's (1985) general qualities of talent development to better understand the characteristics that benefit both areas of these students' lives. These qualities include a strong interest and emotional commitment to a particular talent field or fields, the desire to reach a high level of attainment, and the willingness to invest great amounts of time and effort necessary for reaching high levels of achievement. These students may spend years finding and maintaining a balance in order to fully commit to the demands of these characteristics across multiple areas.

An early and competitive admissions process for top collegiate music programs further increases pressure on this decision. Typically spanning the majority of the senior year of high school, applications for auditions are often due by December–January, with auditions occurring between January and March. Assuming that minimum university admissions requirements are met, admittance to music programs relies heavily on the audition results. Future music majors typically begin their senior year having already narrowed down their college searches with audition music chosen and nearly mastered. The level of foresight, organization, and motivation required to make this possible is unique and impressive.

By this point, families, teachers, and music programs have likely invested a great deal into instruments, private lessons, competition fees, and travel. In addition, by this stage in their development, the student will often have developed a strong personal relationship with a music teacher(s) with whom he or she may have studied for many years. In my experience, this collective investment can weigh heavily on an already complicated decision-making process for students with multiple potentials.

WHY CHOOSE?

Multipotentiality in gifted students faced with career decisions may leave them feeling paralyzed by an abundance of choice (Elijah, 2011). These students may also feel external pressure to pursue one career over another, thereby forsaking interest and ability in other areas. Further, the choice to pursue a major and plan a career outside of music often feels like a decision to relinquish one's hard-earned identity as a musician (Muratori & Smith, 2015). Undoubtedly, there are circumstances in which it is possible to retain performance opportunities in college at a level that would allow preservation of the musician identity. But, often, the logistics of higher education in another academic area and the demands of many college majors do not allow for the continuation of serious musical study. Further, although many universities allow non-music majors to audition for particular ensembles, these students will compete for positions against music majors who, by nature of their degree program, spend hours each day practicing and improving their skills. These non-major students may not be competitive under these circumstances and, importantly, may find it increasingly difficult to participate at the level to which they were accustomed. However, as you will see in the resources section of this chapter, there is a slow shift in higher education—particularly at highly selective institutions—that is making it easier to pursue rigorous interdisciplinary degrees to accommodate students with abilities in seemingly disparate fields.

EXAMPLE FROM THE FIELD: THE DRIVEN ACADEMIC MUSICIAN

Over the years, I have had the privilege of working with many exceedingly talented students. One particularly bright student was especially enthusiastic and motivated in the classroom as well as with his music, keeping him on a steeply positive track. At an early age, Eric was a fine pianist, classical percussionist, and composer. He attended a large public high school in a suburban area of the North Texas region. Throughout middle and high school, he was highly involved in concert and marching band, percussion ensembles (both classical and marching), concert band, and solo competitions. He participated in multiple national solo and ensemble competitions and was quite successful, earning a first-place title. In addition, he maintained a stellar academic record and was accepted to his top choices for highly selective colleges.

In his words, "It'd be impossible to talk about my life or my education without talking about music. It's been so many things for me: my inspiration, my motivation, my therapy." Upon graduation from high school—having been accepted to the University of Chicago, Princeton, Columbia, and Harvard—his future seemed boundless, as if he could do nearly anything he desired. The limitless options left him feeling "everywhere," a feeling he would carry with him into his first years of college. He explained that his major choice and career aspirations changed on a daily basis, and they always had. Music was the one consistent aspect of his life, and "the practice room and the grand piano were always ready and there for me." So, his choice to major in a different area was, as he said, "ridiculously tough."

He had the crucial support of his parents, who, when discussing the possibility of majoring in music, did not counter with the usual sentiments of how difficult it is to make a living as a musician or question him as to whether he realized how much hard work it would entail. Instead, they lovingly told him that he would need to start practicing a lot more. Eric viewed this decision as a choice between two good things. He decided that he had the self-discipline to maintain music as a part of his life while pursuing a major in another area. After all, he had proven himself capable of dividing his time between the two areas during high school. The next step was choosing a college that would allow him to do so.

Although Eric believed that his peers likely assumed that he chose Harvard simply for its prestige, he claimed his choice was due to the availability of quality music ensembles in which he could participate as a nonmusic major. He was able to be a part of The Harvard Undergraduate Drummers (THUD), the timpanist for the Dunster House Opera, and a member of the Harvard-Radcliffe Orchestra. He maintained that although he could have obtained as good an education at other schools to which he was accepted, he chose Harvard after visiting campus and sitting in on a rehearsal because it was the only place that he felt he "could keep music as fully a part of my life as I wanted it to be."

YOU ARE THEIR GREATEST RESOURCE

So often, educational decisions are not clear-cut for these unique students. The choice between music and another major can feel absolute and permanent, and often carries great emotional consequence. However, parents and guardians may play a crucial part in assisting with this decision by encouraging students to:

>> engage in candid conversations about life or career goals and how their interests or college majors may enable them to meet those goals;

>> seek out conversations with their music teachers about this decision, as they know firsthand the rewards and challenges related to being a professional musician and music educator;

>> plan ahead in order to apply to college early and complete necessary auditions so that, should they decide to major in music, no time is lost by missing a required audition; and

>> consider institutions that offer supportive options for non-music majors to stay involved in private lessons, ensemble participation, or a music minor.

The achievements of such gifted students may elicit a hands-off approach as many assume that these students will easily surmount this challenge as they have others before. Although they may eventually do exactly that, the difficult decisions and related emotions they will encounter along the way should be addressed. Conversations with parents or guardians, teachers, and counselors will help these students to make the necessary difficult choices and assist in the transition through their changing identity.

RESOURCES

There are an increasing number of innovative degree and dual-degree programs that allow for rigorous academic and musical pursuits. Here are three:

» Carnegie Mellon's School of Music, along with the School of Computer Science and Department of Electrical and Computer Engineering, offers a Bachelor of Science and Master of Science degree in music and technology. These programs offer students a breadth of experience in music, computer science, and engineering. For more information, visit https://www.cmu.edu/cfa/music.

» The Peabody Conservatory and Johns Hopkins University offer advanced students a 5-year, double-degree program from Peabody and either the Krieger School of Arts & Sciences or the Whiting School of Engineering. For more information, visit https://peabody.jhu.edu.

» Harvard College offers a 5-year joint bachelor's and master's degree option for advanced music students who also seek a rigorous liberal arts education. Along with their undergraduate requirements, Harvard students complete requirements for a master's degree in music from either the New England Conservatory or Berklee College of Music. For more information, visit https://college.harvard.edu/admissions/application-process/dual-degree-music-programs.

REFLECTION QUESTIONS

1. Identify driving forces. What are the student's career and/or life goals?
2. Reflect on the student's goals and interests. Are there commonalities? Is there a way to combine his or her multiple abilities and interests into a fulfilling major and career?
3. What are the student's concerns about making a college major choice? In what ways can those concerns be mitigated?

4. What hardships does the student believe that he or she will encounter with his or her top major choices? In what ways can you prepare for those hardships ahead of time?

REFERENCES

Bloom, B. S. (Ed.). (1985). *Developing talent in young people*. New York, NY: Ballantine.

Elijah, K. (2011). Meeting the guidance and counseling needs of gifted students in school settings. *Journal of School Counseling, 9*(14).

Muratori, M. C., & Smith, C. K. (2015). Guiding the talent and career development of the gifted individual. *Journal of Counseling & Development, 93*, 173–182.

CHAPTER 4

SEVEN WAYS PARENTS HELP CHILDREN UNLEASH THEIR TALENTS

by Kenneth A. Kiewra

Amadeus Mozart and Pablo Picasso were child prodigies, mastering their domains along with the best of adults. However, these extraordinary performers represent just the tip of the child prodigy iceberg. I've investigated talent development in various domains, from ice skating to chess, to determine how some youngsters get to be so good so fast and what talent development roles their parents play (Kiewra, 2019).

On the surface, it might seem that talent is born. Mozart played the piano at age 3 and composed at age 6. Picasso, the child, drew like an adult. Look deeper, though, and we see that talent is made. Mozart and Picasso had fathers who were expert instructors in their sons' talent areas and who diligently guided their practice.

So, how is talent made? Often, behind every talented individual are parents pushing the right buttons and doing all they can to nurture talent. The following are seven ways that parents help children unleash their talents.

1. DISCOVER A CHILD'S ELEMENT

All of us have talent potential in certain areas of biological strength, and talent is most likely to blossom when we discover and toil in our true element (Robinson, 2009). My oldest son showed traits as a youngster that helped me discover his element. He had a strong memory and was unbeatable in strategic games like tic-tac-toe and checkers. Given these characteristics, I reasoned that he might enjoy and succeed in chess. Chess was indeed his element. Today he is an International Chess Master and professional chess coach.

Parents should offer their children varying opportunities (a talent menu), observe their interests and strengths, and then feed those. One twirling parent I studied agreed: "Parents need to look at what a child's desire is. Matching training to that desire can be a beautiful thing. But, if parents make a child do something that *they* want the child to do, then it can be ugly" (Kiewra & Witte, 2015, p. 18).

2. PROVIDE AN EARLY START

In my own study of talented youth, eventual national and world-class chess players, baton twirlers, figure skaters, and musicians were routinely introduced to their talent domain when they were 3–5 years old (Witte, Kiewra, Kasson, & Perry, 2015). Moreover, many were "born" into the talent domain, as their parents were already accomplished players, coaches, or enthusiasts. The same holds true for former athlete and golf fanatic Earl Woods, who gave Tiger his first club when Tiger was just 7 months old and had Tiger sit in his high chair in the garage to watch his father hit golf balls into a net. Before Tiger turned 2, he and his father were practicing golf regularly on the course.

Time, practice, and biological development are distinct advantages to an early start. Youngsters can commit more time to their talent area when they are not busy with school and homework. The sooner one begins, the more practice hours one can log. And, practice in childhood can sometimes produce greater physical development and brain growth than practice in adulthood (Ericsson & Pool, 2016). All of these advantages accumulate and multiply quickly.

Take hockey for example. Rosters of elite junior and professional hockey teams in Canada are littered with players whose birthdays primarily fall in the first three months of the calendar year. This is not an astrological phenomenon, but one that fits with the January 1st cut-off age for junior hockey. In short, players born earlier in a particular calendar year have a physical advantage over players born later in that same calendar year. That early physical advantage leads to more playing time, which leads to greater skill development. That skill development advantage, in turn, leads to other advantages down the road, such as working with better teams and coaches. Early advantages accumulate (Gladwell, 2008).

3. ESTABLISH A CENTER OF EXCELLENCE

One small British road and surrounding neighborhood produced more outstanding table tennis players in the 1980s than all of the other roads throughout England combined because of a charismatic schoolteacher. This teacher was an elite and avid table tennis player and opened an afterschool program in a dilapidated facility for neighborhood kids. All of the kids had keys and near round-the-clock access. In a short time, this facility became a Ping-Pong center of excellence (Syed, 2010).

Such centers of excellence are fairly widespread. New York City is a center of excellence for chess and was the starting point for world champion Bobby Fischer and other chess prodigies. Similarly, Milwaukee, with its Olympic-sized skating oval, has long been a center of speed skating excellence (Ott Schacht & Kiewra, 2018). When kids grow up in such areas, they have access to elite coaches and other competitors who can push them and help them grow. Parents should look in their own backyards for such talent development opportunities.

Enterprising parents can also establish their own centers of excellence. National High School Rodeo Champion Jayde Atkins was raised on a ranch in Broken Bow, NE, that her parents outfitted with horses, barns, a training apparatus, and trailers she needed to be become a rodeo star (Kiewra & Witte, 2018).

4. FACILITATE PRACTICE

An enriched early environment might jump-start a child on the road to Carnegie Hall, but it takes practice, practice, and more practice to deliver him. Talented musicians like Mozart and artists like Picasso, despite their early talents, practiced arduously for 10 or more years before completing a significant work (Weisberg, 1993). Years of practice are, of course, necessary in other talent domains—such as chess, swimming, baton twirling, and figure skating—to achieve mastery (Witte et al., 2015).

Practice, though, cannot be casual; it must be deliberate (Ericsson & Poole, 2016). This means that learners must work purposefully and repeatedly on challenging skills outside of their comfort zones. Josh Waitzkin (2007) credited his world-class rise in two domains to deliberate practice. As a chess competitor, Josh didn't practice by just playing a lot of games. Instead, he painstakingly studied the variations that arose from a single chess position for days. Later, as a martial artist, Josh deliberately practiced against stronger competitors, asking them to target his weaknesses so that he could strengthen them. And, when he broke his dominant hand, he practiced fighting with the other hand to make that one equally dominant.

Parents often go to great lengths to ensure their talented children can practice. In my studies, the parent of a twirler rented an indoor tennis court so her daughter could practice when gym space was unavailable; another built a great room with an extra-high ceiling in her home so that her daughter could practice indoors during inclement weather (Kiewra & Witte, 2015).

5. ARRANGE INSTRUCTION

Getting budding talent to bloom also depends on securing a series of teachers who can help the child build early interest, hone technical skills, and establish a lasting relationship with the talent domain (Bloom, 1985). All of the young stars I studied worked with a series of coaches (Kiewra, 2019). Often, a parent serves as the child's first coach and introduces the child to the talent domain in a playful way. In some cases, parents, particularly those who are accomplished in their own right, continue on as technical coaches. Nearly all of the twirler moms I studied were professional twirling coaches. One chess parent was merely a recreational player when his son caught the chess bug. This father studied chess on his own about 20 hours a week in order to teach his son.

Most parents, though, eventually enlist master teachers to teach their children, often at the suggestion of the former coach. Master teachers are International Grandmasters, national or world champion twirlers, skaters with Olympic experience, and musicians employed at leading universities or conservatories.

Securing elite coaching does not come easily or cheaply. One skating family relocated hundreds of miles from their home so their son could work with a top coach. The parent of a violinist flew with her son across the country every week so that he could study with a top-flight music coach. Lessons, meanwhile, are expensive. To pay for top coaches, many families make sacrifices, such as borrowing money, forgoing retirement savings, living in smaller homes, and taking second jobs. A skating mom said bluntly: "This is an ungodly expensive sport. It really is. I can't tell you how many times we remortgaged our house" (Witte et al., 2015, p. 90).

6. SUPPORT SINGLENESS OF PURPOSE

Long and daily practice sessions, lessons with mentors, and numerous competitions leave talented individuals with little time for outside activities. But, most prefer it that way. They have a singleness of purpose. When I asked chess parents why their talented kids spent so much time on chess, all credited the child's chess passion. One parent remarked:

> He is passionate about it, just thrilled by it. It gives him a lot of joy and satisfaction, and he's not really happy when he's not playing. If someone were to take chess away from him, he just wouldn't be a complete person. We once took chess away and he was miserable; it was like yanking out the soul. (Kiewra, O'Connor, McCrudden, & Liu, 2006, p. 103)

To most people, such single-mindedness seems unnatural or unhealthy. Still, a pinpoint focus is the hallmark of talent. Talented individuals simply practice a lot because they want to and like to practice. Their hard work and singleness of purpose is the product of a rage to learn and master (Winner, 1996).

Parents play a central role in their children's single-minded pursuit of talent. They are often high achievers themselves, and they espouse and model a hard-work ethic. They strive for excellence, set no limits, and teach that no goal is impossible. They also support their children's single-mindedness by being fully committed to talent-nurturing themselves.

7. MAKE A FULL COMMITMENT

In Poker terms, talent parents are all in. They recognize the rarity of their child's talent and their responsibility to nurture it. One parent said, "I've made a commitment to him that as long as he continues to work and grow and do his best, we'll use whatever resources we have to get him where he wants to go" (Kiewra et al., 2006, p. 104).

These committed parents take on roles beyond normal parenthood. They act as coach, accountant, fund raiser, secretary, hairdresser, costume designer, press agent, travel agent, travel companion, medical assistant, dietician, chauffeur, school liaison, videographer, and practice monitor. No job is too big or too small. Parents often described their collective duties as a second or full-time job.

The parent of a young writer and international speaker who quit her job to foster her daughter's talent said, "It's a full-time job—sometimes even more than full-time—and can be hard. But the reason I keep doing it is that I don't just manage somebody. The person I manage is my daughter" (Witte et al., 2015, p. 91).

FINAL THOUGHTS

The road to excellence is passable for those who discover their element, gain early access to the talent domain, link to a center of excellence, engage in deliberate practice, work with top coaches, and have a singleness of purpose.

No child, though, can complete this journey alone. A fully committed parent must help at every turn. But, regardless of how far the road is traveled, parents contend that the joys and benefits from talent development come as much from the journey as the destination. One twirling parent remarked, "[My daughter] has learned many life skills along the way that have nothing to do with twirling a baton" (Kiewra & Witte, 2015, p. 17). Another parent remarked, "I have no regrets because every single thing that I did [to help develop talent] has brought [my son] into my life. I felt lucky to share this with my son" (Kiewra & Witte, 2013, p. 159). Finally, a chess parent described why he has nurtured talent: "Because he's my son and I love him and I want him to be whatever he can be. And, if that happens to be chess . . . then that's what I want for him. I want him to be happy. . . . And I love his chess too" (Kiewra et al., 2006, p. 105).

REFLECTION QUESTIONS

1. This chapter emphasized the supporting role parents play in talent development. How might schools and communities play the supporting role instead, as was the case in the film *Knights of the South Bronx* about poverty-stricken kids becoming chess champions?
2. It might seem that talent development can only occur in well-off families—not true. How might any family find the resources necessary to raise a tennis, music, or geography star?
3. Explain why talent is a continuum and why all parents should be interested in talent development.
4. Explain this statement: There are no exceptional children, only exceptional conditions.
5. Explain why talent development is good for those traveling the talent path and, ultimately, good for the world at large.

REFERENCES

Bloom, B. S. (Ed.). (1985). *Developing talent in young people.* New York, NY: Ballantine.

Ericsson, A., & Pool, R. (2016). *Peak: Secrets from the new science of expertise.* New York, NY: Houghton Mifflin Harcourt.

Gladwell, M. (2008). *Outliers: The story of success.* New York, NY: Little, Brown.

Kiewra, K. A. (2019). *Nurturing children's talents: A guide for parents.* Santa Barbara, CA: Praeger.

Kiewra, K. A., O'Connor, T., McCrudden, M., & Liu, X. (2006). Developing young chess masters: A collective case study. In T. Redman (Ed.), *Chess and education: Essays from the Koltanowski conference* (pp. 98–108). Richardson, TX: Chess Program at The University of Texas at Dallas.

Kiewra, K. A., & Witte, A. L. (2013). How to parent chess talent: Classic and modern stories. In M. F. Shaughnessy (Ed.), *The nurturing of talents, skills, and abilities* (pp. 139–162). Hauppauge, NY: NOVA Science.

Kiewra, K. A., & Witte, A. L. (2015). How to parent baton twirling talent: Four success stories. *Talent Development and Excellence, 7,* 13–27.

Kiewra, K. A., & Witte, A. L. (2018). Prodigies of the prairie: The talent development stories of four elite Nebraska youth performers. *Roeper Review, 40,* 176–190.

Ott Schacht, C. L., & Kiewra, K. A. (2018). The fastest humans on earth: Environmental surroundings and family influences that spark talent development in Olympic speed skaters. *Roeper Review, 40,* 21–35.

Robinson, K. (2009). *The element: How finding your passion changes everything.* New York, NY: Penguin.

Syed, M. (2010). *Bounce: Mozart, Federer, Picasso, Beckham, and the science of success.* New York, NY: HarperCollins.

Waitzkin, J. (2007). *The art of learning: An inner journey to optimal performance.* New York, NY: Free Press.

Weisberg, R. W. (1993). *Creativity: Beyond the myth of genius.* New York, NY: Freeman.

Winner, E. (1996). The rage to master: The decisive role of talent in the visual arts. In K. A. Ericsson (Ed.), *The road to excellence: The acquisition of expert performance in the arts and sciences, sports and games* (pp. 271–301). Mahwah, NJ: Erlbaum.

Witte, A., Kiewra, K. A., Kasson, S. C., & Perry, K. (2015). Parenting talent: A qualitative investigation of the roles parents play in talent development. *Roeper Review, 37,* 84–96.

PART II

EARLY CHILDHOOD

A quote by poet Charles Péguy could easily be a founding principle for raising and nurturing young gifted learners. He said, "One must always tell what one sees. Above all, which is more difficult, one must always see what one sees." This presents an important question for any adults who work with young gifted learners: We may indeed tell what we see, but do we really see what we see? What might we find if we look more deeply—with more openness, care, and sensitivity?

The authors in this section answer that question by sharing what they have discovered through researching, teaching, and parenting young gifted students. They describe the challenges children face every day—too much pressure to conform in traditional classrooms; too many constraints in how they can learn; an insensitivity to learning style differences; intense emotional sensitivities that baffle teachers and even some parents; and uneven development in abilities, sensibilities, and social and emotional growth.

The chapters assembled here demonstrate the urgency of advocating for young gifted students in their earliest and most formative years of life. They offer practical guidance for families and teachers who want to understand what giftedness looks like in young children and how they can support it. What are the different ways giftedness reveals itself, and in what situations? What mitigating factors might affect how children experience and express their abilities and passions? What drives children's curiosity and makes them feel free? What limits and entraps them?

The authors show how children's giftedness may be misconstrued by adults who do not understand them and may even hold them back. Learning to "see what one sees" encourages an inquiring, open mind in recognizing the unique personality and characteristics of young gifted children and their special needs at home and at school. Learning to "tell what one sees" guides parents to create friendly relationships with teachers that invite a mutual sharing of observations and information, and collaborative efforts to address the changing needs of children intellectually, emotionally, and socially.

Addressing parents as well as teachers, the authors explore many strategies that stimulate creative thinking and learning and enliven the hearts and minds of young gifted children. This kind of learning embraces play—imaginative play, word play, games, visualization, humor, or arts explorations. For learning should not always be a serious business as it so often seems to be in schools, but should elicit the deep joy of discovery and wide-open curiosity that characterizes children's first years of life.

—Joan Franklin Smutny

CHAPTER 5

THE PIVOTAL ROLE OF PARENTS IN EXPANDING THE WORLD OF YOUNG GIFTED CHILDREN

by Joan Franklin Smutny

There are no seven wonders of the world in the eyes of a child. There are seven million.

—Walt Streightiff

One of the greatest joys known to parents of very young children is the wonder in children's faces when they encounter something new. A large shaggy dog is every bit as extraordinary as a praying mantis clinging to a leaf. Their determination to touch, feel, and taste whatever they can get their hands on comes from a deeply felt need to be fully in the world. Parents often remark that taking their young children on outings changes their own experience of the world around them. They remember the sense of awe and delight they had growing up, and it comes back to them in the company of their children.

I mention this because young gifted students begin life deeply engaged with their surroundings and drawn to its many mysteries. There are ways that parents can keep this curiosity and hunger for learning alive, even in cases in which schools or social pressures seem to dampen these tendencies.

BETWEEN HOME AND THE OUTSIDE WORLD: "GIFTED PROGRAMS" BY PARENTS

Parents often ask what they can do for their gifted children in a time of reduced or eliminated funding for gifted education. I tell them that there is a "gifted program" waiting to happen in their own homes and communities. A useful start is to couple at-home explorations of children's interests with related activities outside of the home. Gifted learners love discovering links between new dinosaur facts they've learned at home and the full-scale skeletons in a field museum, or between their knowledge of constellations and the local planetarium where they can search for them in a winter sky. Helping gifted learners to think of questions they want to answer or ideas they want to test makes the experience more inquiry-based, active, and far more meaningful.

Through online searches and networking, parents can find resources focused on specific fields—literature, music, the arts, science, technology, nature study, and more. In recent years, workshops in STEM and STEAM (science, technology, engineering, art, and math) have proliferated across the country, encouraging children to integrate subjects and materials—an engineering project with metal sculpturing, for instance. The Maker Movement, which owes its inventiveness and momentum to the innovative do-it-yourselfers, technological developments, and popular Maker Faire events, has led children away from an excessive use of screens to a more creative, hands-on mode of tinkering, designing, crafting, and engineering. As professionals and enthusiasts share their project ideas and successes online, parents today can often find even the most obscure interest represented at a Makerspace or STEAM event in learning centers, libraries, museums, and other local places.

EXHIBITS (MUSEUMS, AQUARIUMS, OBSERVATORIES)

Museums, aquariums, and planetariums offer a host of youth events that would appeal to young gifted learners. To make the most of a museum trip, parents can select and research a few exhibits. By limiting the number of exhibits, children can take their time, observe closely, ask questions, and write/draw/design their responses to what they've learned. If live rain forest frogs have arrived at the aquarium, for example, find out what frogs will be featured and what events or workshops the institution offers. Young learners are highly inquisitive beings and will relish the chance to pose questions: "Why do most of these frogs live in trees? Why are they more colorful than the ones I see where we live? How did the monkey frog get its name?" Whether parents are preparing for a visit to the art museum, the field museum, or a planetarium, children connect to the experience more deeply if they've had a chance to learn enough beforehand to feel curious—whether it's a cubist painting, a constellation, or an amphibian. Books from the library, family discussions, and online searches bring mysteries for young children to investigate at exhibits and then explore later—through writing, drawing, designing, modeling, and building.

NATURE ADVENTURES

The natural world offers some of the richest resources for young gifted children, whether they be on a distant mountain or in a forest near home. American cities and towns conceal many pockets of nature where young children can experience the wonder of growing things and moving creatures. Local organizations and Internet searches provide leads for outdoor adventures and workshops. Consider possibilities such as these:

» Botanical gardens or ecology centers frequently offer activities for young children, sometimes in the form of spring or summer camps that introduce art, conservation, birding, and botany. Ecology centers also train volunteers to assist in special efforts to improve habitats by pulling up invasive species and planting native plants. Children learn about local flora and fauna, soil types, and pollinators; they sketch or paint their findings to design creative guidebooks.

» Nature walks allow children to use all of their senses, develop observation, listen for bird songs and calls, learn how to walk respectfully in a wild place, look for plant and animal species, and use binoculars. Families can find free apps at the Cornell Lab of Ornithology (http://www.birds.cornell.edu/k12) that support children's knowledge and identification skills, and give them a chance to contribute to the Lab's database and participate as "citizen scientists."

» Wildlife rehabilitation centers provide unique opportunities for young children who love animals and wish to volunteer. Parents can find these centers online and consult their local Audubon organizations for information. Learning how to work responsibly with wildlife thrills young children with a gift for this kind of work.

COMMUNITY RESOURCES

Parents who cannot easily take their children far from home can still find valuable resources in their immediate community. Clubs of various kinds, workshops, and open studios often meet in local spaces—some in private homes and churches—offering free or moderately priced classes. Here are some examples of valuable community resources:

» **Libraries.** Having a relationship with the local library is vital for young gifted children, most of whom love words and books of all kinds. I always encourage parents to go to a library event where young children can experience the social and theatrical process of reading. A story or poem comes alive when shared and performed. Try to have a reading period every day or at specific times in the week and use library visits to explore a variety of genres, including books that children might not ordinarily pick up: poetry, stories, nonfiction, humor, and biographies. Do oral readings together to share poems, humorous stories, and writings with wordplay they can understand and enjoy. Explore other library offerings: parent-child book clubs; STEAM Lab; workshops in coding, robotics, arts and crafts; LEGO club; and chess programs.

» **Studios.** Explore dance, art, and music studios. Look for innovative programs that include more than formal instruction. Young talented children need technique, but many need creative experiences as well. If the budget is tight, inquire about scholarships and other art opportunities in the area. Network with other parents to see what local families are doing and what sorts of informal talent support might exist in the neighborhood.

» **Community centers.** The advantage of community centers is the variety of offerings. If a young child is particularly skilled in a subject or talent area, parents can sometimes negotiate for a higher level class. In some cases, teachers can accommodate different levels because of an open classroom format. In Makerspaces or STEAM workshops, children can progress at their own pace and level, while receiving instruction and support from professionals and assistants.

For young people with limited resources, community programs are havens for discovering new talents.

THE HOME: A PLACE FOR
CURIOSITY AND WONDER

In my experience with families, I've noticed that parents who
are curious about many things and follow their passions in life foster these same qualities in their children. Real learning begins with
curiosity and a deep hunger to know. Young gifted children may have
different interests from their parents, but they often discover these
interests in a home in which exploring the world around them is a
way of life. E. Paul Torrance (2002) emphasized the importance of
not being "afraid to fall in love with something."

A home environment that reflects and supports young children's
interests is as important as the places parents take their children.
Consider some of these questions:

» Are there places where your children can work on something they love—quietly, away from electronic noise?

» Do they have reading places/reading times?

» Do your children have sufficient supplies or the right kind
of supplies to explore their interests or discover new ones?

» Are there areas where the family can keep and use instruments like microscopes and binoculars or where they can
perform simple tests or experiments?

» Are there art materials and other odds and ends (e.g., bottle
tops, colored wire, and other "found" objects) that children
can use to create things?

Having a home that embraces different family interests—a
makeshift laboratory for the budding scientist, an art-making place,
a quiet nook for reading and writing—gives young children joy in
expanding their mastery and skill. It also means that they can begin
to guide their own learning, increase their competence in planning
and completing projects, and achieve goals that matter to them.

A FINAL NOTE

Expanding the world of young gifted children through at-home learning and related experiences beyond the home is immensely strengthening. Open exploration gives them confidence and resiliency as active learners. For parents, this kind of enrichment offers proof and hope that the confining circumstances of school or society cannot stifle their children's curiosity or stop them from discovering new interests and embarking on their own adventures.

REFLECTION QUESTIONS

1. How have online resources changed the way parents seek new opportunities for their young gifted children?
2. How can parents collaborate more with each other to design new learning opportunities for their children?
3. What sorts of at-home materials and activities help prepare gifted young children for events/classes/workshops in different fields (e.g., technology, arts, ecology, literacy, etc.)?
4. What long-term steps can parents take to enrich their children's learning and provide the creative spaces children need to develop specific talent areas?

REFERENCE

Torrance, E. P. (2002). *The manifesto: A guide to developing a creative career*. Westport, CT: Ablex.

CHAPTER 6

THE IMPORTANCE OF PARENT INTUITION AND OBSERVATION IN RECOGNIZING HIGHLY CREATIVE YOUNG CHILDREN

by Kathryn P. Haydon

In my work with hundreds of families, I have observed one common truth: Parents are the experts on their own children, especially when it comes to giftedness. Parents often observe certain characteristics in their children and view them as positive traits until those same characteristics are regarded negatively in school. Although there may be outside pressure not to accept a "gifted" or "highly creative" label, sometimes the label is the one thing that can save a child from being misinterpreted and misidentified at home and at school.

RECOGNIZING THE HIGHLY CREATIVE CHILD

Sometimes it's not easy for highly creative children to "comply" with a regular curriculum, even at the preschool age. They are wired to explore, experiment, build, imagine, and create. If forced at a young age into a diet heavy on rote learning and directed work, they may struggle. It's not that these children can't do the work; it's that the work does not engage their depth of thinking, ability to make connections, and need to contribute original ideas. Their needs are so much more complex than what a traditional classroom can meet, especially if they are inclined toward a self-driven pursuit of knowledge. See Table 6.1 for a list of characteristics of these highly creative thinkers.

TABLE 6.1
CHARACTERISTICS OF HIGHLY CREATIVE THINKERS
(DAVIS, 2004; HAYDON & HARVEY, 2015)

Creative Strength	Negative Interpretation
Original	Disobedient; divergent
Curious inquiry	Challenges authority; goes off on his or her own; busy; asks too many questions
Sense of humor	Immature; disruptive; class clown
Energetic	Fidgets; hyperactive; disobedient; inattentive
Intense thinker	Daydreams; spaces out; slow with rote work; slow or forgetful with daily tasks such as getting ready; talks to self
Open-minded	Indecisive; stops work in the middle to move on to something else
Loves a challenge	Complicated; resists "easy" or rote work; makes simple things harder than they "need" to be; distracted when doing rote work; wastes time
Needs to be alone	Not always with the group; antisocial; moody; plays alone; poor social skills
Sensitive	Needy; clingy; insecure
Inventive	Strange; nonconforming; doesn't do assignments the "right" way

CREATIVE TRAITS IN ACTION

Talia's story shows the traits of a highly creative preschooler in action. In general, Talia was a sweet, helpful, and independent yet generally obedient 3-year-old. She had a beautiful personality, loved to share her insightful thoughts with adults, had a rich imagination that usually involved her stuffed animals, and was quite helpful around the house. She loved to explore and she learned effectively when she pursued her interests. For example, she taught herself to read at age 2, among many other things.

Talia had strong ideas about what she wanted to explore. She resisted being confined to small spaces, and most often only the vast variety and peace of the outdoors could fully engage and calm her. She didn't want to do things other kids were doing, and sometimes her mother despaired at group events when she left the group activity to do her own thing.

She created new uses for toys or skipped over the toys to make original use of their shipping boxes instead. With careful observation, however, it was clear that every activity that Talia pursued was embedded within a discovery process, an opportunity for deep exploration.

She vehemently resisted prescriptive—or pre-scripted—activities. For example, if the art project in preschool was to glue eyes, nose, and mouth onto a page in a certain way to create a monster, she wouldn't do it. That was too prescriptive. But if the teacher provided red, yellow, and blue paints with brushes and paper, she would eagerly experiment with abstract markings, watching how colors mixed and lines formed on the canvas. Every move she made demonstrated a hunger for knowledge and a deep desire to integrate that knowledge through her own imagination and power to originate.

Talia had one year of preschool under her belt in a nurturing classroom with a veteran teacher who gave the children plenty of freedom to explore, create, and direct their own learning. The following year, she matriculated to the next class, and teachers began to say that she had serious behavior problems. She was not following directions, would run out of the classroom and ask to go home, and wasn't participating in the lessons on colors, numbers, and letters.

Her teachers knew that Talia had taught herself to read a year earlier, was already reading *Magic Tree House* chapter books independently, could write, and had an extensive knowledge of geography, including all of the U.S. states and capitals. However, they would approach her parents at drop-off and say, "Talia did not participate in the letter lesson today." Or, they would share "good" news: "Talia learned something today along with all of the other children. She didn't know the word *dog* and learned to read it." (To please the teachers, Talia had pretended not to know the word *dog*, although it was one of her favorite words to write at home.)

The school suggested bringing in a behavior specialist to evaluate Talia because she was running out of the classroom and didn't follow directions. Her parents met with the teachers and shared their experiences: Talia was a highly creative, rapid, self-taught learner, and didn't exhibit behavior problems at home.

It was then that the parents realized that, based on her learning style, a traditional preschool or kindergarten might not be the right fit for Talia. They felt that it would be cruel to both teacher and student for her to sit through hours of learning to read, write, and do basic math when she had already learned these skills on her own at an early age. Soon, they had Talia take an IQ test with a psychologist who had extensive experience with gifted children, and she fell within the profoundly gifted range.

For a profoundly creative thinker such as Talia, rote academic work often does not engage learning. It can sometimes do more harm than good, forcing a child to numb her mind in order to comply with repetitive tasks. A creative learning setting, with ample freedom to explore, may be a better environment that won't choke creative pursuits or a love of learning (Goertzel, Goertzel, Goertzel, & Hansen, 2004). Talia's parents worked hard to find the right setting that year, and they continued to seek out educational settings that valued Talia's intrinsic motivation to learn deeply.

ANALYSIS

In analyzing Talia's case, one of the most important factors was that her parents understood her creative traits—originality, imagination, curiosity, and energy—and they viewed these *as strengths*. They actively looked for ways to support these characteristics as part of Talia's identity, rather than to make her shed them in order to follow a typical, prescribed path.

For parents, an alternative route to education is not an easy road to take, but it's a road that supports the child in the long term. Sometimes unique educational options require great sacrifice—socially, financially, or career-wise. But when children don't fit into a traditional setting, they need a firm foundation from which to grow and a healthy self-confidence that helps them to accept themselves and feel confident in their own skin.

In hindsight, Talia's original classroom could have become a place where she thrived, even with her different rate of development. The first step would have been a willingness on the part of the teachers to acknowledge the needs of the individual child. The second step would have been the flexibility to meet Talia where she was, even if her learning style and abilities seemed out of sync with the standardized program. This might have included structuring the classroom differently, with more independent centers and theme-based explorations, exempting Talia from lessons in content areas in which she demonstrated mastery, and acknowledging creative strengths as positive traits to be nurtured rather than negative traits to be controlled.

CONCLUSION: FORTITUDE AND OPENNESS

Open, flowing communication between home and school is absolutely essential to meet the unique needs of creative learners. Therefore, each member of the child's learning team must be an active, open-minded, and willing collaborator.

Teachers should try to avoid making generalized assumptions. They are in a strong position to unlock the potential of their gifted and creative students, but must be open and willing to evaluate the suitability of their classroom practices for students. Parents need to know their children, understand their strengths, and have the fortitude to stand by these strengths even when the characteristics are called deficits by others.

There is tremendous pressure today for kids to conform, academically and socially. For gifted, creative kids, this is often not possible or prudent. Highly creative children are unique, and the only way for them to thrive long-term is for those around them to accept their uniqueness. They will still need to do what is required to be successful, but they may need different routes to get there.

REFLECTION QUESTIONS

1. Looking at Table 6.1, what are all of the creative strengths that your child exhibits?
2. Out of all of his or her creative strengths, which one shines the brightest at home?
3. Are any of these creative strengths subject to a negative interpretation in other settings, like at school or in after-school classes?
4. What are the characteristics of these settings that seem to change a strength into a challenge? Is it the structure of the environment . . . the processes and practices . . . the attitudes of the other people involved?

5. What might be changed to bring out your child's creative strengths in these settings?

REFERENCES

Davis, G. A. (2004). *Creativity is forever* (5th ed.). Dubuque, IA: Kendall Hunt.

Goertzel, V., Goertzel, M. G., Goertzel, T. G., & Hansen, A. M. W. (2004). *Cradles of eminence: Childhoods of more than 700 famous men and women* (2nd ed.). Scottsdale, AZ: Great Potential Press.

Haydon, K. P., & Harvey, J. (2015). *Creativity for everybody.* New York, NY: Sparkitivity.

CHAPTER 7

DEVELOPING THE YOUNG GIFTED CHILD'S MATHEMATICAL MIND

by Carol Fisher

When people talk about mathematics, they frequently refer to the computational aspects of mathematics. Those rooted in innumeracy will easily say, "I can't balance my checkbook" or "I can never figure the tip." Parents of gifted children often say, "My 5-year-old can multiply," "My 4-year-old can add numbers in her head," and "My second grader is doing fourth-grade math."

Schools seem firmly rooted in the emphasis on computational mastery and seldom seem to have time to develop other areas of mathematical thinking, such as real-world problem solving and the application of mathematical concepts. All too often, children seem to do well in math in the early grades because they easily memorize the facts and the algorithms needed for computation.

However, merely learning arithmetic algorithms is not sufficient preparation for solving real-world problems. Even computational situations such as balancing a checkbook and figuring a tip are grounded in understanding the application of the computation. In the real world, you are rarely given all of the information you need, requiring data collection from a variety of resources. There are usually several viable strategies to approaching the problem. Life has no answer key.

MATH IN DAILY ROUTINES

Luckily, there are opportunities for young children to practice mathematical thinking at home every day. References to time, for example, lend themselves to real-life problem solving and often take the form of typical phrases: "You have one more minute," "We are leaving at 8:00 for school," or "It takes 45 minutes to get to Grandma's house." There is more to the subject of time than being able to successfully read a digital or analog timepiece.

What other daily routines can be discussed mathematically? Sequencing and patterns are the foundations of algebraic thinking. Recipes, anything involving money, weather, sports statistics, and shopping, whether at the grocery or toy store, provide parents with many opportunities to share mathematics with their children.

BUILDING MATERIALS

Recent studies (e.g., Stannard, Wolfgang, Jones, & Phelps, 2001) confirm that children who actively play with blocks do better when they attempt higher mathematics, such as algebra and calculus. Geometry concepts, such as balance, visual spatiality, and symmetry, are embedded in blocks.

The beautiful thing about building materials is that you can engage in mathematical discourse with your child: "What are you making? How did you make this part hang over the section below? How did you decide which blocks to use?" As children begin to use exploded view drawings—directions that show how parts should be assembled—parents' questions can continue to elicit mathematical discourse. Questions can promote solution justification, strategy formation, pattern recognition, conjecture formation, and perseverance.

In addition to LEGO bricks and K'nex, other building sets designed to further mathematical thinking include the following.

FOR AGES 3, 4, AND UP

> » Geoblocks: hardwood blocks in an array of metric sizes and pattern blocks, including cubes, rectangular prisms, and triangular prisms
> » GoldieBlox: construction sets designed to introduce young girls to engineering with wheels, axles, hinges, levers, pulleys, and gears
> » KEVA Planks: structures built by stacking planks with no glue or connectors

» Magformers: 3-D structures created with magnetic 2-D pieces

» Squigz: colorful, flexible "suction" construction parts that stick to each other and any flat, nonporous surface

» Colorful Shape Tetris Montessori Geometry Building Block Toy: wooden peg board with shapes to arrange in a variety of ways on the pegs

FOR AGES 5 AND UP

» Q-Ba-Maze: translucent cubes to set up complex marble runs

» ZomeTool: colored struts and balls/nodes inspired by Buckminster Fuller's dome geometry

PUZZLES

Like building materials, puzzles develop spatial visualization, perseverance, and, in many cases, creativity. In fact, research (Jirout & Newcombe, 2015) has found that children who play with puzzles between 26 and 46 months of age have better spatial skills when assessed at 54 months of age. And, early puzzle play has been found to lay the groundwork for future STEM (science, technology, engineering, and math) abilities.

A variety of other puzzles with roots in two-dimensional and three-dimensional geometry also challenge mathematical thinking. These include Fractiles, Pentominoes, tangrams, Tessel-Gons, Ball of Whacks, X-Ball, Y-Ball, star ball, and rhombi.

FAMILY GAME NIGHTS

Whether children are conscious of it or not, game playing involves analyzing, predicting, decision making, and evaluation. Even a simple game of tic-tac-toe or checkers involves a great deal of strategy if you wish to be successful. The best games maintain interest and strategically challenge both the child and the parent (or any other family members who wish to play). During game play, parents can also stimulate the child's mathematical thinking by asking open-ended questions such as "Why?" and "How?"

Intriguing games that incorporate mathematical and spatial concepts include the following.

FOR AGES 3 AND UP

» *Enchanted Forest*: an adventure to be the first to tell the king where the fairy tale treasures are hidden
» *Labyrinth*: a board game with continually shifting walls that make it challenging to get the treasures
» *Rivers, Roads & Rails*: an ever-changing matching game that creates intricate networks for transportation
» *Robot Face Race*: a game with the goal of finding the one robot that matches the particular attributes rolled (color of face, eyes, nose, and mouth) before one's opponent
» *Spot It!*: a game that uses visual perception to find the one matching image on two cards

FOR AGES 8 AND UP

» *Logic Dots*: challenges players to use deductive reasoning to find the "Golden Dot."
» *Tic Tac Two*: a challenging strategy game in which players play a piece or move the grid
» *Otrio*: looks like tic-tac-toe but is far more complex
» *Prime Climb*: built on arithmetic and prime numbers, requiring strategies so opponents don't beat players to 101
» *Dr. Eureka*: speed logic game in which players race to solve the formula by moving molecules from tube to tube without touching them
» *Rock Me Archimedes*: combines balance with strategy
» *Newton*: a twist on a familiar concept (the game *Connect 4*), but the colors in the columns are constantly moving
» *Suspend*: hand-eye coordination works in conjunction with strategy for an exciting balancing game

No matter what puzzles parents choose, from pots and pans to tessellation puzzles, from simple counting books to those examining fractals and googols, from a deck of cards to complex, three-dimensional challenges, parents' interactions with their children are key.

In today's school environment, it's even more critical than ever for parents to provide support for mathematical thinking. Parents should play with their children when they are young, letting the children guide the exploration. As children get older, parents should encourage more independent play but can still interact with their children by asking questions, providing feedback, or playing games with them.

INCORPORATE MATH INTO READING TIME!

Reading a bedtime story is a common practice in many households. Why not incorporate math literature into reading time? Children's literature is an effective tool for mathematics instruction because it (Burns, 2019):

» incorporates stories into the teaching and learning of mathematics
» introduces math concepts and contexts in a motivating manner
» acts as a source for generating problems and building problem solving skills
» helps build a conceptual understanding of math skills through illustrations (para. 2)

These books provide encounters with mathematical concepts and vocabulary in the context of something familiar—a story.

MATH CONCEPTS
Books for younger children:
- » *The Very Hungry Caterpillar, 1, 2, 3, to the Zoo, 10 Little Rubber Ducks, Rooster's Off to See the World,* and *The Secret Birthday Message* by Eric Carle
- » *Anno's Counting Book* by Mitsumasa Anno
- » *Shape Up!: Fun With Triangles and Other Polygons, If You Were an Inch or a Centimeter,* and *You Can, Toucan, Math* by David Adler
- » *Actual Size* and *Biggest, Strongest, Fastest* by Steve Jenkins
- » *Ten Little Caterpillars* by Bill Martin Jr.

Books for ages 6 and up:
- » *A Cloak for the Dreamer* by Aileen Friedman
- » *How Do You Lift a Lion?, Is a Blue Whale the Biggest Thing There Is?,* and *What's Faster Than a Speeding Cheetah?* by Robert E. Wells
- » *Sea Squares* and *Wild Fibonacci: Nature's Secret Code Revealed* by Joy N. Hulme
- » *The Greedy Triangle, How Many Feet? How Many Tails?: A Book of Math Riddles,* and *Spaghetti and Meatballs for All* by Marilyn Burns
- » *Edgar Allan Poe's Pies: Math Puzzles in Classic Poems* by J. Patrick Lewis
- » *Bees, Snails, and Peacock Tails* by Betsy Franco
- » *How Tall, How Short, How Far Away* by David A. Adler

Books for ages 8 and up:
- » *G Is for Googol: A Math Alphabet, If You Hopped Like a Frog, Millions to Measure,* and *On Beyond a Million* by David M. Schwartz
- » *The Book of Think: Or How to Solve a Problem Twice Your Size, The I Hate Mathematics! Book, Math for Smarty Pants,* and *The $1.00 Word Riddle Book* by Marilyn Burns
- » *The Adventures of Penrose the Mathematical Cat, Fractals, Googols, and Other Mathematical Tales, Math for Kids and Other People Too!, Math Stuff,* and *Math Talk: Mathematical Ideas in Poems for Two Voices* by Theoni Pappas

» *The Boy Who Reversed Himself* by William Sleator
» *The Number Devil: A Mathematical Adventure* by Hans Magnus Enzensberger
» *Coincidences, Chaos, and All That Math Jazz: Making Light of Weighty Ideas* by Edward B. Burger
» *The Rabbit Problem* by Emily Gravett
» *The Math Instinct: Why You're a Mathematical Genius (Along With Lobster, Birds, Cats, and Dogs)* by Keith Devlin

CULTURAL TALES

Books for younger children:
» *Two Ways to Count to Ten: A Liberian Folk Tale* by Ruby Dee
» *My Granny Went to Market: A Round-the-World Counting Rhyme* by Stella Blackstone
» *Paper Crane* by Molly Bang

Books for ages 8 and up:
» *The King's Chessboard* by David Birch
» *One Grain of Rice: A Mathematic Folktale* by Demi
» *Amelia to Zora: Twenty-Six Women Who Changed the World* by Cynthia Chin-Lee
» *Sweet Clara and the Freedom Quilt* by Deborah Hopkinson
» *The Man Who Counted: A Collection of Mathematical Adventures* by Malba Tahan
» *The Toothpaste Millionaire* by Jean Merrill
» *Hidden Figures: The American Dream and the Untold Story of the Black Women Mathematicians Who Helped Win the Space Race* by Margot Lee Shetterly

REFLECTION QUESTIONS

1. Why is it important for children to develop mathematical thinking skills beyond computation?
2. How can you incorporate already learned computational skills into mathematical problem solving?
3. What are some thoughtful mathematics questions you might ask children during daily routines?
4. How do games support mathematical thinking?

5. How can the inclusion of math literature introduce or extend concepts and provide contexts for mathematical thinking skills?

REFERENCES

Burns, M. (2019). *Integrating math and language arts.* Retrieved from http://teacher.scholastic.com/reading/bestpractices/math.htm

Jirout, J. J., & Newcombe, N. S. (2015). Building blocks for developing spatial skills: Evidence from a large, representative U.S. sample. *Psychological Science, 26,* 302–310.

Stannard, L., Wolfgang, C. H., Jones, I., & Phelps, P. (2001). A longitudinal study of the predictive relations among construction play and mathematical achievement. *Early Child Development and Care, 167,* 115–125.

CHAPTER 8

SOCIAL-EMOTIONAL CHARACTERISTICS OF YOUNG GIFTED CHILDREN

by Ellen Honeck

There are a variety of definitions related to giftedness. Recognizing that the definitions vary by affiliation, school, and state, this chapter focuses specifically on a definition related to the whole person. Annemarie Roeper (1982) defined giftedness as "a greater awareness, a greater sensitivity, and a greater ability to understand and to transform perceptions into intellectual and emotional experiences" (p. 21).

Gifted children have a variety of identifying characteristics. These characteristics are present across cognitive and affective domains and manifest themselves differently among individuals. The focus of the following characteristics is the social-emotional aspect of young gifted children, ages 3–8 (see Table 8.1).

Children, particularly young children, demonstrate characteristics of giftedness in many different ways. These characteristics manifest based on gender, experiences, cultural identity, personal passions and interests, and family or community.

Gifted children develop asynchronously, meaning some areas are more advanced than others and do not develop at the same time (e.g., a child advanced in number sense may be average or below average in literacy skills). This asynchrony is present in young gifted children and can pose challenges when addressing social-emotional characteristics. A child may have an in-depth conversation about dinosaurs with an adult and then turn around and hit a classmate for not sharing a toy. Asynchrony adds another dimension for building a repertoire of strategies in working with young gifted children.

TABLE 8.1
SOCIAL-EMOTIONAL CHARACTERISTICS

Characteristics	Possible Manifestations of Characteristic
High degree of sensitivity and empathy	Knows what everyone else is doing and feeling; understands the depth of issues
Perfectionism	May not finish a project because it doesn't look as good as the child envisions; may shut down; becomes frustrated; feels unsuccessful
Excellent/keen sense of humor	Has the ability to pick up on adult humor at an early age; understands the use of puns; plays with language
Feeling of being different	Playmates may be older peers; struggles to find chronological peers; recognizes that he or she doesn't "fit in"
Intensity	May be focused on learning everything there is to learn about a topic; may come across as being serious
Heightened sensory awareness	May be sensitive to touch, sounds, sights, and smells, which may result in only wearing clothes with no tags and needing a quiet environment; has sensory overload when a vast arrays of colors or items are used; feels ill when walking by a department store perfume counter or a food court at the mall
Idealism	Wants everyone to get along; believes no problem is too big, and there is a solution; believes everything can be worked out
Sense of justice	Thinks each person should be treated equally
Advanced levels of moral judgment	Focuses on family or community even though peers may still be focused on self
High expectations of self and others	Expects everyone to live up to behavior guidelines
Early development of inner locus of control	Participates in activities for him- or herself, not others; believes external rewards don't matter
Awareness of society and global community	Understands his or her place in a larger community and world

Note. Table adapted from multiple sources (Johnsen, 2018; Smutny & von Fremd, 2009; Van Tassel-Baska & Baska, 2019).

Parents are ideally suited to address their child's exhibited characteristics and develop strategies that support him or her. As children grow, their needs change and strategies must be modified or adapted. As experts in their own children's giftedness, parents need to work with teachers and caregivers to determine what techniques work best at various stages of development.

There are a few strategies that are universally applied when addressing social-emotional characteristics of gifted children. Cross (2018) provided the following strategies:

» teaching the child to anticipate and understand how he or she reacts to events and situations;

» providing techniques and strategies to either change the reaction or deal with his or her reaction;

» guiding the child in dealing with the difficulties and as he or she develops strategies; and

» communicating with teachers and other caregivers to understand the child and the goals for the child.

By using a variety of strategies to meet the social and emotional needs of the child, there is better chance of him or her developing appropriate coping skills.

CHILDREN YOU MAY KNOW

HIGH DEGREE OF SENSITIVITY

Brian, age 7, has always been a sensitive child. He demonstrates genuine care for his peers and adults and is considered a friend by all of his classmates. He has a well-developed sense of right and wrong. When Brian does something "wrong," he immediately internalizes his "failure." Any sign of a raised voice or disappointment from an adult leads him to find a corner of the room, cover his face, cry, and shut himself off from others. This is difficult for the adults who want to discuss the situation with him or ask for reasons behind the inappropriate behavior. Sometimes he becomes so upset that he refuses to listen, cooperate, or engage, resulting in the appearance of sullen refusal to deal with the consequences of his actions.

Brian displays a variety of characteristics but most prominently a high degree of sensitivity and empathy, high expectations of self and others, an inner locus of control (i.e., the belief that his choices control his abilities and the outcome of a situation), and perfectionism related to behavior and idealism. At-home strategies include talking to Brian with a soft voice, providing time to allow him to calm down, and having him identify what he did "wrong." Brian needs the adults in his life to have a great deal of patience, to provide an identified space for him to go to so that he can spend the time he needs to calm himself down, and to have an awareness that he needs some time alone (Clark, 2013). Discussion can happen after he has calmed down, focusing on his behavior and future choices (Fonseca, 2016).

Brian's teachers need to understand how sensitivity translates to certain behaviors. Providing teachers with this information helps them to recognize that the behavior is the internalized consequences of the unacceptable behavior rather than defiance toward adults.

At school, Brian's teachers must be patient and build a trusting relationship with him. When an incident does happen, a quiet, private place to talk is best. Brian needs reinforcement that it was his behavior that was unacceptable and that the teacher still likes him. Brian thrives on trusting relationships, and it is important that these develop with the adults in his life.

AWARENESS OF SOCIETY AND THE GLOBAL COMMUNITY

Samantha, age 8, cannot be in the room when a news story is on the television or radio. She becomes consumed with the problems presented in the stories and tries to develop solutions to complex, sometimes inexplicable issues. Her immediate response is a deeply felt empathy that quickly becomes paralyzing. The level of sadness is difficult for her to deal with, and she struggles to continue with her daily routines. Samantha becomes withdrawn and frightened, feeling powerless in an out-of-control world.

Samantha displays an awareness of society and global community, advanced levels of moral judgment, a high degree of sensitivity and empathy, idealism, a sense of justice, and intensity. At home, if possible, her parents should avoid media outlets and discussions about current events while she is around. However, it is important for Samantha to develop an understanding that bad things happen in the world that she has no control over. Events and information need to be discussed in consumable amounts or through books with a focus on positive, age-appropriate ways that she can help (Halsted, 2009). Community service projects will provide strategies or solutions for helping her feel that she can contribute to a cause. Projects need to be age-appropriate and may include making sympathy cards for victims and thank-you cards for first responders; gathering supplies for a disaster drive; making blankets, hats, or scarves; or raising money for an organization (Kaye, 2010).

In school, teachers need to be aware of Samantha's deep response to issues. When issues arise in the classroom, she can be given the opportunity to remove herself from the discussion. Using journals can provide Samantha with an outlet for discussing issues or concerns as well as provide the teacher insights into her thinking (Galbraith & Delisle, 2015). Class service-learning projects provide her with the ability to contribute to an organization and a way to focus on making a difference. Communication with teachers and other adults in her life will be beneficial in her development of additional personal strategies.

HEIGHTENED SENSORY AWARENESS

Genell, age 4, is extremely sensitive to her environment. She is aware of every color, sound, and scent within the classroom. She was in the gym at school one day when the fire alarm went off for a routine drill. She was so affected by the sensory overload that she refused to return to the gym at the conclusion of the drill. For several months after the incident, Genell became physically ill upon entering the gym.

Genell has a heightened sensory awareness, intensity, and an inner locus of control. At home, Genell does best in an environment without a variety of stimuli and needs some quiet time in an environment that works for her. Discussion of loud noises and the purposes of the sounds will help Genell with the recognition of the importance of the sounds. Her parents can talk with Genell to find out what was happening at the time the alarm went off: Was there something specific that would have helped her? What was she thinking when she walked back into the gym? Recognizing the specifics of the incident will help Genell and her parents develop strategies for dealing with future events.

At school, teachers need to understand that this was a traumatizing event. In the future when there is a scheduled drill, someone can remove Genell from the building prior to the alarm going off or warn her that it is coming, and keep the communication with her parents open. Patience is critical in working with Genell. Providing encouragement while she is given time to acclimate herself to the gym will be needed (Silverman, 2000). Before participating fully in the class, she may need to stand in the doorway or enter the gym for increasing amounts of time. This process may take a couple of days to months. Adults need to be patient with her and recognize that she experienced a traumatic event and needs guidance and support in addressing this situation.

SUMMARY

Parents of gifted children act as guides, supports, inspirations, and advocates for them. Manifestations of giftedness in young children are often puzzling: their responses seem amplified, their interests all-consuming, and their needs insatiable. At other times, they may be delightfully engaged and brimming with enthusiasm. Without a guide or manual for such situations, parents sometimes feel as if they are on an uncharted course. With the ideas and strategies discussed in this chapter, parents, caregivers, and teachers can help children steer their social and emotional issues successfully.

REFLECTION QUESTIONS

1. What social-emotional characteristics resonate with you and children you know?
2. Select a recommendation or strategy that you can apply to your child or a child you work with. Discuss how you would implement it within your setting.
3. Reflect on your perspectives related to the social-emotional characteristics in Table 8.1. Are there elements that reinforced your thinking, changes you need to make in your thinking, or topics you want to learn more about?

REFERENCES

Clark, B. (2013). *Growing up gifted: Developing the potential of children at home and at school* (8th ed.). Pearson.

Cross, T. L. (2018). *On the social and emotional lives of gifted children* (5th ed.). Waco, TX: Prufrock Press.

Fonseca, C. (2016). *Emotional intensity in gifted students: Helping kids cope with explosive feelings* (2nd ed.). Waco, TX: Prufrock Press.

Halsted, J. (2009). *Some of my best friends are books: Guiding gifted readers* (3rd ed.). Scottsdale, AZ: Great Potential Press.

Johnsen, S. K. (Ed.). (2018). *Identifying gifted students: A practical guide* (3rd ed). Waco, TX: Prufrock Press.

Kaye, C. (2010). *The complete guide to service learning: Proven, practical ways to engage students in civic responsibility, academic curriculum, and social action* (2nd ed.). Minneapolis, MN: Free Spirit.

Galbraith, J., & Delisle, J. (2015). *When gifted kids don't have all of the answers: How to meet their social and emotional needs.* Minneapolis, MN: Free Spirit.

Roeper, A. (1982). How the gifted cope with their emotions. *Roeper Review, 5*(2), 21–24.

Silverman, L. K. (Ed.). (2000). *Counseling the gifted and talented.* Denver, CO: Love.

Smutny, J. (2001). *Stand up for your gifted child: How to make the most of kids' strengths at school and at home.* Minneapolis, MN: Free Spirit.

Smutny, J., & von Fremd, S. E. (2009). *Igniting creativity in gifted learners, K–6: Strategies for every teacher.* Thousand Oaks, CA: Corwin Press.

VanTassel-Baska, J., & Baska, A. (2019). *Curriculum planning and instructional design for gifted learners* (3rd ed.). Waco, TX: Prufrock Press.

CHAPTER 9

WHAT EVERY PARENT AND EARLY CHILDHOOD EDUCATOR SHOULD KNOW ABOUT YOUNG HIGH-ABILITY LEARNERS

by Robin M. Schader

See that little girl on the playground, over by the edge of the grass, all by herself? She's looking down at the ground, scratching in the dirt with a small branch, not engaged with the rest of the class. Maybe she's yours? When the teacher rings the chime to come back inside, she has to go over and touch the girl's arm to get her attention. Without glancing up, the girl silently shakes her head, not ready to join the group.

What about the eager boy bouncing up and down on his chair, throwing his arms in the air, begging to answer every question? His responses are so atypical that often his classmates (and sometimes the adults, as well) don't understand his answers could be correct. To the question "What is a ceiling?", he might happily squeal, "It seals up a room!" At home, he rarely does what his mother asks him to do, especially in the way his mother has asked that it be done. If corrected, he stubbornly continues doing it his way. This child's unusual train of thought can confuse and disrupt the best of plans.

Are you familiar with the *Sesame Street* song that starts with "One of these things is not like the other; one of these things just doesn't belong"? The words of the song ask the listener to look at a group of objects and, as part of the game, explain what it is that makes one thing different from the rest. Whether or not it's conscious, parents, caregivers, and teachers do the same exercise with children, looking for indicators that a child is not "fitting in" with peers.

Differences can be apparent in a wide variety of areas; however, in most cases, teachers and parents are looking for problems or learning difficulties that need to be addressed because the earlier a problem is discovered and diagnosed, the more likely an intervention or remediation will be successful.

Interestingly—and importantly—the same is true for exceptional abilities: The earlier they are noticed, encouraged, and supported, the more likely those abilities will develop into special talents or skills. Yet, especially in young children, high abilities and how to nurture them are rarely a topic of conversation among parents and educators, which means that the very differences that can be clues to potential talents may not be appropriately recognized and understood.

WHY HIGH ABILITIES CAN BE MISSED

Early signs of high potential can go unseen simply because, in the hustle and bustle of daily life, we aren't looking for them. The earliest indicators may be small, they may not be recognized, and they may be misunderstood. When observing differences, we tend to explain them in familiar terms. For example, when a young child is cranky and out of control in the afternoon, we often go through a mental checklist of what could be wrong. Because of habit, we may not recognize the child's frustration in trying to figure out a new, intriguing, but challenging puzzle. If we look past the common causes (e.g., hungry, wet, tired) and observe what's really happening (attempting a new puzzle), we have an opportunity to help the child "stay in the struggle" and problem solve, and then cheer on the success.

THE EARLIEST INDICATORS MAY BE SMALL

Yes, there are children who begin to read at the age of 3, who have prodigious memories and can name all of the countries and capitals in the world, or who play the piano and compose pieces when very young. It's true these special gifts do need nurturing and should not be ignored. In their early stages, though, exceptional abil-

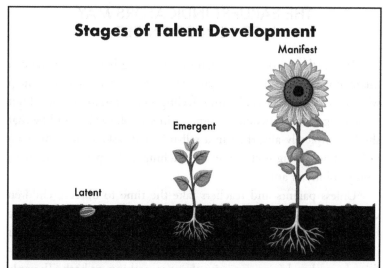

Figure 9.1. Stages of development. Adapted from *Applying Gifted Education Pedagogy in the General Education Classroom: Professional Development Module*, by D. E. Burns et al., 2004, Storrs, CT: The National Research Center on the Gifted and Talented. Design, Ryan Ward. Adapted with permission.

ities are not always so obvious. Emerging abilities can be like tiny, tender shoots beginning to poke through the soil. They are fragile and susceptible to the climate around them, and they require attention, encouragement, and support to grow. Figure 9.1 is a helpful illustration of the different stages of developing talent. A latent seed will not begin to germinate until the conditions are right. The barely visible emergent talent needs careful, sensitive tending, and the more obvious and strong manifest talent requires qualitatively different care and feeding. Gifts don't grow on their own.

A child who notices and remembers details (e.g., "No, Mom, this isn't the way we go. We need to turn at Wilson Street!" or "Somebody painted that house yellow, but it's supposed to be blue like before!") is showing small signs that need to be encouraged. Don't pass up the chance to add to the discussion with your own observations and continue to follow up when you get home. Pull out a map or draw your own. Talk about alternate routes. Talk about what you usually see. Bring out Dr. Seuss's book *And to Think That I Saw It on Mulberry Street*. This child could be an emerging cartographer or systems engineer.

THE EARLIEST INDICATORS MAY
NOT BE RECOGNIZED

That little girl on the playground scraping her stick in the dirt might not be comfortable playing with others. She may need help with social skills. Possibly she's feeling embarrassed or sad about something that happened at home or in school. Or it could be that she is completely absorbed in a self-initiated task, such as drawing figures, uncovering rocks, or even watching and experimenting with a busy colony of ants.

Unless parents and teachers take the time to observe children carefully and repeatedly, we may assume nothing special is unfolding because we aren't actually seeing the child in the moment. The loner child could be having social problems, or such a child could be satisfying his or her driving curiosity about something, or both. The only way to know is to keep our eyes and minds open to the possibility that there can be multiple reasons for behaviors.

In thinking about exceptional abilities in young children, parents and teachers might discount a particular child, wondering, "How can that child be considered high ability when she doesn't follow instructions and can't even keep track of her shoes?" or "That child can't be gifted because he doesn't even know his math facts."

In response, Drs. Sally Reis and Joseph Renzulli (2009), who are well-known for their research in enrichment, learning, and giftedness, referred to the diagram they call "the atom" (see Figure 9.2). They noted that gifted behaviors can be observed ICP (in certain people), ACT (at certain times), and UCC (under certain circumstances), because not all children, even those children with pronounced gifts, show their gifts at all times and under all circumstances. That also means that a child might reveal his or her abilities only at certain times and under certain circumstances. As adults, it behooves us to find those times and circumstances when a child can shine.

THE EARLIEST INDICATORS MAY
BE MISUNDERSTOOD

The eager, active, imaginative, opinionated boy mentioned at the beginning of this chapter could, under some circumstances, be

Figure 9.2. An atom of optimal learning. From "The Schoolwide Enrichment Model: A Focus on Student Strengths and Interests" by S. M. Reis and J. S. Renzulli, in *Systems and Models for Developing Programs for the Gifted and Talented* (2nd ed., p. 326), by J. S. Renzulli, E. J. Gubbins, K. S. McMillen, R. D. Eckert, and C. A. Little (Eds.), 2009, Waco, TX: Prufrock Press. Copyright 2009 by Prufrock Press. Reprinted with permission.

described as hyperactive, stubborn, defiant, argumentative, and willful. When his perspectives and contributions are ignored or negated, he puts up a fight and rarely backs down. How easy it is to see this child through the lens of "problem" rather than the lens of "promise" or "potential," particularly when the clock is ticking and parents or teachers are trying to deal with other children as well. It takes a lot of patience to see through the stubbornness and discover what the child is trying to say.

What every parent and early childhood educator needs to know about high-ability learners is that under some circumstances and at certain times, they could be mistaken for children with the types of problems that require intervention with remediation and/or therapies.

The following are seven characteristics that describe potential problems, such as sensory integration issues, autism spectrum disorders (ASD), hyperactivity, and/or emotional disorders. Confusingly, the very same characteristics on this list are also among those used to identify children of promise. The characteristics include:

> intense reactions to noise, pain, or frustration;

> sustained attention span;

» difficulty transitioning;
» high activity level;
» ability to solve problems in unique ways;
» vivid imagination (i.e., imaginary companions); and
» high sensitivity and awareness.

What if these characteristics or behaviors evoke images of children you know? Observe and record some of the specific behaviors for discussion with teachers, professionals, or other sympathetic parents and include the times and circumstances of what you note. For example, "I first noticed her interest in . . . when . . ." or "When he is very focused on something (like building blocks), he totally ignores everything else—even dinner!" or "He's sure tuned in when the two of us are working on categorizing insects. He learns so fast I'm amazed, yet when he's in a group of kids he spaces out."

NURTURING CHILDREN'S GIFTS

Children learn more and remember it better when learning is fun, and there's no end to what meaningful, appropriate, and sincere encouragement can do to bring out the best in a child. Realistically speaking, raising a high-ability child is a long and challenging journey—one that's difficult to do alone, so reach out to others for support. Look through the wealth of information on the National Association for Gifted Children (NAGC) website at https://www. nagc.org/resources-publications/resources-parents. These resources were compiled by experts, parents, and teachers across the nation who are dealing with (and who have dealt with) situations similar to yours. Be open to discovering the many ways that the individual abilities of young children can be nurtured and celebrated.

REFLECTION QUESTIONS

1. Do you and your child's teacher talk about when your child is at his or her personal best? How could including such a perspective help build positive, meaningful discussions that will lead to increased engagement and learning?

2. When do you see the light in your child's eyes? Think about the times and circumstances when this is true.

3. Why is noting when a child's eyes are bright and shiny (think of it as "Eye-Q") as important as IQ when talking about abilities, interests, and readiness to learn?

REFERENCES

Burns, D. E., Gubbins, E. J., Reis, S. M., Westberg, K. L., Dinnocenti, S. T., & Tieso, C. L. (2004). *Applying gifted education pedagogy in the general education classroom: Professional development module* (PDMCD04) [CD Rom]. Storrs: University of Connecticut, The National Research Center on the Gifted and Talented.

Reis, S. M., & Renzulli, J. S. (2009). The schoolwide enrichment model: A focus on student strengths and interests. In J. S. Renzulli, E. J. Gubbins, K. S. McMillen, R. D. Eckert, and C. A. Little (Eds.), *Systems and models for developing programs for the gifted and talented* (2nd ed., p. 326). Waco, TX: Prufrock Press.

CHAPTER 10

DEVELOPMENTALLY APPROPRIATE PRACTICE AND GIFTED STUDENTS

by Christy D. McGee

The concept of Developmentally Appropriate Practice (DAP) requires educators to use only those strategies for teaching and discipline that are appropriate for the age of the child. Makes sense, doesn't it? Everyone should want children to be working at a level that challenges them but is not overwhelming. But here is the problem: The underlying assumption of this concept is that those who work with preschool- and primary-age children actually know what is developmentally appropriate for the typical child, as indicated by research in the area of child development. Unfortunately, this presumption of practitioner knowledge is not always evident in practice. DAP begins with proper assessment of using established criteria to ascertain whether children meet, fall below, or exceed those norms. In other words, the basic tenet of developmentally appropriate practice rests on the practitioner's knowledge of child development and appropriate teaching strategies when working with young children. In order to thoroughly understand DAP, the National Association for the Education of Young Children (NAEYC, 2009) developed essential understandings of DAP. They are:

» knowledge and understanding of child development and learning that includes characteristics related to the age of the child that can predict "what experiences are likely to best promote children's learning and development" (p. 9);

» awareness of each individual child in order to best respond and/or adapt to various needs; and

» understanding of the child's social and cultural background in order to best communicate with the child and family in a respectful manner.

Additionally, NAEYC (2009) established 12 Core Principles of Child Development and Learning that inform practice:

1. All areas of development and learning are important.
2. Learning and development follow sequences.
3. Development and learning proceed at varying rates.
4. Development and learning result from an interaction of maturation and experience.
5. Early experiences have profound effects on development and learning.
6. Development proceeds toward greater complexity, self-regulation, and symbolic or representational capacities.
7. Children develop best when they have secure relationships.
8. Development and learning occur in and are influenced by multiple social and cultural contexts.
9. Children learn in a variety of ways.
10. Play is an important vehicle for developing self-regulation, and promoting language, cognition, and social competence.
11. Development and learning advance when children are challenged.
12. Children's experiences shape their motivation and approaches to learning.

It is critical that practitioners use appropriate teaching strategies, and that parents are aware of these practices. A list of such strategies include (NAEYC, 2009):

» creating a caring community of learners,
» teaching to enhance development and learning,
» planning curriculum to achieve important goals,
» assessing children's development and learning, and
» establishing reciprocal relationships with families.

This overview of the background information necessary to understand developmentally appropriate practices for young children leads to the question: How should DAP affect young gifted children? Although NAEYC (2009) discussed the importance of the critical issues of the shortage of quality care for infant and toddler populations, vulnerable groups of immigrant children, and children with special needs, including those with disabilities and/or challenging behavior, the needs of young gifted children are not specifically addressed. Unfortunately, many early childhood practitioners are unaware of what that might mean for the gifted child.

To assist parents and childcare providers, McGee and Hughes (2011) created a questionnaire to assist parents and professionals in the identification and support of young gifted children. This instrument (see Figure 10.1) is intended to be a springboard for parents and educators of young children. More intense observations and consultation with appropriate psychometricians is highly advised.

Most practitioners quickly realize when a child is not developing at a typical age-group pace and implement strategies to assist the child in "catching up" to peers. Students performing above typical development levels do not always get the same understanding and support. The practitioner may not realize that supporting the child with advanced atypical development is just as important as assisting those who fall below the typical criteria for the age group. Parents and practitioners may not understand that advanced children must be provided with activities that challenge them to continue to grow in the area(s) in which their gifts lie, or they may realize that a child is advanced but do not have the teaching tools or strategies to appropriately meet his or her needs. Only when parents and practitioners begin to understand that gifted children are atypical and that they need to think outside the box in order to support them appropriately will many of these children find success in school and home settings. Now, this does not mean that all gifted children are not being taught using appropriate strategies; it does mean that although some children have teachers and parents who understand their special needs, others do not.

Many students with talents and academic gifts are not receiving the support they need to be successful. In the *2014–2015 State of the Nation in Gifted Education* (National Association for Gifted Children [NACC], 2015), alarming statistics and practices for gifted students were revealed:

> » 28 states have no gifted education performance indicators on their report cards.
> » 19 states do not monitor or audit local gifted programs, 22 do not require districts to submit gifted education plans, and only 11 produce an annual report on gifted education services in the state.

The purpose of this questionnaire is to help professionals and parents become aware of children who may show characteristics that are more advanced than those of their peers. This questionnaire does not identify giftedness but allows for discussion about educational opportunities to develop abilities in the areas that the child may excel.

There are no right answers. Gifted children will not show all of the characteristics described in this questionnaire. Several answers that differ from peers' answers may indicate that a child has particular needs that should receive extra support.

Some of these questions may be considered "negative traits" of giftedness or disabilities, such as colic, hypersensitivity to surroundings, touch, and noise. These traits, in conjunction with other traits, may be indicators of a child's highly developed neurological and cognitive system.

Child's Name: _____

Birth Date: _____ Date: _____

1. How old is the child?

2. Is s/he often mistaken for being older?

3. Do you notice the child having strong interests in particular objects, topics, or actions? If so, describe them.

4. At what age did the child first start saying words?

5. Was the child particularly alert as an infant?

6. Did the child have colic or was the child really fussy and hard to soothe?

7. At what age did the child start walking?

8. Did/does the child have an imaginary playmate?

9. Has the child learned to read? If so, when?

10. Is the child concerned about "grown up" issues, such as death or time?

11. Does the child seek out challenging activities, such as complicated puzzles, word plays, or games with multiple steps?

12. Does the child prefer to be with older children or adults?

13. Is the child particularly emotional?

14. Does the child often create games or rules of his/her own?

15. Is the child highly curious?

16. Is the child aware of, and concerned about, larger community and world problems?

17. Is the child extraordinarily creative? In what area(s)?

18. Does the child ask questions beyond "Why?" such as "What if?" or "How does?"

19. Can the child focus for long periods of time on tasks of interest (not including television or video games)?

20. Is the child often aware of small details that others do not observe?

21. Can the child conduct an involved conversation with adults?

Figure 10.1. Questionnaire for parents and professionals supporting young children (McGee & Hughes, 2011).

» Only 7 states require school districts to report on gifted student achievement/performance.

» 13 states expressly prohibit students from entering Kindergarten early and 19 states leave such decisions to local school districts.

» 4 states prohibit proficiency-based promotion or the advancement of students by subject, and 14 states leave decisions to school districts.

» 19 of 29 responding states require teachers in gifted programs to hold a specialized credential or endorsement.

» Only 10 of 40 states report requiring school districts to have a dedicated gifted and talented administrator. (pp. 2–3)

These results concerning the interest in and support of gifted children reveal that the concept of implementing DAP by parents and teachers should be appealing, and—if implemented properly—more gifted children would be challenged in their educational settings. However, it seems that developmentally appropriate strategies and teaching are viewed as involving typical or struggling children and not those who exceed what is considered typical development. This practice must give way to meeting the needs of all students.

Further, these results reveal an appalling lack of interest in this nation's young gifted population. U.S. education officials moan over the poor performance on the National Assessment of Educational Progress (NAEP; see https://nces.ed.gov/nationsreportcard) tests but continue to fail to support our brightest students with developmentally appropriate practice that would be work toward meeting their needs. Such practices would include acceleration in all its forms, flexible homogeneous grouping, curriculum compacting, and pull-out and specialized classes (NAGC, 2015). The point is that if practitioners were taught the importance of supporting gifted learners using accepted developmentally appropriate practice, then practitioners could assure parents that their children would be meeting their highest potential.

REFLECTION QUESTIONS

1. Explain the term *developmentally appropriate practice* and discuss how it pertains to gifted students.
2. Discuss how parents and practitioners might use the Questionnaire for Parents and Professionals Supporting Young Children (Figure 10.1) in assisting in determining if a child may be advanced in his or her development?
3. Analyze the statistical information from the *2014–2015 State of the Nation in Gifted Education* (NAGC, 2015) to determine how many states are, or are not, supporting gifted education.
4. What could your parent group do to advance the education of gifted children?

REFERENCES

McGee, C. D., & Hughes, C. E. (2011). Identifying young gifted learners. *Young Children, 66,* 104–109.

National Association for Gifted Children. (2015). *2014–2015 state of the nation in gifted education: Turning a blind eye: Neglecting the needs of the gifted and talented through limited accountability, oversight, and reporting.* Retrieved from https://www.nagc.org/sites/default/files/key%20reports/2014-2015%20State%20of%20the%20Nation.pdf

National Association for the Education of Young Children. (2009). *Developmentally appropriate practice in early childhood programs serving children from birth through age 8* [Position statement]. Retrieved from https://www.naeyc.org/sites/default/files/globally-shared/downloads/PDFs/resources/position-statements/PSDAP.pdf

PART III
SOCIAL-EMOTIONAL LEARNING

I would not be surprised if readers skip other sections to read this one first. Working in a center for gifted studies, I receive more phone calls and e-mails from parents than anyone else. Certainly, many of those communications focus on cognitive issues or lack of challenge; however, the majority touch on some social and/or emotional concern:

> » When my son doesn't earn an A, he is beside himself with worry and self-doubt. What can I do?
> » How can I convince my daughter that it's okay to make mistakes—or even fail?
> » My 8-year-old worries so much about world issues that he's losing sleep at night. Any suggestions?
> » My middle schooler is a loner. I know she wants friends, but there is no one around who gets her. Can you help?
> » I hear about grit, resilience, and mindset, but how can I make my teenager understand their importance?
> » All I want is for my child to be happy. Do you have any ideas?

The list goes on and on. Parents tend to focus on their children as whole beings—not just as students. Unfortunately, not all schools have the people resources or even the time to go beyond what happens in the classroom. Parents must be proactive.

This section serves as a rich resource for pertinent, research-based information regarding the social-emotional needs and issues of gifted and advanced learners. Better yet, each author has focused on practical strategies for home and school to address those issues. Topics range from perfectionism and managing anxiety, to the importance of failure and finding a therapist. Some of the top names in the field share parenting tips (including the "don'ts"—which are just as important as the "do's") to raise happy, productive people. Also included are the critical skills necessary for advanced learners to thrive. Each chapter concisely explores research and presents the reader with the most important concepts.

In my experience, educators love children and young people. Just because their time and resources may be limited does not mean that they don't care about all of the needs of their students, including the social and emotional ones. I hope readers can share what they learn with their children's educators. That partnership is incredibly important.

—Tracy Ford Inman

CHAPTER 11

30 THINGS GIFTED KIDS AND THEIR PARENTS NEED TO KNOW

by Deb Douglas

The father of a recently identified gifted 6-year-old asked, "What should I tell my daughter?" That's not an unusual question. As parents, we want to be straightforward with our children about their giftedness, but we often get conflicting messages about what to say. Will our kids become self-centered if we tell them they are gifted? Is knowing they're gifted helpful or harmful? Is it even okay to use the word *gifted*?

More than 30 years ago gifted students' number one gripe was that no one explained giftedness (Galbraith, 1985). Not much has changed. In 2016, more than 300 gifted teens from around the country were surveyed during self-advocacy workshops (Douglas, 2017). Less than 25% said that their parents had talked with them about being gifted. In fact, 33% said no one had explained giftedness to them. Although students want to have that conversation, parents struggle with knowing exactly what to say.

On the following pages, experts on the lives of gifted children share nuggets of wisdom—a total of 30 beliefs that help every parent share "giftedness" with their child.

MORE THAN AN ENGAGING LESSON
BY GEORGE BETTS

On August 14, 1966, I thought I knew everything. I had graduated from college and was preparing to teach my first class. Wanting to catch the students' attention, I walked into the room dressed as a historical figure and conducted the class in character. They were mesmerized. At the end of class, however, a student named Kathy asked if I had a minute to answer a question. "Mr. Betts, my stepdad beat up my mom last night. What should I do?" In that instant, I recognized that I didn't know everything.

Kathy and many other learners taught me that they needed more than just an engaging lesson. I've learned the importance of social-emotional development. Tell kids:

1. Giftedness lies within you, 365 days a year, and not only the 180 days of the school year.
2. Do all you can to surround yourself with a positive, nourishing environment.
3. Find your group of true peers who will inspire, support, and encourage you.
4. Find your passion and engage in it. That process can grow into a passion for passions.
5. A nourishing environment, true peers, and engagement in your passion will help you develop a positive self-concept and true self-esteem.

DREAMS DEFERRED: CULTURALLY AND LINGUISTICALLY DIVERSE STUDENTS
BY JOY LAWSON DAVIS

In more than 30 years in gifted education, I've spent many hours listening to gifted learners and their families, all remarkable human beings. As members of communities for whom low expectations may be the norm, they are challenged to help others see and value their gifts. These observations may help others from culturally diverse groups overcome the many challenges they will face:

1. Parents: To help your students overcome any bias they may experience in schools and communities, help them focus on their dreams rather than on the negative messages they may receive.
2. Students: Prove the naysayers wrong. Demonstrate in your actions that those who don't believe in your potential are wrong. Use their negatives to build your courage, and use that courage to propel you forward into the future.
3. Parents: Learn as much as you can about giftedness and school services, so you can advocate for increased access to services.

4. Students: Keep your family informed of activities and opportunities for gifted students. Ask questions to get access to the information you need.

5. Students: Seek out role models and mentors who can provide real-life examples of overcoming barriers to help you accomplish your dreams.

FROM A TEACHER, CONFIDANTE, AND DAD
BY JAMES R. DELISLE

In my 42 years working with gifted kids, I've learned a few things from them:

1. Acknowledge your children's minds and also their hearts. They are more than the sum of their abilities. Gifted students are smart, but they are also deep, with emotions and insights that often surpass their chronological ages.

2. Embrace their intensities as assets to be treasured, not liabilities to be eliminated. When your children's intense feelings come fully alive, don't ask, "Why do you always get so worked up about things?" Instead, say, "It's not easy to be as sensitive as you are, is it?"

3. Encourage your gifted children to explore their passions, not yours. When they tell you that they want to be a writer when they grow up, don't say, "You'll never make any money at that." Instead, ask why that career interests them so much.

4. Teach your kids to advocate for themselves. If something isn't working at school, they need to consider what they can do to address the situation. If your children use the right words and approach, most teachers will listen.

5. Remember: You never outgrow your giftedness. Gifted kids grow up to become gifted adults, perhaps as you did. Embrace this reality with gusto and joy.

FROM A COUNSELOR'S PERSPECTIVE
BY JEAN SUNDE PETERSON

In my research studies of gifted youth, hidden distress emerged as a common concern. Many told neither parents nor teachers of their sadness, anxiety, or fear, instead feeling they needed to "figure it out" themselves.

1. Gifted kids must learn to ask for help—for social, emotional, and academic concerns. They can teach the adults around them about their stressors, doubts, and limitations.

2. Having opportunities in school to meet with intellectual peers to discuss growing up helps develop expressive language, which is likely to benefit future relationships in the workplace, in partnerships, in parenting, and with peers.

3. Knowing that struggle has a purpose may be helpful during crises. Through struggle, we develop resilience and gain confidence in our ability to persevere. It may lead to greater self-awareness, altruism, compassion, and vision.

4. Achievement level is not a guarantee of success in college and in adulthood. Yet many adults try to predict the future based on how gifted kids are succeeding during the school years.

5. Process (the doing) is as important as product (what is produced)—perhaps even more important. Being able to appreciate and enjoy the journey without being preoccupied with the destination (and evaluation) contributes to life satisfaction.

FIVE "COMMANDMENTS" FOR THE GIFTED
BY KAREN B. ROGERS

As I look back on my life, my husband's life, and the lives of our three gifted children, I'm aware of five lessons that may predict a gifted child's ability to succeed personally and professionally:

1. Know thyself. Students should figure out how far their capabilities extend, what they are good at, and which areas are not strengths. Understanding themselves as learners will make them less likely to question whether or not they are "really gifted."

2. Know thy institutions. By third grade, students can begin to identify the hurdles that could hinder their learning. Developing appropriate negotiating skills will allow them to circumvent the "school game."

3. Know thy peers. Gifted students are often frustrated during group work. We can help them realize why team work is important, what they can gain from it, and when to negotiate with the teacher about working on their own.

4. Know thy community. Students can identify community projects where they can work with all ages and ability levels—developing their communication skills, recognizing others' strengths, and learning to be a follower at times.

5. Know thy education pathway. Before middle school, students can begin to determine if they need to shorten the time spent in K–12 before moving on to postsecondary work. There are ways they can bypass what they already know and compact out of curriculum standards they have already mastered.

FOSTER AN HONEST AND FACTUAL DIALOGUE
BY DEB DOUGLAS

Talking with our kids about their giftedness isn't a one-and-done deal. We must consider it an ongoing conversation about all of the possibilities and potential problems they may encounter.

1. Being gifted is not what you *do*, but who you *are*. It's not how well you do in school, what you become someday, or what you can contribute to society, but rather it's a unique set of characteristics you have that may morph over time.

2. Remember that although you may be *better at* some things than others your age, that doesn't mean you're *better than* they are.

3. There are many ways to be gifted, and gifted people are not all alike. Each one has a combination of exceptionalities—a mixture that is different for every person.

4. Being gifted means you may have different educational needs than some of your classmates. You can help your teachers and parents know when the challenge feels right, when it's too tough, and when it's too easy.

5. Being gifted doesn't mean your life will always be a breeze, but it's part of what makes you uniquely wonderful.

We empower our children to follow their dreams when we help them reflect on their individual gifts, understand their rights and responsibilities, connect with others who can provide support, and explore the wonderful, wide world of opportunities.

REFLECTION QUESTIONS

1. Why is it important for children to understand their giftedness?
2. What can you do to help your child overcome any stigma associated with giftedness?
3. How can you teach your child to advocate for himself?
4. Why is it important to separate the child from his or her grades, accomplishments, and achievements?

REFERENCES

Galbraith, J. (1985). The eight great gripes of gifted kids: Responding to special needs. *Roeper Review, 8*(1), 15–18.

Douglas, D. (2017). *The power of self-advocacy for gifted learners: Teaching the four essential steps to success.* Minneapolis, MN: Free Spirit.

CHAPTER 12

MAKING HAPPINESS AND HEALTH A PRIORITY

by Micah N. Bruce-Davis

"What do you want to be when you grow up?" Adults often ask children this question, expecting answers like "doctor," "lawyer," or "engineer." However, teenager Logan LaPlante (as cited in TEDx Talks, 2013) argued that adults should not focus on their children's careers, but rather on how to help them grow up to be happy and healthy individuals. Frustrated and stressed out with his schooling experience, several years ago Logan and his family hacked his education—coining the term *hackschooling*—and decided to incorporate Walsh's (2011) eight ways of well-being into their lives: exercise, nutrition and diet, time in nature, relationships, recreation and enjoyable activities, relaxation and stress management, religious and spiritual involvement, and contributions and service. This major lifestyle shift also opened up opportunities for Logan to intern at a custom baseball company and to work on his competitive skiing career.

Although hackschooling isn't for everyone, there are many ways families can incorporate well-being practices into family life. Concerns over grades, getting homework completed, and managing busy schedules can be overwhelming for parents and children. So, in addition to making plans for their child's educational goals, parents should consider setting well-being goals to create a happy and healthy family.

SPEND TIME IN NATURE

With increased access to technology and fears of dangers that lie outside of the home, people are spending less time in nature. In

Last Child in the Woods, Richard Louv (2008) argued that children are suffering from "nature-deficit disorder" and that children require nature to support their development. He claimed that alienation from nature results in diminished use of the senses, attention difficulties, and higher rates of physical and emotional illnesses. Research (Wells & Evans, 2003) also suggests that the presence of nearby nature can moderate or buffer the impact of life stress on children. Time in nature supports the development of senses as children learn to look more carefully, listen more closely, and smell more deeply. Natural environments offer silence to process thoughts or soothe emotions.

PRACTICE RELAXATION AND STRESS MANAGEMENT

Stress and worry have become major concerns for parents and children. There are frequent reports of the hazards of stress on the human body. Although some stress can lead to positive change, excessive stress has been shown to have detrimental health effects. Children can learn at an early age to manage stress. Mindfulness training and breathing techniques are two ways to help children deal with stress.

Mindfulness training in schools has led to decreased anxiety, less rumination, and improved optimism (Bostic et al., 2015). School mindfulness programs focus on quieting the mind, mindful attention, managing negative emotions and thinking, and stress reduction.

Training in mindfulness may be particularly interesting to gifted students, especially in how the body functions with stress or emotions. Questions such as "What happens in the brain when we are angry?" or "Why do my hands get sweaty when I'm nervous?" can spark curiosity and wonder.

At home, parents can work with their children on building mindfulness skills for them to use throughout the day. For example, families might start their mornings by taking 10 deep breaths together, listening to mindfulness meditations on the way to school, or having everyone close their eyes for 2 minutes and listen for all of the sounds they hear.

ENGAGE IN RECREATION AND ENJOYABLE ACTIVITIES

Children often have a full schedule of activities outside of school. Learning a new sport or how to play a musical instrument is often enjoyable; however, children don't always tell their parents if they aren't enjoying an activity. As children engage in schoolwork or extracurricular activities, parents should look for activities that spark the most joy in their child and encourage a playful approach to the work. Additionally, parents should try to incorporate playfulness into everyday activities, such as cooking or tidying up.

OTHER WELL-BEING PRACTICES TO INCLUDE

Walsh (2011) suggested considering an additional five well-being practices to improve physical and mental health:

1. **Exercise.** Encourage children to play outside each day. Take daily family walks or try a new sport.
2. **Nutrition and diet.** Cook family meals. Have an experimental meal with new fruits and vegetables once a week.
3. **Relationships.** Engage your child in pleasurable activities so she can meet other children with similar interests.
4. **Religious and spiritual involvement.** Discuss belief systems as a family.
5. **Contribution and service.** Find ways to be of service that are motivated by being helpful, not by obligation. Cook meals for neighbors. Encourage children to make new buddies on the playground. Join a local civic group for a clean-up day.

CREATE NEW HABITS

Ultimately, the key to success is to make well-being practices a priority and family habit. Even by taking small steps, such as designating a weekly "no electronics/spend time in nature" day, starting each day with a short meditation practice, or instituting a family game night, parents can help children develop not only their academic skills and talents but also their whole being.

REFLECTION QUESTIONS

1. Which well-being practices do you currently engage in with your family? What role do you think this plays in your family's overall happiness and health?

2. Are there additional opportunities for you to incorporate well-being practices? What are some obstacles? How can you plan to overcome those obstacles?

3. How might you adapt these practices to fit your family best?

4. For your child/children: What is something that we do as a family that makes you smile? Why do you think it makes you smile?

5. After trying a well-being practice, debrief with your child/children: How does your body feel (e.g., relaxed, energized)? How does your mind feel (e.g., clear, rested, excited)? What about this activity did you like? What about this activity was different/awkward/uncomfortable? Do you want to do this activity again? Why or why not?

REFERENCES

Bostic, J. Q., Nevarez, M. D., Potter, M. P., Prince, J. B., Benningfield, M. M., & Aguirre, B. A. (2015). Being present at school: Implementing mindfulness in schools. *Child and Adolescent Psychiatric Clinics of North America, 24,* 245–259.

Louv, R. (2008). *Last child in the woods: Saving our children from nature-deficit disorder.* Chapel Hill, NC: Algonquin Books.

TEDx Talks. (2013). *Hackschooling makes me happy | Logan LaPlante | TEDxUniversityofNevada* [Video file]. Retrieved from https://www.youtube.com/watch?v=h11u3vtcpaY

Walsh, R. (2011). Lifestyle and mental health. *American Psychologist, 66,* 579–592.

Wells, N. M., & Evans, G. W. (2003). Nearby nature: A buffer of life stress among rural children. *Environment and Behavior, 35,* 311–330.

CHAPTER 13

TEACHING YOUR CHILD TO FAIL

by Diana Reeves

"They won't stick together! I quit!"—Aaron, age 3

"This isn't supposed to look like this. It looks terrible. I don't feel well."—LeToya, age 8

"I really messed up in honors algebra; I'm going for 'dumb math' next term."—Eric, age 16

"So the rest of the girls thought I was harassing them, and they complained to the teacher. I was really upset. I didn't want to disappoint my parents."—Addi, age 14

All of these kids have experienced failure in one way or another. How they dealt with it depended largely upon the ways that their families and teachers prepared them to cope with the disappointment, frustration, and, yes, learning opportunities inherent in not achieving a desired outcome. Who among us has never failed—in a job, in a relationship, or on the tennis court? Winner worship is embedded early. Society suggests that the ultimate put-down is "loser" and failure is the ultimate f-word. But we could pay a terrible price for our loser loathing: What better way to avoid failing than to never enter the fray?

Fear of failure begins early in life and is common among high achievers (Callard-Szulgit, 2012). From their earliest years, many gifted children are successful in almost everything they try because they are underchallenged, and, paradoxically, they become failure-avoidant. And, when we parents always encourage our children to get the highest grade or to be the best, we may be discouraging them from seeking challenges that are optimal for their level of possible accomplishment. The adults in their lives also need to take risks and to model a growth mindset prepared to cope with all possible outcomes (Haimovitz, & Dweck, 2016).

EMBRACE MISTAKES

High-level achievement should be encouraged; however, it is important to teach how to set priorities and to model taking time to reflect on the value of mistakes. Learning to set achievable goals is a big part of avoiding failure (Brown, 2007). Teaching task commitment, or sticking with something until it is successfully completed, can be a delicate dance.

Children need to learn when to let go of a project but also need to realize that very few masterpieces were created on the first try. When projects are displayed or graded, it is always useful to have students respond to these questions:

> » What have you done?
> » What did you learn?
> » What would you have done or learned with more time?
> » What will you do differently next time?

When things go wrong, these mistakes can be corrected and can serve as a learning experience. This process is popularly referred to as "failing forward" (Maxwell, 2000). A candid admission that you are wrong is the first step in getting it right the next time. Xiaodong Lin-Siegler, a researcher at Columbia University's Teachers College, hit it right on the head with her observation that "failure needs to give people a chance to regroup and rewind" (as cited in Fattal, 2018).

MANAGE TIME

We can't do everything that we would like to do. Not everything worth doing can be done equally well. Read that last sentence over again, slowly, especially if you tend to aim for perfection in all that you attempt. With the hurried pace and information overload that pervades most of our lives, children need to practice time management. Making mistakes often means that a problem has not been thoroughly thought through. Mistakes often result from reacting to a perceived lack of options or not having begun the task in enough time to allow for successful completion.

When teaching our children to fail safely, we need to pay specific attention to sharing with them how we, as adults, make decisions by previewing outcomes, evaluating choices, and reviewing previous mistakes. When you include your children in family planning and decision making, they can learn to take the baby steps necessary to begin to plan for themselves. Maintaining a household calendar with input from all family members will assure that priorities can be established, overscheduling can be avoided, and free time can be preserved. Many teachers would argue that learning how to set aside both a place and a time to focus on assignments is the most valuable aspect of homework. High schoolers learning how to successfully integrate school commitments and early employment opportunities will be much better prepared to cope with the challenges of college scheduling (Heinrich, 2018).

ABSORB DISAPPOINTMENT AND MODEL RESILIENCE

An important part of surviving failure is the development of resilience. Resilient people can absorb disappointment because of a belief in themselves and a connection to others. A resilient child has confidence in her decision-making ability. Parents who can demonstrate their failures and intentionally share their thoughts and feelings about them model resilient behavior, sometimes called *grit*. They teach their children how to cope with disappointment while remaining passionate and persevering. Grit predicts success, and you can learn to be gritty (Duckworth, 2013). When parents can find the words to walk their children through life's catastrophes—making transparent their feelings of despair, disappointment, grief, or pain—children learn that parents are not perfect and that events are frequently uncontrollable. Teaching children how to regain hope and deal with change will prevent them from seeing failure as a permanent condition.

It's a parent's responsibility to set clear limits and to follow through with appropriate consequences. Everyone needs to agree upon an acceptable level of performance or behavior, *before the task is undertaken!* When the definition of success has been agreed upon ahead of time, it is far easier to hit the mark. If it is important to take out the trash every day without being asked and to separate the recyclables into three different containers, the magic of doing a good job is dispelled. Kids can learn that failure can often be avoided by attending early on to the criteria of success.

Children need to learn to accept responsibility for their mistakes, rather than being prevented from doing so by well-meaning parents who wish to shield them from any negative experiences. How many of us qualify as Zamboni Parents—human ice-resurfacers, attempting to smooth over life's experiences so that no child of ours will stumble or fall (Farragher, 2019, para. 11)? A child who refuses to wear boots in the snow will not suffer irreparable harm from sitting through the school day in wet sneakers. Competitions that provide all participants with a prize stand as testament to our reluctance to have our children experience what Patz (2010) described as "the pain of dashed expectations" (para. 2). If allowed to fail, children develop problem solving skills, creative thinking ability, coping skills, and the ability to collaborate. As Roy Baumeister, a Florida State University researcher, asserted, "Success leads to feeling good about yourself, not the other way around" (as cited in Patz, 2010).

DEVELOP ISLANDS OF COMPETENCE

Psychologist Robert Brooks (2007) suggested helping your child develop "islands of competence" in order to build self-esteem (p. 11). Being very good at something—and knowing that you are good at it—can reinforce confidence and self-worth when encountering difficulties or roadblocks.

In a family or classroom, knowing the personal strengths and weaknesses of each member can be valuable in fostering cooperation and teamwork. Adults do this all of the time. We hire someone to help us with our taxes if we lack the time or talent to do them well. Children need to understand that no one can do everything perfectly, that some failure is unavoidable, and that examination of mistakes can lead to improvement and correction the next time.

SEPARATE FAILURE FROM THE CHILD

Anyone who has failed in some way needs to feel that he belongs and that he can still make a difference in the world. Separating the failure from the child is a place to start. Reinforcing that "No matter what you say or do, there is nothing that will stop me from loving you" is a preventative vaccine that should be administered early on, with booster shots given periodically throughout the rest of one's life.

SHARE AND CARE

Teaching children to cope with failure requires that we reveal ourselves—our manners of decision making, habits of dealing with frustration, and entrenched patterns of thought. Just as we aim to teach the whole child, we must aim to teach from the whole of ourselves.

Our inner resources register deeply with our children. If anything can prepare a child for life's inevitable failures, it is time spent in the presence of loving adults who are willing to share their wisdom and care enough to provide meaningful guidance.

REFLECTION QUESTIONS

1. Describe a childhood failure. Why do you remember it still?
2. What is worth doing, even if you fail?
3. In your experience, how are failure and forgiveness linked?

REFERENCES

Brooks, R. (2007). The search for islands of competence: A metaphor for hope and strength. *Reclaiming Children and Youth, 16*(1), 11–13.

Brown, B. (2007). *I thought it was just me (but it isn't): Making the journey from "what will people think?" to "I am enough."* New York, NY: Avery.

Callard-Szulgit, R. (2012). *Perfectionism and gifted children* (2nd ed.). Lanham, MD: Rowman & Littlefield Education.

Duckworth, A. L. (2013). *Grit: The power of passion and perseverance* [Video file]. Retrieved from https://www.ted.com/talks/angela_lee_duckworth_grit_the_power_of_passion_and_perseverance?language=en

Farragher, T. (2019). As high schoolers await college acceptance letters, one counselor has some advice. *The Boston Globe.* Retrieved from https://www.bostonglobe.com/metro/2019/02/19/high-schoolers-await-college-acceptance-letters-one-counselor-has-some-advice/O4buGGaM9Fgcagulwi0wZL/story.html

Fattal, I. (2018). The value of failing. *The Atlantic.* Retrieved from https://www.theatlantic.com/education/archive/2018/04/the-value-of-failing/558848

Haimovitz, K., & Dweck, C. (2016). Parents' views of failure predict children's fixed and growth mind-sets. *Psychological Science, 27,* 859–869.

Heinrich, A. (2018). *7 effective time management tips for college students* [Web log post]. Retrieved from https://www.rasmussen.edu/student-experience/college-life/time-management-tips-college

Maxwell, J. (2000). *Failing forward: Turning mistakes into stepping stones for success.* Nashville, TN: Nelson.

Patz, A. (2010, October 11). Failure is an option: Teaching your child to cope. *Parents Magazine.* Retrieved from https://www.parents.com/kids/development/behavioral/failure-is-an-option

CHAPTER 14

THE IT FACTOR: FINDING A THERAPIST FOR YOUR GIFTED CHILD

by Alessa Giampaolo Keener

Growing up can be tough for some smart children, but the questions have long been asked: Does being gifted offer an inoculation against mental health problems? Or, does high intelligence lead to more serious difficulties coping with life's challenges? Unfortunately, no definitive answer exists, but we do know that decades of studies demonstrate "there is not enough evidence to conclude whether or not gifted adolescents *per se* have a higher than average risk" of committing suicide (Cross, 2018, p. 230).

TYPICAL TEEN BEHAVIOR OR CAUSE FOR CONCERN?

The American Academy of Child and Adolescent Psychiatry (2015) offered helpful advice in spotting the difference between normal developmental changes and when certain behaviors are a warning sign to seek help immediately. Behavioral warning signs can include:

» self-injury, such as cutting or suicide threats;
» hurting younger children or animals;
» lying, stealing, or damaging other people's property;
» excessive defiance of authority;
» drug or alcohol use; and
» sexually acting out.

THE IT FACTOR

Rarely do mental health professionals receive extensive instruction in the special developmental needs of gifted children, so finding an appropriate mental health professional to work with a family can be difficult.

Just as no one list of characteristics apply to all gifted children, it becomes difficult to quantify what a therapist needs to know to effectively work with a gifted child. Parents who have walked the road of mental health treatment often refer to the "It Factor," an elusive quality that seems to set their children's social-emotional needs apart from those of typically developing age peers. But, what is "it"—asynchrony, intensity, an analytical nature, perfectionism, or a combination of these behaviors?

Understanding the It Factor goes beyond a therapist rattling off a checklist of gifted traits. It requires an appreciation for how a child's level of intelligence may be correlated to the depth of his or her problem and how treatment goals should be developed.

Social anxiety, for example, can have a variety of causes. For one child, an advanced level of intelligence may feed into his social isolation from same-age peers. For another child, a move to a new school may displace her former "star smart student status," leaving her unsure of how to fit into her new social setting. Counselors who take the time to look for an intersection of contributing factors are best equipped to help a child client develop the most impactful coping skills.

HOW TO FIND A THERAPIST

STEP 1

Obtain a list of participating mental health providers from your insurance company's behavioral health division. Families without insurance may find low-cost therapeutic options through their local department of social services.

STEP 2

Narrow down your list by must-have criteria, such as how far you're willing to travel, the gender of the therapist, and the type of therapist you want to work with, such as a licensed psychologist, a clinical social worker, or a psychiatrist with a medical degree who can prescribe medications.

STEP 3

Schedule a telephone interview with a potential therapist before the first appointment. Prepare a few questions relating to giftedness that will help you evaluate if the therapist possesses essential skills necessary for successful treatment, such as empathy, respect, genuineness, collaboration, and boundaries. Because you will not have the benefit of seeing changes in body language during your conversation, keep your ear open for changes in tone of voice that may indicate impatience, rather than true understanding for the nature of your interview questions.

INTERVIEWING A THERAPIST

EMPATHY

Try asking: *Are you gifted?* A therapist does not need to be as gifted as your child in order to understand her thoughts, feelings, life experiences, or struggles. However, child clients must feel heard if you expect them to open up and talk about their problems. Simply echoing back statements does not demonstrate empathy. Neither does unintended condescension nor minimizing the child's problem.

One gifted teen reported his experience with a therapist who lacked the ability to build empathy with him (Giampaolo Keener & Taylor, 2012). He told his mother,

> I'm not going back to someone who tells me, "You have so much going for you. Anyone would trade places with you in a heartbeat." If she doesn't understand that gifted kids can be depressed, there's no way she can help me.

RESPECT

Try asking: *My child's IQ is ___. In your opinion, how does high intelligence impact a child's ability to cope with depression/anxiety/etc.?* In order for a healthy and productive therapist-client relationship to form, children must feel as though they have fundamental worth in their therapist's eyes. The child client needs to know that he is seen as more than an IQ number. Worth, however, must be tempered by a healthy dose of caring reality (Wampold, 2018). Many gifted people may find it difficult to feel true self-worth or make adequate treatment progress when they're placed on a pedestal or when another adult believes they need a lesson in humility.

A Colorado mom experienced the unhelpful effects of what happens with a therapist who has too much respect for a gifted child (Giampaolo Keener & Taylor, 2012). The mom explained:

> At the age of 4, my daughter had behavioral problems at school and wasn't able to get along with peers. She played games with the therapist every week for 2 years, but the therapist couldn't see the 2e issues, not even the Asperger's that was eventually diagnosed by someone else. The therapist believed my kid was an Indigo Child—this other-worldly being with special spiritual powers—and this was something to accept. I don't think she was doing enough for my kid, so we left.

GENUINENESS

Try asking: *What have you found to be the most challenging behaviors of gifted kids?*

Like it or not, we all hold certain personal biases and stereotypes in life. But, certain professions call on people to temporarily set aside those beliefs while they do their job. Perhaps no job requires this more than mental health professionals.

Mindful awareness of how one interacts with a client takes great effort and discipline (Staemmler, 2011). Some therapists working with gifted children may need to remind themselves that a highly or profoundly gifted 7-year-old is capable of a qualitatively different type of conversation than the vast majority of same-age child clients. Others must suspend their personal judgment on issues such as grade-skipping and pushy parents in order to accept their child client and what she brings to the therapy relationship. Gently inquiring about a therapist's mindful awareness will alert you to whether the therapist can work in therapeutic relationships as bias-free as possible.

COLLABORATION AND BOUNDARIES

Try asking: *What do you see as my role, as the parent in the therapeutic process?* Seeking therapy for your child creates a need for a functional three-way relationship. Parents of minor children have the right and responsibility to be part of the therapeutic process, but the child's age will determine how much the parent is involved (American Academy of Pediatrics, 2009). Parents should also keep in mind that once a child client turns 18, the Federal Health Insurance Portability and Accountability Act of 1996 allows the client to block parents from receiving therapy updates, even if the parent pays for the care.

Negotiating confidentiality and disclosure boundaries should occur at the start of therapy. Child clients should be fully aware that, legally, a therapist must report any suspicion that a child is being abused or has thoughts of harming himself, herself, or another person. Other privacy ground rules should be jointly agreed upon by the child, parent, and therapist.

COLLABORATION AND GOAL SETTING

Try asking: *What are your thoughts about underachievement?* Immediately addressing a child's most glaring behavioral issue will not necessarily provide meaningful treatment for a more deeply rooted problem. Despite extensive training, licensed mental health professionals do not have a crystal ball that allows them to know your child's precise problem within 10 minutes of the first session. Depending upon the age of the child, a good therapist may assign homework for the child to list 3–5 top problems she is currently experiencing. By prioritizing the list in a team fashion, the therapist begins to build trust by showing he is interested in hearing what the child has to say. Additionally, therapists should seek periodic feedback during the therapeutic process, from both the child and parent, in order to gauge if progress is being made (Wampold, 2018).

Good communication between the parent, child, and therapist also offers assurance against what some call "the snow effect" (Giampaolo Keener & Taylor, 2012):

> Therapists need to know how not to get played. A gifted kid will figure out what the exit criteria are and then systemat-

ically go about meeting them. Then the mom gets called in and told that there is no longer any reason to be meeting, patient healed. Or the gifted kid likes said therapist or likes the game and purposefully does not make progress in order to continue meeting. It takes a bright, intuitive person to handle a gifted child.

PARTING THOUGHTS

Mental health treatment goals will vary from child client to child client, but generally speaking, patients work with their therapists to develop effective and healthy coping skills (Wampold, 2018). Before productive work can be accomplished, however, a good working relationship must first be established between the gifted child, the parent, and the therapist. That relationship begins with a clear and mutual understanding of who the child is—from name to gender and age, to family dynamics, including ethnicity and socioeconomic background. The child's identity and how it contributes to her current problem is also affected by her level of intelligence—that ever-elusive It Factor. Therapists open to acknowledging and discussing the It Factor may prove to be the best fit for your child.

THERAPY APPROACHES

COGNITIVE BEHAVIORAL THERAPY
» Works to change poor thinking patterns in order to change habits and behaviors
» Ages 10 and up
» Helps with anxiety, depression, and childhood mood disorders

DIALECTICAL BEHAVIORAL THERAPY
» Focuses on personal responsibility in dealing with conflict and negative emotions
» Ages 14 and up
» Helps with borderline personality disorder

PLAY THERAPY
» Uses traditional toys and games to help children learn to recognize and talk about their feelings and how to manage them better
» Ages 4–12
» Helps with anger, conflict management, and coping skills

ART THERAPY
» Uses different media to help clients express their inner feelings while developing greater insight
» Ages 4–18
» Helps with stress and dealing with traumatic experiences

BEHAVIOR PLANS
» Establish a contract for changing negative behavior; criteria define acceptable behavior and specific consequences for a variety of infractions
» Ages 4–18
» Help modify behavior

RESOURCES

» HealthyChildren.org (https://www.healthychildren.org), a website hosted by the American Academy of Pediatrics, offers thousands of resources to support the physical, mental, and social health and well-being of your children, from infants to young adults.
» The National Alliance on Mental Illness (https://www.nami.org), the nation's largest grassroots mental health organization, offers free online resources, a telephone help line, and community-based resources in every state.
» Supporting Emotional Needs of the Gifted (https://www.sengifted.org): Join an 8-week SENG Model Parent Group and participate in guided discussions about motivation, discipline, stress management, and peer relationships.

REFLECTION QUESTIONS

1. Have you discussed therapy with your child? How receptive is your child to the idea of meeting with a counselor to work on issues that may be a problem right now?
2. What is one question you think is important to ask a therapist during the interview process? What type of answer would help you feel confident that the therapist understands the It Factor?
3. How well do you cope with situations in which you do not know all of the details that relate to your child and a struggle he or she may be having? How will you respond to confidential boundaries established by the therapist and your child?
4. What are your personal experiences with mental health counseling? Is it a topic you are comfortable talking about with other people, or do you feel like therapy is a matter not to be discussed outside of the family?

REFERENCES

American Academy of Child and Adolescent Psychiatry. (2015). *When to seek help for your child*. Retrieved from https://www.aacap.org/AACAP/Families_and_Youth/Facts_for_Families/FFF-Guide/When-To-Seek-Help-For-Your-Child-024.aspx

American Academy of Pediatrics. (2009). Adolescent consent and confidentiality. *Pediatrics in Review, 30*, 457–459.

Cross, T. L. (2018). *On the social and emotional lives of gifted children* (5th ed.). Waco, TX: Prufrock Press.

Giampaolo Keener, A., & Taylor, S. T. (2012, July). *Best fit: Finding a therapist for your gifted child*. Paper presented at the annual meeting of Supporting Emotional Needs of the Gifted, Milwaukee, WI.

Staemmler, F.-M. (2011). *Empathy in psychotherapy: How therapists and clients understand each other*. New York, NY: Springer.

Wampold, B. E. (2018). *The basics of psychotherapy: An introduction to theory and practice* (2nd ed.). Washington, DC: American Psychological Association.

CHAPTER 15

DO'S AND DON'TS FOR MOTIVATING YOUR HIGH-ABILITY CHILD

by Del Siegle and D. Betsy McCoach

Perhaps no issue frustrates parents of gifted students more than seeing their progeny fail to engage in and embrace learning opportunities. There is no silver bullet that is guaranteed to improve students' motivation. Given its intrinsic nature, the will to engage in challenging and meaningful tasks must come from within. However, there are several strategies that have proven to be helpful motivation kick-starters. In this chapter, we offer tips for improving motivation as well as pitfalls to avoid.

Individuals who are motivated tend to believe they have the necessary skills to be successful at a task. They also value the task and see it as meaningful. Finally, they believe that if they attempt the task, their efforts will be supported. These three beliefs engender motivation. Based on these principles, we offer the following do's and don'ts to successfully navigate your parenting journey and increase or maintain your child's motivation levels.

AVOID SABOTAGING YOUR CHILD'S SUCCESS

Be careful of—even inadvertently—sabotaging your children's perceptions about themselves, their peers, and their teachers.

DO

> » Model a growth mindset. Help your child understand that with effort and practice she becomes more skilled.

» Let your child struggle a bit, but monitor to avoid total frustration. Learning to overcome challenges increases confidence.

» Present a united front with your partner. Although you may disagree with your partner, work out your differences privately. This avoids having your child pit you against your partner.

» Show that you value education and teachers. To be successful in school, children need to view school and their teachers as valuable and supportive.

DON'T

» Use "est" words—e.g., *best, brightest, prettiest, fastest*. Being the best doesn't leave room for growth, and the pressure to remain the best can be paralyzing for some children.

» Swoop in, rescue, and provide unnecessary assistance—otherwise your child will never feel challenge. Unnecessary assistance can rob your child of the joy of succeeding at a difficult task.

» Let your children play parents against one another. Gifted children can be skillful at manipulating parents to get their way.

» Criticize teachers in front of your children. Children who respect their teachers have a more positive attitude toward school.

UNDERSTAND CAUSE AND EFFECT

Gifted children need to understand that they control their own destinies: They succeed because they have the skills and put forth effort, and failures may be attributed to lack of effort.

DO

» Help your child analyze success or failures—e.g., "Did we study the right things?" or "What was on the test that we didn't study?" Take time to discuss what is working and what is not working.

» Counsel your child to reflect on difficult situations and discuss ways to change the environment to fit her needs or adjust her behavior to the existing environment. The secret to success is discerning which situations are under one's control and which are not.

» Help your child break down projects and map out tasks. Through planning, children can visualize a task coming to fruition. Visualizing the steps needed to accomplish a large project makes it appear more manageable.

» Model curiosity and creativity about the world around you. Help your child develop a wonder and appreciation for the world around her.

DON'T

» Allow him to blame others for his lack of success—e.g., "The teacher just doesn't like me." Help him take responsibility for finding ways to be successful.

» Intervene and solve problems for your child. Rather, involve and engage her, so she is part of the solution. She can develop problem-solving skills that are useful throughout her life.

» Assume that because your child is gifted, he intuitively knows how to organize tasks or manage projects. Some students need help developing organizational strategies.

» Ignore opportunities to demonstrate how to transform your child's curiosity into action. Rather, suggest, "Let's look up your question on the Internet." Asking questions is important. Seeking the answers to those questions is more important.

FIND MEANINGFULNESS

Even at a very young age, gifted and talented students need to find meaning in their lives and the tasks they encounter.

DO

» Support your child in exploring what is personally interesting to him. Help your child see how he can apply his interests to school projects.

» Recognize that children's motivation is linked to what they view as useful. When they value or enjoy an activity, they are intrinsically motivated. Help them apply what they learn in school to their life.

» Help your child see beyond the immediate activity to long-term outcomes. Philosopher Friedrich Nietzsche said, "The future influences the present as much as the past."

» Share your child's interests with the teacher or school, and find ways to incorporate those interests into school projects.

» Find peers or other role models with whom your child can relate. Relating to others who have struggled and succeeded increases confidence.

DON'T

» Force your child to pursue interests that you like or feel she should pursue because "all of the kids are doing it." Expose your child to the world around her, but follow up on interests that attract her.

» Overly focus on external rewards systems as the way to motivate your child. Offering rewards can be motivating; however, keep them small and strive to minimize them.

» Set goals for your child that you value but have little or no meaning to him. Learn what is valuable to him and help him set goals based on those values.

» Be afraid to let the teacher know what your child cares about. You can help your child's teacher recognize her interests and relate them to school assignments.

» Foster an environment of unhealthy perfectionism. Rather, find examples of famous role models who struggled but persevered to success. Help your child appreciate improvement in his performance without being paralyzed by needing to be perfect.

DISCUSS GIFTS AND ABILITIES

High-ability children must understand that they have gifts and talents . . . but it's up to them to put forth effort, persevere, and accept challenges to grow.

DO

» Help your child see that no one is born a Nobel Prize winner—it takes effort to succeed. Talents need to be developed; it takes effort and practice to reach eminence.

» Find challenging and stimulating opportunities to improve skills and develop talents. Your child is more likely to embrace a challenging and stimulating activity than one that is simply challenging.

» Encourage your child to take risks; share struggles and successes. Share with your child your own experiences of overcoming difficult situations.

» Document your child's growth and review periodically to build confidence. Children often fail to recognize the strides they are making.

DON'T

» Devalue the importance of working hard and putting forth effort.

» Overlook the fact that your child needs to learn basic study skills, such as outlining, note-taking, and identifying main points—even though she has a good memory and fast processing skills. Some children naturally develop these skills; others need assistance.

» Imply that giftedness is tied to perfect performance. Learning from mistakes leads to success. Never say "I thought you were gifted!" when your child makes a mistake, even in jest. Such comments can lead to heightened insecurity, and your child may decide it's better not to attempt a difficult task than to attempt, fail, and no longer "be gifted."

» Forget to sit down with your child to review examples of previous work to provide a visual marker of his growth—to build self-confidence and higher self-efficacy.

LISTEN AND SUPPORT INTERESTS

Gifted children want their voices to be heard.

DO

» Listen to what your child has on her mind. Gifted children often see the complexities of the world and need opportunities to share their thoughts and concerns.

» Be an active, empathetic listener by saying such things as "So it sounds like you are feeling . . ." or "What I hear you say is . . . ." Individuals don't always directly state their concerns. By actively reflecting on what your child says, you and he can better understand issues that are concerning him.

» Provide compliments that are genuine, specific, and earned. For example, say "I like the colors you chose here" or "You are providing good supporting sentences for your topic sentence in your opening paragraph." Drawing attention to specific skills helps your child recognize and appreciate her growth in them.

DON'T

» Solve her problems for her. Give her the space and time to talk it out and problem solve independently, but with support.

» Be distracted, dismissive, or interruptive when he is trying to share his feelings or point of view. Sometimes he just needs to be heard.

» Compliment your child in a general way ("good job") for underperforming or for unchallenging tasks. Specific compliments, rather than general compliments, will better help her appreciate the talents she has developed.

All of us are works in progress. Children refine their interests and talents as they mature. What one child finds interesting and motivating may not appeal to another, and there is no guarantee that children will have the same interests as their parents. We can encourage our children to explore and appreciate the world around them and support their pursuit of the interests they develop. We can also help them to develop resilience by showing them that failure is an inevitable, but temporary state.

REFLECTION QUESTIONS

1. What obligation do children have to develop their talents?
2. How can we encourage children to pursue excellence without becoming paralyzed by perfectionism?
3. In what ways can we share children's interests with the school?
4. How do we recognize the importance of effort while helping children appreciate their giftedness?
5. How do parents subtly sabotage their children's motivation?

CHAPTER 16

MANAGEMENT OF ANXIETY IN YOUNG PEOPLE BEGINS AT HOME

by Sal Mendaglio

Parents of gifted children are often concerned about their children's anxiety—and with good reason. Experiencing anxiety is distressing and debilitating. Recently, a study using data from the 2016 National Survey of Children's Health reported that 7.1% of children aged 3–17 had current anxiety problems, and, of these, 59.3% had received treatment in the previous year (Ghandour et al., 2019). Although research on anxiety does not indicate the number of gifted children included in studies, it is reasonable to assume that representative samples include children who are gifted.

Regrettably, children do not always communicate their anxiety directly or explicitly. The expression of anxiety—or lack of expression—depends largely on the child's makeup and may occur in different ways. Some children cry or behave aggressively, while others withdraw from the situation. Although the mode of expression of anxiety varies, there are sources applicable to all children as well as those that are unique to gifted children.

SOURCES OF ANXIETY FOR CHILDREN

Forty years of counseling experience supports research findings that a parent's anxiety is a strong predictor of a child's anxiety (Borelli, Rasmussen, St. John, West, & Piacentini, 2015). In addition to parental anxiety, several parent-child situations have been observed which may contribute to childhood anxiety:

» inconsistent parenting, which creates unpredictability for children;

» a child's not knowing whether a behavior is acceptable;

» parental conflict in the presence of children, including both arguments unrelated to children and disagreements regarding parenting;

» discussion of adult matters, such as issues related to other family members, medical concerns, and current events, in the child's presence; and

» parental criticism and disapproval.

Of these, criticism and disapproval are among the most pervasive sources of anxiety in children and require special attention (Nelemans, Hale, Branje, Hawk, & Meus, 2014). Parents are the most influential people in children's lives, and parental approval is a primary motivating force for children: Children want their parents' approval 24/7.

However, in raising children, parents find occasions when they must communicate disapproval of their children's choices. Even if done in a gentle, loving manner, behavior correction is a form of disapproval and may create anxiety in the child. This means that normal parenting, in itself, can create a certain amount of anxiety in children. This is *necessary anxiety*, which cannot be avoided. However, parents can avoid *unnecessary anxiety*, which is caused by their own feelings of frustration and anger in parent-child interactions. In this regard, two factors are important: manner of expression and intensity. A child's experience of anxiety may be ameliorated by the home psychological environment. For example, warm, nurturing, forgiving, and gentle parental correction of misbehavior leads to low-intensity anxiety; rough correction leads to high-intensity anxiety.

SOURCES OF ANXIETY FOR GIFTED CHILDREN

Although some sources of anxiety are common to all children, parents and teachers of gifted children need to know that research has identified potential sources unique to giftedness. These include *social coping*, in which gifted children feel different or are identified as different by their peers, leading to their experience of social rejection (Ersoy & Uysal, 2018). Gifted children may also experience the *big-fish-little-pond effect*, which refers to the deflated self-concept gifted children may feel when moving from mixed-ability to similar-ability programming (Becker & Neumann, 2016). The stress associated with high-level programs can interfere with success (Suldo, Shaunessy-Dedrick, Ferron, & Dedrick, 2018). *Hitting the wall* is a shock that occurs with the first educational encounter that requires that gifted children put forth more effort to achieve than they have in the past (Mendaglio, 2010).

Giftedness itself can be another source of anxiety (Mendaglio, 2012). Social-emotional characteristics of gifted individuals that may contribute to anxiety include the following:

» **Heightened sensitivity—greater awareness of the physical, social, and intrapersonal environments.** Heightened sensitivity enables one to vicariously experience the emotions and moods of others. Thus, gifted children are so keenly aware when adults and peers are happy, anxious, or stressed that, at times, they feel what others are feeling. They are also highly aware of disapproval and may feel responsible when parents, especially, are unhappy. Essentially, gifted children feel what all children feel, but some have more intense feelings because they see and sense the nuances of communication and demeanor.

» **Analytical attitude—propensity to question, evaluate, and judge everything and everyone one encounters.** Gifted children may face a negative response when they question or challenge people in authority, such as parents and teachers. For example, when a gifted child corrects a teacher's error, the reaction may not be gratitude but rather defensiveness and disapproval. Society and its agents (parents and educators) generally expect conformity and compliance. Questioning may be perceived as resistance and defiance, predisposing gifted children to external conflict.

» **Self-criticism—constant review of one's own attributes and behaviors.** Whereas the analytic attitude scrutinizes the external environment, self-criticism evaluates the intrapersonal environment. When gifted children turn their intelligence onto themselves, they tend to focus on deficits rather than accomplishments. Viewing oneself through a critical lens can result in disapproval of self and internal conflict.

WHAT SHOULD PARENTS DO?

RECOGNIZE ANXIETY

The first challenge parents face is to recognize anxiety in their children. When a child uses statements such as "I am afraid," parents can easily understand their child is anxious and can respond with reassurance. However, anxiety is not always obvious and may be expressed in a variety of ways. It is important for parents to remember that outbursts or overreactions may not always be simply "bad" behavior, but rather a sign of emotional distress.

AVOID/REDUCE OVERREACTIONS

Not just children overreact; parents overreact, too. Parental overreactions commonly occur when a parent communicates a request to a child and the child does not respond. This may occur in trivial situations. For example, a parent might ask a child to load the dishwasher, and the child responds with "in a minute." After patiently waiting, when the child continues to resist, the parent repeats the request. With repetitions, irritation turns to frustration and anger. Parents should monitor their reactions to a child's behavior and minimize emotional overreactions whenever possible.

RESPOND EFFECTIVELY TO NEGATIVE EMOTIONS

Lastly, parents of gifted children have another dimension to consider: how they will respond to the negative emotions their gifted child expresses resulting from a heightened sensitivity, analytical attitude, and/or self-criticism. The natural reaction is for parents to want to reduce painful emotions or to problem solve. For example, a child may come home after school stating what a horrible day it was because she was ignored by her friends. There may or may not be tears. In such situations, parents often describe a pattern that includes a combination of sympathy and problem solving: "I'm sorry that happened to you. Now, let's talk about how to handle/prevent it." When parents attempt to convince the child that the situation she experienced was not that bad or to solve the problem with reasoning, they minimize the importance of her experience. Emotions cannot be "fixed" through reasoning.

When children are in distress, it is recommended that parents avoid denial and demonstrate acceptance of the felt emotion. Other responses trivialize their child's experience and will likely intensify and prolong negative emotion. Parents will not add fuel to the fire if they display an attitude of acceptance, which tends to remove oxygen from emotionally charged situations. The fire will soon extinguish on its own. Then, parents may give the child space, thereby providing an opportunity to learn to self-calm.

CONCLUSION

There are numerous sources of anxiety in young people. However, parents are most influential in their children's lives, and, unlike external influencers, parents have opportunities to control the anxiety that they may be unwittingly creating in their children. By reducing the anxiety at home, parents can create a significant positive change in their children's sense of personal security. In addition, parents of gifted children, who tend to be gifted themselves, can draw on their own experiences to help children understand how giftedness itself may cause anxiety. When parents increase their understanding of giftedness, engage in honest self-analysis, and model mindful and intentional practices, their gifted children are the beneficiaries.

REFLECTION QUESTIONS

1. How would you rate your level of anxiety while interacting with your child?
2. How frequently do you overreact to your child's trivial misbehavior?
3. How often is your child within earshot when adults are experiencing conflict?

REFERENCES

Becker, M., & Neumann, M. (2016). Context-related changes in academic self-concept development: On the long-term persistence of big-fish-little-pond effects. *Learning and Instruction, 45,* 31–39.

Borelli, J. L., Rasmussen, H. F., St. John, H. K., West, J. L., & Piacentini, J. C. (2015). Parental reactivity and the link between parent and child anxiety symptoms. *Journal of Child & Family Studies, 24,* 3130–3144.

Ersoy, E., & Uysal, R. (2018). Opinions of school psychological counselors on giftedness and gifted students' education. *American Journal of Qualitative Research, 2,* 120–142.

Ghandour, R. M., Sherman, L. J., Vladutiu, C. J., Lynch, S. E., Bitsko, R. H., & Blumberg, S. J. (2019). Prevalence and treatment of depression, anxiety, and conduct problems in US children. *Journal of Pediatrics, 206,* 256–267.

Mendaglio, S. (2010). Anxiety in gifted students. In J. C. Cassady (Ed.), *Anxiety in schools: The causes, consequences, and solutions for academic anxieties* (pp. 153–177). New York, NY: Lang.

Mendaglio, S. (2012). Gifted adolescents' adjustment problems: A universal with special characteristics perspectives. In A. Zeigler, C. Fischer, H. Stoeger, & M. Reutlinger. (Eds.), *Gifted education as a lifelong challenge: Essays in honour of Franz J. Monks* (pp. 57–68). Zurich: Lit Verla.

Nelemans, S. A., Hale, W. W., III, Branje, S. J. T., Hawk, S. T., & Meus, W. H. J. (2014). Maternal criticism and adolescent depressive and generalized anxiety disorder symptoms: A 6-year longitudinal community study. *Journal of Abnormal Child Psychology, 42,* 755–766.

Suldo, S. M., Shaunessy-Dedrick, E., Ferron, J., & Dedrick, R. F. (2018). Predictors of success among high school students in Advanced Placement and International Baccalaureate programs. *Gifted Child Quarterly, 62,* 350–373.

CHAPTER 17

PERFECTIONISM: HELPING GIFTED CHILDREN LEARN HEALTHY STRATEGIES AND CREATE REALISTIC EXPECTATIONS

by Hope E. Wilson and Jill L. Adelson

One of the most common concerns of parents and teachers of gifted children is perfectionism. Gifted children often have nearly impossibly high expectations of themselves in academic and other settings, causing high levels of anxiety (Margot & Rinn, 2016). There are several ways in which perfectionism may manifest in children and many strategies for parents and teachers to help their students.

HEALTHY AND UNHEALTHY PERFECTIONISM

Although perfectionism can be a frustrating and overwhelming experience for parents and teachers, it can also have positive benefits for students. Perfectionism can be classified as healthy or unhealthy (Adelson & Wilson, 2009). Although unhealthy perfectionism can be associated with stress, unyielding expectations, risk avoidance, and procrastination, healthy perfectionism is associated with high levels of achievement and dedication to academic performance. Students who exhibit healthy perfectionism have high expectations for their work, high levels of motivation to complete tasks, and high self-confidence in their abilities to reach those goals. Therefore, it is the aim of interventions to help children transition from unhealthy to healthy perfectionism.

It is important to note that unhealthy perfectionism has been associated with depression and anxiety disorders, greater levels of violence and substance abuse, and eating disorders (Accordino, Accordino, & Slaney, 2000). This topic is complex and outside of the scope of this chapter, but when serious concerns about a child's mental health arise, it is imperative to seek help from a mental health professional. You can find local mental health professionals using the American Psychological Association (APA) Psychologist Locator at https://locator.apa.org, or by contacting your health insurance to locate a provider.

Additionally, parents and educators should be aware that perfectionism can be manifested in certain situations at certain times. Rather than think of perfectionism as a trait of the student, we recommended becoming aware of perfectionistic behaviors or tendencies and when/how they are manifested.

PERFECTIONISM AND GIFTED CHILDREN

Although perfectionism, both healthy and unhealthy, affects many populations (notably athletes, musicians, and performers), it poses special concerns for gifted students. Facing unchallenging schoolwork, many gifted children have been able to achieve perfect (or near-perfect) scores on assignments with relatively little effort. The expectation of mistake-free achievement often becomes reinforced by teachers, parents, and even peer groups. Thus, it is the high ability and achievement of gifted students that puts them at particular risk for perfectionistic behaviors and tendencies.

WHAT DOES PERFECTIONISM LOOK LIKE?

Most people are familiar with "overachieving" perfectionism, but perfectionism may also manifest itself as procrastination or risk-avoidance. Although these are presented as separate profiles, many gifted children fit multiple categories, and their perfectionistic behaviors/profiles may vary by area (e.g., homework, extracurricular activities, school projects).

THE ACADEMIC ACHIEVER

Achievers are primarily characterized by high expectations for their academic performance, with a strong focus on external evaluations, such as grades. Academic Achievers are often emotionally upset and extremely disappointed with grades that are less than the very top levels of performance. They often engage in dichotomous thinking. A gifted child, for example, may consider scoring 89% on a spelling test "failing." They also often generalize poor performance on one assignment or in one class to their overall level of intelligence or self-worth. In this case, they may believe that scoring 89% on one test means "I must not be very smart" or "I am terrible at spelling." To help Academic Achievers, parents can deemphasize grades and external evaluations, focusing instead on growth, learning, and the satisfaction from completing projects and homework—before the grades are returned or work is evaluated.

THE AGGRAVATED ACCURACY ASSESSOR

Aggravated Accuracy Assessors focus on mistakes and spend inordinate amounts of time attempting to create "perfect" work. These children often spend longer on their homework than is healthy, to the detriment of other activities, such as socializing with friends and family, participating in extracurricular activities, and even sleeping. These workaholic tendencies can add stress to family dynamics. Aggravated Accuracy Assessors often have difficulty relaxing standards, and they may refuse to submit a rough draft or may rewrite class notes with neater handwriting. Some strategies for helping these students are to model mistakes, provide examples of imperfections in role models from books and movies, and stick to schedules that limit time spent on assignments allowing for a healthy balance of activities.

THE RISK EVADER

When faced with exacting standards and the possibility of not being successful on the first attempt, Risk Evaders will often disengage. For example, a musically talented child may not audition for a solo in the school concert to avoid the potential disappointment of not being selected. Alternatively, a high school student may avoid Advanced Placement or honors classes, worrying that she might not be able to achieve high grades in more challenging classes. At younger ages, Risk Evaders may avoid answering questions in class or completing assignments. Parents and teachers can work to create safe environments for these children to take academic risks, and adults should praise attempts, rather than the outcomes, of these endeavors.

THE CONTROLLING IMAGE MANAGER

Controlling Image Managers are focused on the perceptions of others and attempt to preserve the appearance of perfection or high levels of success. This can easily create conflicts with peers when students quit playing or throw a game when it appears that they will lose. These children may also be overly concerned with the appearance of the final product, rather than the growth and learning that occurs through the process. Parents and teachers can help Controlling Image Managers by modeling good sportsmanship and helping children develop pride in the process and effort rather than the final product.

THE PROCRASTINATING PERFECTIONIST

Faced with looming (and often insurmountable) expectations and the fear of not meeting them, the Procrastinating Perfectionist will delay beginning his work. Children may fall into this habit as a way to avoid risk or preserve their image. If they wait until the last minute and rush through their work, then they have an excuse for a lapse in quality. Other children may procrastinate due to anxiety about their project. They may have difficulty breaking the project into manageable pieces or be paralyzed by the fear that their performance will not live up to their expectations. Parents and teachers can help Procrastinating Perfectionists by clearly communicating timelines, as well as working with children to divide large tasks into manageable goals and smaller deadlines to combat procrastination.

WHAT CAN TEACHERS DO?

Although teachers can feel frustrated and unsupported when teaching children who display perfectionistic tendencies, several simple interventions may be useful. Teachers can work to create a safe classroom environment for students to take academic risks by modeling mistakes. That is, teachers can explicitly call out errors they themselves make and model how to deal with it. Teachers can also focus praise on attempting difficult tasks, effort put into achievement, and individual student growth, rather than evaluation of the final product or grades. Additionally, they can avoid such dichotomous phrases and labeling as "You're so smart!" or "You are really good at math!" For many classes of gifted learners, it may be preferable to refrain from recognizing honor roll or other grade-based achievements to lessen the competition among students.

WHAT CAN PARENTS DO?

Parents of gifted students who display perfectionistic tendencies also face challenges. To help children move from unhealthy to healthy perfectionism, parents can foster a process-based, rather than performance-based, home learning environment. Specifically, helping children to take pride in a job well done, the learning completed, and the growth experienced, instead of emphasizing a final evaluation or grade, can mitigate unhealthy perfectionism. This can be as simple as celebrating the learning at the end of the marking period—before the report cards come home. Additionally, parents can encourage and model participation in fun activities outside of traditional areas of strength, such as bowling, karaoke, or dancing to popular music. These activities can help children embrace mistakes as learning experiences. Finally, parents can work to establish clear communications to help develop partnerships with teachers, so everyone can work together for the success of students.

FINAL THOUGHTS

Although unhealthy perfectionism is a common concern for gifted children, parents and teachers can help children learn healthy strategies for excelling academically. Children with unhealthy perfectionistic behaviors can fit several profiles, each of which presents unique challenges that can be met through simple interventions.

REFLECTION QUESTIONS

1. Does your child display healthy or unhealthy perfectionistic behaviors?
2. Which of the profiles of perfectionism seem to match with your child's behaviors and tendencies?
3. What can you do, as a parent, to help your child with perfectionistic tendencies?
4. How can you change your family's routines and habits to help prevent unhealthy perfectionistic behaviors?

REFERENCES

Accordino, D. B., Accordino, M. P., & Slaney, R. B. (2000). An investigation of perfectionism, mental health, achievement, and achievement motivation in adolescents. *Psychology in the Schools, 37*, 535.

Adelson, J. L., & Wilson, H. E. (2009). *Letting go of perfect: Overcoming perfectionism in kids*. Waco, TX: Prufrock Press.

Margot, K. C., & Rinn, A. N. (2016). Perfectionism in gifted adolescents. *Journal of Advanced Academics, 27*, 190–209.

CHAPTER 18

TOP 10 PSYCHOSOCIAL SKILLS TO CULTIVATE IN YOUR GIFTED CHILD

by Paula Olszewski-Kubilius

I am often asked by parents what are the most important things to do for a gifted child. I always interpret this to mean, "What can I do at home to help my child reach her full potential and be successful and happy?" That is a difficult question as so many factors are involved in talent development, and many of them are beyond our absolute control. Also, how success and happiness are defined or measured varies from one family and individual to the next. But over the years, I have developed a list of characteristics that I have come to believe are some of the most important ones for parents to cultivate so as to help gifted children realize their dreams (notice I said *their* dreams and not their *parents'* dreams). My list is based on the research literature in the field, as well as my own experience as an administrator of gifted programs and as a parent.

GRIT

This is a concept that psychologist Angela Duckworth (2016) developed and promoted. She and her colleagues defined it as perseverance and passion for long-term goals. Grit involves working assiduously in a talent domain over time, including maintaining effort despite failures, plateaus, and setbacks. Grit may emerge early in a young aspiring musician or artist or develop later as a high school student commits to the study of medicine or political science.

How does one develop or cultivate grit? Although research has not specifically focused on this, finding one's passions seems to be key, which takes time and deliberate searching. Parents can help by exposing children to a wide range of fields and topics of study through informal (e.g., trips to museums) and formal (e.g., enrichment courses) learning experiences. We do this a lot with young children, but it is important to help middle school and high school students also investigate fields and careers to find their passions. Helping students understand that people who make creative contributions to society were in it for the long haul and that creative breakthroughs do not come out of the blue without commitment and hard work over extended periods of time is also crucial. Children can begin to get a picture of this by reading about the lives of eminent individuals and seeing that there were ups and downs, great triumphs, and some failures along the way—and that the development of their abilities and talents was a lifelong journey.

SELF-CONTROL

This is another characteristic that Duckworth (2016) talked about. She defined it as the regulation of behavior, attention, and emotion to meet personal goals and standards. Self-control is what enables a student to stay focused on a day-to-day basis to meet the many smaller goals that are involved in reaching big life goals. Self-control is involved in working consistently to get good grades in a course even if it is not that interesting and choosing to do homework instead of socializing with friends, even though the latter is much more fun. It boils down to a willingness to do what it takes to get the job done even if the activity (e.g., practice) is not always that enjoyable. Self-control involves being able to delay immediate gratification so as to remain focused on a larger goal. This is an important skill to model and teach your child. There are many things in life that we all do that are a means to an end—a necessary step on the path toward more autonomous and enjoyable activities. Too many gifted children miss out on challenging and engaging opportunities because they are unwilling to work to get the grades that are needed to qualify or be selected for such opportunities. Like it or not, teachers will often choose students who are willing to work hard and make the most out of a special class or opportunity rather than a child who is very bright but does not demonstrate effort.

FINDING MEANINGFULNESS IN LEARNING

Del Siegle (2013), a leading expert on underachievement of gifted children, emphasized, "making school more meaningful . . . is among the most promising strategies for reversing academic under-achievement" (p. 98). Even if your child is achieving satisfactorily, making learning more personal and meaningful can only enhance motivation and commitment. How do we do this as parents? One way is to encourage students to pursue their interests outside of school via formal programs or learning on their own at home. Rather than directly teaching their child, parents can assume a supportive role, providing resources, supplies, and encouragement and connecting children to other adults (e.g., career professionals) who can be helpful to them. Parents can request that teachers help students understand why learning something is important and how it will be helpful to them in the future (e.g., How might I use algebra or geometry in the future? Why is it important to understand world history?). With a little bit of research on their own, parents can help students understand the connection between subjects in school and future careers and professions, or how understanding in one subject is necessary as a prerequisite for more advanced study later.

DEVELOPING APPROPRIATE ATTITUDES TOWARD WORK AND ABILITY

Ability and talent have to be combined with a strong work ethic and commitment to study or practice in order for students to be successful in achieving their career and life goals. Carol Dweck (2006), a psychologist, has popularized the idea of *mindsets* or beliefs about intelligence and ability. According to her, a *growth mindset*—a belief that ability, including intelligence, can change, grow, and improve with practice and study—is crucial for sustaining a long-term commitment to the development of one's talents. In contrast, a *fixed mindset*—a belief that one is born with a certain amount of ability or intelligence that is fixed and immutable—can hinder performance and achievement even among the most talented individuals. Research by Dweck and others shows that children who hold a growth mindset about their abilities and intelligence will persist through difficult times and rebound from setbacks (e.g., poor grades, not being selected for a program) more readily. How do parents cultivate a growth mindset? According to Dweck, the messages we give children about their performances and grades, specifically the type of praise, can influence their beliefs. Praise that focuses on recognizing and rewarding hard work and feedback that is centered on improvement and growth will promote healthy attitudes toward both ability and effort.

ENJOYMENT OF SOLITUDE

A consistent finding within the research literature on giftedness is the value of developing the ability to enjoy spending time alone. Historical accounts of the lives of individuals who make creative contributions to society reveal that often, this alone time was a result of difficult circumstances. Whether self-imposed or the result of external conditions, this alone time was used productively by individuals—to pursue independent projects, read broadly, write in journals, practice musical instruments, make art, or study (Olszewski-Kubilius, Worrell, & Subotnik, 2017).

How can parents cultivate enjoyment of solitude in children? It is challenging in current times because children can always remain connected to friends through social media. Modeling of independent pursuits helps, as well as encouragement and facilitation of a quiet place to do their work, study, practice, engage in hobbies, dabble in new interests, or just retreat for reflective thought. Parents can stress the importance of down time to recharge and rejuvenate, set rules or guidelines for phone and Internet use during family dinners or events, and show through their own actions how to balance productive use of solitary time with social activities.

RESILIENCY

One of the important facts about highly successful individuals is that although they achieved great renown for their creative contributions to society, their paths to success were not always easy (Olszewski-Kubilius et al., 2017). Many encountered significant challenges in childhood, including loss of a parent, instability in their family life, poverty, or racism. Often they found refuge in their talent domain—playing music, writing stories, or reading broadly and voraciously. Even when they were in their professional careers, their success was not instant or consistent. They typically had significant failures along the way, including loss of a job, work that was rejected or panned by critics, or business ventures that failed. Yet, they came back from these failures and persevered. Children need to know that success and failure often go hand in hand. In fact, you often cannot get more of one without more of the other. Michael Jordan expressed this when he said:

> I have missed more than 9,000 shots in my career. I have lost almost 300 games. On 26 occasions I have been entrusted to take the game winning shot . . . and I missed. I have failed over and over and over again in my life. And that's precisely why I succeed. (as cited in Nike, 2006)

OPTIMISM

Related to resiliency is what psychologist Maureen Neihart (2008) referred to as one's explanatory style—or how individuals explain their success or failure. Neihart said that explanatory style has three dimensions: permanence (whether the cause of an event is viewed as temporary or enduring forever), pervasiveness (projecting causes across many situations), and personalization (whether oneself or an external event is responsible for the loss or failure). Children who are optimistic are more likely to believe that setbacks or failure are temporary and will persevere because they have hope that things will change for the better—and they can bring about some of that change (e.g., study harder). Optimists also tend to limit the effects of failures rather than perceiving them as major catastrophes. In response to a poor grade, an optimist may say that her teacher has high expectations or the test was very hard rather than concluding that all teachers are unfair. As a result, an optimistic child can find a solution and way to improve the outcome rather than dissolving into hopelessness. Neihart said that pessimists blame themselves when things go badly and do not take credit when they work out well. Optimists do the opposite. They take credit for successes and recognize the role of outside factors (at least partially) in disappointing outcomes. The goal is to help children be accountable for their failures and address any areas of weaknesses without losing confidence to try again. The good news is that optimism can be taught! Parents can help children by actively shaping their explanatory style for successes and failures (e.g., teaching them to entertain multiple explanations for a poor performance).

BEING AN AUTONOMOUS, AUTODIDACTIC LEARNER

This includes a number of skills such as being able to initiate learning independently, setting individual learning goals and following through on them, identifying what one needs to learn and do in order to complete a project, being able to monitor and evaluate the success of one's learning, and accessing the appropriate resources needed for learning, such as seeking help from knowledgeable others. Although the learning that takes place in school is critical to developing the talents of gifted children, much of it is determined and dictated, at least in part, by a teacher and often is on topics children need to study that may not particularly engage or interest them. Outside of school is often where passions can be pursued. The ability and desire to learn things that are not required for school, coupled with the motivation to pursue these assiduously, are critical for the development of talent. Some researchers and scholars within the field of gifted education believe that not all that is necessary to develop ability into talent can realistically be done in schools, and learning outside of school is not just supplemental but fundamental. Parents can model autonomous learning, helping children decide on projects and goals and connecting children to activities that allow them to practice independent learning (e.g., competitions). They might also help by alerting teachers to a child's significant interests and pursuits outside of school, thereby giving the teacher an opportunity to capitalize on and connect learning at home with learning within school.

LEARNING TO DEAL WITH STRESS AND CONTROL ANXIETY

Any athlete performing at a national level or performing artists such as dancers, musicians, and actors will tell you that a key to their success is learning to deal with stress and anxiety. It is not that elite performers do not feel stress and anxiety; however, they practice and develop techniques (e.g., breathing to reduce physical manifestations of stress or anxiety) and strategies (e.g., overpreparation) to reduce it (Neihart, 2008; Peters, 2013). Often, they are taught these techniques by coaches, sports psychologists, other performers, mentors, and teachers. Performing arts schools and training facilities for elite athletes recognize both the positive and negative aspects of stress on performance and how to capitalize on or mitigate these stressors in order to enable peak performances. In the academic domains, we do very little of this even though scientists, literary scholars, mathematicians, and business entrepreneurs are often similarly involved in competitive (e.g., for grants, contracts, awards) or performance (e.g., presentations) situations. Also, there is stress and anxiety that comes from producing creative work, such as a story, piece of art, original song, or scholarly paper, and having it judged and evaluated by the gatekeepers, such as journal reviewers, art critics, or book reviewers, in a field. In short, everyone who works at the highest levels of achievement and creativity will encounter and need to learn to deal with stress and anxiety. As parents, we can begin early to help children with these feelings so that rather than shying away from a challenging course that requires oral presentations, choosing not to run for a school office because it involves making a public speech, or not submitting a story or art piece to a competition, students embrace these as opportunities to learn from and view them as stepping stones toward the accomplishment of their goals.

WORKING ON THE EDGE OF ONE'S COMPETENCY

This is one of Maureen Neihart's (2008) seven habits of top performers. It refers to being willing to work at something for which success or high achievement is not guaranteed. We all know the importance of challenge in producing growth. Athletes improve their game when they play against better athletes. Musicians improve their technique when they perform with other highly skilled musicians. Students improve their arguments when engaged in discussions with other students who challenge their ideas and assertions. It is not always easy, however, to put yourself into situations that require you to work on the edge of your existing competencies, so many students steer clear of these, preferring to continue doing what they are good at and confident they will succeed at. Neihart suggested that parents help children discern reasonable risks to take in terms of opportunities to grow and improve significantly, help children identify ways to prepare for the challenge, and facilitate reflection on the outcome afterwards. Getting comfortable with risk-taking is critical to enabling a child to reach the highest levels of performance he or she desires.

FINAL THOUGHTS

My two daughters are now grown, and as I look back at those years of parenting, I realize that my most important role in their lives was serving as their emotional coach. I have learned that this takes a great deal of time and effort and is even more important than any teaching activity or academic learning experience I could provide or access for them. I have also learned that it is a lifelong role and that every individual can continue to grow in self-understanding and gain social and emotional maturity and competence.

REFLECTION QUESTIONS

1. Of the 10 skills listed in this chapter, which ones do you think your child needs the most assistance with? How might you help your child make progress on that skill?
2. What are your reactions to your child when she brings home a disappointing grade or performance? In what ways might you reframe your reactions to facilitate a growth mindset for your child? What else might you do to promote growth mindsets?

3. How can you approach homework and school projects at home to facilitate your child becoming a more independent, autonomous learner? What else might parents do to cultivate independent learning skills?
4. How would you characterize your child's explanatory style? What messages or examples might you use with your child to build optimism and hope?

REFERENCES

Duckworth, A. (2016). *Grit: The power of passion and perseverance.* New York, NY: Scribner.

Dweck, C. S. (2006). *Mindset: The new psychology of success.* New York, NY: Random House.

Neihart, M. (2008). *Peak performance for smart kids: Strategies for ensuring school success.* Waco, TX: Prufrock Press.

Nike. (2006). *Failure* [Video file]. Retrieved from https://www.you tube.com/watch?v=45mMioJ5szc

Olszewski-Kubilius, P., Worrell, F. C., & Subotnik, R. F. (2017). The role of the family in talent development. In S. F. Pfeiffer & M. Foley-Nicpon (Eds.), *APA Handbook on Giftedness and Talent* (pp. 465–477). Washington, DC: American Psychological Association.

Peters, D. (2013). *Make your worrier a warrior. A guide to conquering your child's fears.* Tuscon, AZ: Great Potential Press.

Siegle, D. (2013). *The underachieving gifted child: Recognizing, understanding, and reversing underachievement.* Waco, TX: Prufrock Press.

PART IV
CREATIVITY

The authors in this section of the book offer a rich tapestry of ideas for opening the creative minds of gifted children and young people. In schools that provide it, creativity tends to focus more on the cognitive aspect—in particular, models and techniques that help children solve problems and expand thought. This is immensely valuable, but creativity embraces many other elements as well, among them the rich world of the arts and the imagination. As parents become versatile in using the different models and resources at home, children become adept at applying them, whether to a mathematical puzzle or free verse poem.

The parents, teachers, and researchers featured in this section have discovered innovative methods for unlocking the imagination of gifted learners, and they have done so in the face of the many constraints and pressures that so often attend the lives of their creative children. Their research and experience bring new light to the social and emotional difficulties gifted children experience as they try to press forward on their own path. Knowing how to approach issues such as low self-esteem, insecurity, lack of safety, and underachievement is critical if we want to help promising young learners realize their gifts now and in the future.

The many benefits that gifted learners receive from a more creative upbringing and education can barely be counted. Among those explored by the authors in this section are open-endedness, divergent thinking, imagination, artistry, analytical thinking, intuition, immersion in the senses, and depth of feeling. Gifted students thrive in situations that allow multiple responses and out-of-the-box approaches; they hunger for greater exposure to new ideas, knowledge, and catalysts that enable them to challenge the conventional.

In literature, the arts, math, science, and technology, they explore different lines of questioning, nuances of meaning and subtleties of interpretation beyond the level of understanding they would normally acquire.

In so many different and even surprising ways, creativity offers its blessings upon the hearts and minds of gifted students waiting for a new door to open on their world. The freedom to be fully oneself is perhaps the most precious gift that creativity brings to gifted children. Devoting so many hours to fulfilling the demands of the outside world, these children rarely have an opportunity to draw upon this inner world in such an abundant way. As this section reveals, the power of this freedom leads to lives of curiosity and purpose, a maturity and expansiveness of thought, and an enduring resilience in pursuing what they love.

—Joan Franklin Smutny

CHAPTER 19

DISCOVERING CREATIVE THINKING PROCESS SKILLS: A WIN-WIN FOR CHILDREN

by Bonnie Cramond

I remember my daughter telling me that the only things that she really learned in middle school were from Future Problem Solving Program International (FPSPI; https://www.fpspi.org). Although I know she learned more from school than the competition, the FPSPI experience stood out in her mind because it was so different from her other activities. It was the first time someone had taught her *how* to solve problems and to think creatively. What if she had not signed up for FPSPI?

We teach our children manners, what to do in certain emergencies, and other life basics, but most of us do not intentionally teach our children about thinking strategies and creative problem solving. Perhaps this is the case because many of us have never formalized these processes within ourselves, so we don't feel capable of communicating them to others. Another reason may be that we expect schools to teach most of the cognitive skills. Although society considers creativity one of the most important skills today, schools usually lack training about creativity or the processes of creative thinking (Cramond & Fairweather, 2013). Moreover, many schools fail to give students opportunities to use their creative abilities.

Programs and competitions, such as the International Torrance Legacy Creativity Awards (see https://www.centerforgifted.org/tor rance.html), Odyssey of the Mind (OM), Destination Imagination (DI), various inventing programs, and competitions that are specific to certain content areas, afford many students their best opportunities to stretch their creative muscles and see what others their age are doing. (See *The Best Competitions for Talented Kids: Win Scholarships, Big Prize Money, and Recognition* by Frances A. Karnes and Tracy L. Riley for information on various programs catalogued by subject.)

School programs often incorporate some of these competitions, such as FPSPI, DI, and OM, by including lessons on how to think and solve problems along with giving students opportunities to do so. However, there are many school programs lacking any instruction on problem solving or producing creative ideas. When children attend schools without any creativity instruction, parents can step in to help their children learn about the creative process and ideation strategies.

THE CREATIVE PROCESS

Various scholars have described the creative process through definition or as a stage-process model. Perhaps the best-known description of the creative process is one that English social psychologist Graham Wallas (1926/2014) suggested in *The Art of Thought* almost a century ago. He devised a four-stage process model that includes Preparation, Incubation, Illumination, and Verification.

Although each step of the model can take a different amount of time, and is often recursive, other researchers have verified Wallas's (1926/2014) basic process steps through the years (e.g., Policastro & Gardner, 1999). This is usually true whether the person engages in adaptive creativity (solving a problem) or expressive creativity (developing an artistic product). Although we often separate scientific creativity and artistic creativity, researchers have found that people who engage in thinking creatively use the same basic processes (Root-Bernstein & Root-Bernstein, 1999). Although the stimulus and final product may differ between scientific and artistic creativity, there is good reason to think that the two creative processes are similar.

PREPARATION

To guide children through the creative process, we need to instruct them to *prepare* by finding out as much about the problem as possible. For example, a probing question to explore an artistic venture might be "How can I express this idea or emotion most effectively?" Even if the child has a preferred modality, such as painting, there are still questions to determine, such as the type of palette, composition, medium, and size. In finding a solution to a problem, parents can direct children toward thinking about the components of the problem, finding analogies in other fields or nature, looking at the problem from another perspective, or discovering why previous solutions, if any, were unsatisfactory.

For example, it is clear from his many initial sketches that Picasso carefully considered the composition of *Guernica* before he completed the iconic painting. Dean Kamen invented the wheelchair capable of ascending and descending stairs by considering the problem of wheelchair accessibility from different perspectives. Previous attempts to solve this problem required ramps inside buildings to create accessibility. However, that solution was considered unsatisfactory due to the difficulty of putting ramps in old buildings or because the ramps sometimes required an individual to take an inconvenient route. Instead of making buildings accessible to wheelchairs, Kamen asked, "How could I make a wheelchair capable of navigating stairs?"

INCUBATION

Schools often ignore the second step of Wallas's (1926/2014) creativity process model, incubation. Students rarely have adequate time or encouragement to ponder various facets of a problem. Evidence shows, however, that when individuals have time to relax and think of other things after exploring the problem, the solution to the problem often appears. There are many anecdotal stories of this phenomenon, such as when Poincaré (1914/2010) realized the solution to a complex mathematical problem as he was boarding a bus during a vacation. Parents can teach their children that "sleeping on a problem," taking a walk or riding a bike, doing yoga, or relaxing and listening to music may contribute more productively as incubation rather than continuing to push ahead when stumped in problem solving. Torrance's Incubation Model (Torrance & Safter, 1990) is the only curriculum model that actively encourages students to incubate as part of the learning process, yet it is rarely used in instructional settings.

ILLUMINATION

The instantaneous "Aha!" moment that occurs when all of the pieces finally fall into place comprises the third step in Wallas's (1926/2014) model. Neurological evidence shows changes in brain activity that occur during insight (Kounios & Beeman, 2009). This usually happens after a period of some relaxation, and this research validates the practice of teaching children to relax during the creative process.

VERIFICATION

The final step in the Wallas (1926/2014) process model takes place when the creator tests the idea's suitability, soundness, and validity. For an artistic production, verification may occur subjectively through an assessment of the product quality. With a scientific solution, more objective verification may prove the product's workability.

Because the creative process is recursive, the creator may return to a previous stage to discover additional information, find an alternative solution or idea, or amend an initial idea. Returning to a previous stage may occur at any time in the process, so the process may be considered nonlinear. For example, when an "aha!" idea comes first, children need to gather information from the preparation stage and implement a relaxation period to incubate ideas during the learning process. Teaching children the process of creativity provides worthwhile interactions between parents and children. Parents can encourage children to use these skills when they want to solve a problem or create something new, possibly for a competition.

REFLECTION QUESTIONS

1. In *The War of Art: Break Through the Blocks and Win Your Inner Creative Battles*, Pressfield (2002) said, "We're not born with unlimited choices. . . . Our job in this lifetime is not to shape ourselves into some ideal that we imagine we ought to be, but to find out who we already are and become it" (p. 146). In the same way, it is not our job to shape our children into some ideal, but to help them find out who they already are and become it. In what ways

might you help your children find out who they already are
and become that person?

2. What resources are available in your school or community
to help children explore their creativity? (This is not limited
to art and music, but also creative thinking in any area of
human endeavor.)

3. How can you help your children learn to be reflective and
strategic thinkers?

REFERENCES

Cramond, B. L., & Fairweather, E. C. (2013). Future Problem
Solving as education for innovation. In L. V. Shavinina (Ed.),
The Routledge international handbook of innovation education
(pp. 215–226). New York, NY: Routledge.

Kounios, J., & Beeman, M. (2009). The aha! moment: The cognitive neuroscience of insight. *Current Directions in Psychological
Science, 10,* 210–216.

Poincaré, H. (2010). *Science and method.* New York, NY: Cosimo.
(Originally published 1914)

Policastro, E., & Gardner, H. (1999). From case studies to robust
generalizations: An approach to the study of creativity. In
R. J. Sternberg (Ed.), *Handbook of creativity* (pp. 213–225).
Cambridge, England: Cambridge University Press.

Pressfield, S. (2002). *The war of art: Break through the blocks and
win your inner creative battles.* New York, NY: Black Irish
Entertainment.

Root-Bernstein, R. S., & Root-Bernstein, M. (1999). *Sparks of
genius: The thirteen thinking tools of the world's most creative people.* Boston, MA: Houghton Mifflin.

Torrance, E. P., & Safter, H. T. (1990). *The incubation model of teaching: Getting beyond the aha!* New York, NY: Bearly.

Wallas, G. (2014). *The art of thought.* Kent, England: Solis Press.
(Original work published 1926)

CHAPTER 20

MAY THE CREATIVE FORCES BE WITH YOU: UNCOVERING CREATIVE GENIUS

by Patti Garrett Shade and Richard Shade

When your first child enters school, there are lessons to be learned for both parents and children. Many early learning opportunities are accompanied by rules that diminish both creative behaviors and creative thinking. Gifted children acquire content rapidly, and boredom quickly fills the waiting gaps. As your child navigates the grade levels, these cognitive "time outs" can lead to mischievous meanderings! If your child came with an extra dose of creativity, these, more intense, innate behaviors and creative thinking patterns can be misinterpreted as solely nonconforming—leading to disappointments and frictions affecting the teacher-student relationship.

Before formal schooling, gifted children use creativity skills freely when their home is their primary learning environment. Their creativity is fueled by an endless curiosity about the world they live in and the energy they pour into "try, try again" scenarios. However, when they leave the nurturing and protective free-play home environment and enter school, creative children may find they have to leave their creativity tucked away until called upon for a specific activity.

Creativity is not like an IQ score. Creativity is best identified in children by looking for associated behaviors, such as flexibility, playfulness, curiosity, originality, intellectual risk-taking, and persistence. These creative behaviors occur at certain times and under certain conditions in all children. The natural levels of creative abilities vary from child to child much like athletic abilities. Both can be either enhanced or severely squelched—and will only survive in a supportive environment and with frequent opportunities for practice. Creative behaviors must be supported so all children may fully realize the creative genius that resides in each of them.

UNDERSTANDING AND SUPPORTING HIGHLY CREATIVE CHILDREN

Highly creative gifted children have an insatiable drive to participate in the creative process. They are passionate about their process and their desired outcome. They may seem not to want to finish tasks, because in their minds, "It's just not done yet." Or they may not want to start tasks requiring a quick conclusion. They love the creative process and get immersed in their own version of where their ideas are taking them. Creative children need the freedom of time and the freedom of permission to approach a task differently. Then, they can sort out what creatively makes sense to them.

Research has shown that public school teachers prefer courteous, punctual, well-rounded, receptive, and obedient students (Cropley, 1992). The behavior and personality traits common to highly creative children, such as compulsiveness, nonconformity, disorganization, adventurousness, and imagination, are foreign to teachers as demonstrations of creativity. Understandably, parents may feel the same and respond similarly at home.

Additional studies (Westby & Dawson, 1995) indicated that not only do some teachers have a negative interpretation of characteristics associated with creativity, but they also view students who display such behaviors as "unappealing." These facts further support the notion that, in schools, creativity is misunderstood and not recognized as an important behavior. This points to the need for greater awareness and understanding of the oppositional behaviors associated with creativity.

BEHAVIORS OF HIGHLY CREATIVE CHILDREN

How do highly creative students behave? When immersed in creative activities, all children (especially highly creative gifted children) demonstrate more imagination, curiosity, and emotional intensity. To parents, teachers, and classmates, these intensities might "appear" as stubbornness or a lack of interest in the task at hand. Unfortunately, the highly creative children displaying these behaviors may seem oblivious and not recognize how others perceive their ideas or actions. Creative children may also be viewed as resistant, unmotivated, or slow in completing tasks. These behaviors often manifest as irritating, puzzling, annoying, and problematic to others.

Here's a beginning list of 10 creative behaviors exhibited in varying degrees by children:

1. **Intellectually playful:** Has fun tinkering or pondering ideas and concepts.

2. **Makes unusual associations:** Sees analogies between seemingly unlike ideas.

3. **Asks provocative questions:** Stimulates the conversation or discussion with intense "Why not?" or "What if?" questions.

4. **Passionate level of interest:** Displays intense desire to work on or learn about certain things.

5. **Generates many ideas:** Is prolific when asked to come up with ideas.

6. **Relishes off-the-wall humor:** Likes wacky, weird, or unusual humor.

7. **Broad range of interests:** Has eclectic interests to the extreme; often does not complete tasks or excel in one particular area.

8. **Ideas don't fit the norm:** Generates ideas that are often unique and not understood or accepted by peers.

9. **Greater persistence/determination:** Works ceaselessly and tirelessly in area of interest; enjoys working alone.

10. **Stands ground when criticized:** Does not change mind easily or often; holds strong self-beliefs.

Take note of your child's creative behaviors by keeping a journal and starting a collection of his or her works, interesting comments, and interactions at home. Sharing these observations with your child's teachers is a good way to explore attitudes and beliefs about creativity. This can also serve as an "encourager" for teachers to make classroom observations of all students' creative behaviors. This understanding and awareness will assist teachers in responding appropriately to unusual ideas, questions, and behaviors associated with creativity. Teachers' initial responses to students' creative demonstrations can make or break the creative spirit.

Children learn to value their own creative achievements when individuals in both the home and school settings foster a creative learning environment. It is difficult, even for the creatively savvy teacher to fully acknowledge the diversity of creative behaviors exhibited in the classroom. Using a tool such as the Creative Attribute Learning Log (see Figure 20.1) facilitates a more thorough picture of creative behaviors. This tool lists the behaviors next to a virtual seating chart to make tracking less time-consuming. As teachers reflect on the data collected with this instrument, they will notice the more highly creative students and also note behaviors they want to encourage more in other students.

Here are 12 thoughts about creative thinking that children are not typically taught in school that may enhance their understanding of their own creativity (Michalko, 2013):

1. You are creative.
2. Creative thinking is work.
3. You must go through the motions.
4. Your brain is not a computer.
5. There is no one right answer.
6. Never stop with your first good idea.
7. Expect the experts to be negative.
8. Trust your instincts.
9. There is no such thing as failure.
10. You do not see things as they are; you see them as *you* are.
11. Always approach a problem on its own terms.
12. Learn to think unconventionally.

HAPPY VERSUS UNHAPPY CREATIVE CHILD

Happy adults are healthier, more successful, more hardworking, more caring, and more socially engaged (Wade, 2005). Similarly, children immersed in creativity are more happy, playful, smiling, laughing, and engaged. However, when children are creatively unhappy, it may manifest as opposition or rebellion. This behavior also may be masking nervousness, insecurity, and/or a lack of understanding of

Classroom Creative Attribute Learning Log—January 2016			
Creative Behaviors	**Student Names**		
1. Intellectually playful	Logan 1-1-3-2-2	Caleb 3-3-3	Seth 1-1-4-3	Eli 1
2. Unusual associations	Missy 3-3-3	Amare 2-2	Ella	Bruce
3. Provocative questions	Beau	Jayton	Colby	Kaylee
4. Passionate interests	Sam	Zoey	Zack	Bailey 3-2-3-3

Figure 20.1. Classroom creative attribute learning log. From *Curiosita Teaching: Integrating Creative Thinking Into Your 21st Century Classroom*, by P. Shade and R. Shade, 2014, Denver, CO: RASPO Publishing. Copyright 2014 by P. Shade and R. Shade. Reprinted with permission.

a child's own creativity. An insecure creative child may say, "This is boring," or "My teacher doesn't like me."

When parents hear that their creative child is unhappy, it's important to remember that the child may be caught in several paradoxes. He or she may be feeling insecure or genuinely trying to sort out the dichotomy of his or her creative self within the conformity required in formal educational settings. If a creative gifted child seems unhappy, parents might consider these suggestions (Rimm, 2001):

» encourage creative children to be productive in at least one area of creative expression,
» help them find audiences and/or like groups for their performances and products,
» don't label one child in the family "the creative child,"
» find appropriate models and mentors in areas of children's creativity, and
» help children use creative strengths to support weaknesses in other areas.

CHANGING HORIZONS—CHANGING SCHOOLS

The historical dilemma that's held schools back for some time is beginning to fade away. Many schools felt like they had to choose academic achievement (emphasis on content, grades, state test scores, etc.) and not spend much time (if any) on creativity. Today the call for 21st-century skills has challenged schools to figure out how to embrace creativity within the structure of their teaching environments. Future learning schools are empowering students with confidence in their own creative thinking—equipping them to become dynamic, autonomous future workers. Children will seek work where they can use their creative genius to design beautiful artistic or scientific solutions for our world. They will create:

> To create, a person must have knowledge but forget the knowledge, must see unexpected connections in things but not have a mental disorder, must work hard but spend time doing nothing as information incubates, must create many ideas yet most of them are useless, must look at the same thing as everyone else, yet see something different, must desire success but embrace failure, must be persistent but not stubborn and must listen to experts but know how to disregard them. (Michalko, 2011, para. 12)

However, there is more work to be done. More parents and teachers must join together to change the way creativity grows and flourishes in our homes and schools. May the creative forces be with you and your child!

REFLECTION QUESTIONS

1. What experiences did you have when your child first entered school that might be related to your child's creativity?
2. What is your belief about the importance of creativity in schools? In your opinion, what changes are needed in school to foster creativity?
3. Have you noticed your child demonstrating some of the creative behaviors listed in this chapter? What was your response and/or the school's response?
4. Did you have a positive or negative encounter with a teacher due to your creativity? Please share.

5. Why is the development of creativity skillsets and mindsets crucial for the continuous improvement of the world we live in?

REFERENCES

Cropley, A. J. (1992). *More ways than one: Fostering creativity in the classroom.* Norwood, NJ: Ablex.

Michalko, M. (2011). *The twelve things you are not taught in school about creative thinking* [Web log post]. Retrieved from https://creativethinking.net/the-twelve-things-you-are-not-taught-in-school-about-creative-thinking

Rimm, S. B. (2001). *Marching to the beat of a different drummer.* Retrieved from http://www.sylviarimm.com/article_difdrum.html

Shade, P., & Shade, R. (2011). *Curiosita teaching: Integrating creative thinking into your 21st-century classroom.* Marion, IL: Pieces of Learning.

Wade, D. (2005). *So what do you have to do to find happiness?* Retrieved from https://humanistcontemplative.blogspot.com/2008/06/so-what-do-you-have-to-do-to-find.html

Westby, E. L., & Dawson, V. L. (1995). Creativity: Asset or burden in the classroom? *Creativity Research Journal, 8,* 1–10.

CHAPTER 21

CREATIVE THINKING SKILLS FOR ALL SEASONS: A REFLECTION

by Sarah E. Sumners

An often overlooked area of creativity is how it can be used to attain personal triumph in our everyday lives. The role of parents and mentors who nurture everyday creative thinking in children cannot be understated. Academic and everyday life challenges provide the opportunity for parents, teachers, and coaches to foster creative thinking by promoting ideation, analogous and lateral thinking, visualization, group and individual problem solving, and other strategies that teach children how to think creatively.

My parents played this role for me when I was young and then encouraged me to seek out mentors who would support my need for productive creative behaviors during my adolescence and teenage years. These extended parents came in the form of teachers and coaches who taught me important lessons about how to compete in the classroom and on the tennis court—lessons that have served me well from childhood into my adult years.

By modeling creative behaviors related to my academic and athletic challenges, these mentors made it clear to me that every essay, project, game, and opponent presented separate, individual challenges to overcome. Each shot on the tennis court posed specific problems to solve with myriad ways in which to return the ball. My mentors taught me to visualize the game from every angle, consider my opponent's approach, empathize with the movement of the ball, and explore and evaluate as many outcomes as possible. As a result, I was better equipped to determine the course of action my body and my mind needed to take in order to win the point—then, game, set, and match! By practicing these techniques in singles tennis matches, I then applied them to my success as a doubles partner. Ultimately, these creative thinking skills translated from the tennis court to the academic school setting.

Although creative thinking sharpened my competitive edge in a sport, children of all ages can successfully use these skills in a wide variety of competitions. Some competitions, such as the International Torrance Legacy Creativity Awards (https://www.centerfor gifted.org/torrance.html), embrace the need that all children have to express themselves creatively across all areas of learning. By focusing on the highest form of mental thinking, the Torrance Creativity Award program nurtures creativity in children and young people, ages 8–18. The Creative Writing, Visual Arts, Music Composition, and Inventions award categories provide a competitive outlet with minimal resources required. Mentors who model the creative thinking skills needed by children in specific talent areas significantly impact children throughout their school years and beyond, whether in competitions or everyday lives.

REFLECTION QUESTIONS

1. In what ways, when, and where are you most creative? Be specific.
2. In what ways could you modify your home environment to encourage creative thinking?
3. How have mentors, such as parents, teachers, and coaches, impacted your life?
4. How were these mentors different than other adults in your life? What did they do differently?

CHAPTER 22

CREATIVE UNDERACHIEVERS: CHILDREN WHO ARE TOO OUT OF THE BOX

by Sylvia B. Rimm

Educators in the field of gifted education attempt to not only accelerate curriculum for their students, but also encourage and expand students' critical and creative thinking. They often explain this creative approach to students as out-of-the-box thinking. The box is an effective analogy to help children understand how to shift their thinking and learning styles toward taking initiative and becoming more original, questioning, and imaginative.

As a psychologist who specializes in gifted children, I sometimes work with students who do indeed enjoy learning and working out of the box, but struggle with in-the-box assignments, even those at appropriate challenge levels. They say things like, "I would enjoy math if 6 plus 4 could equal something different each time, but we always have to put down the same exact answer. It's boring." These children often have uneven abilities (Rimm, 2008a); although they may enjoy talking, they prefer to write little, and specifically find repetitive study unpleasant, even when it is helpful for their mastery of information. Many of these children underachieve in school (Rimm, 2008b).

Underachieving children are not always creative, and creative children are not always underachievers. However, an alarming number of highly creative children do not achieve to their abilities in school. Parents of those highly creative children frequently conclude with a certain amount of pride that "their children have always seemed to march to the beat of different drummers" (Rimm, 2001, para. 1).

WHAT PARENTS AND TEACHERS CAN DO TO HELP CREATIVE UNDERACHIEVERS

Ideal home and school environments that foster both creativity and achievement include parents and teachers who value creativity within the limits of reasonable conformity. Children are praised and encouraged to work hard, but also for their unusual and critical thinking and production. The creative thinking does not become a device or a manipulation for avoidance of academic or home responsibilities, even when they are not as exciting. If, in any way, creativity takes on a ritualized position of regularly avoiding parents' requirements or the school's expectations, creativity becomes used as "an easy way out" for avoidance of responsibility and achievement. Here are some recommendations for parents and teachers for the prevention and reversal of underachievement in creative children (Rimm, 2008b):

» **As a parent, don't, if at all possible, ally with children against a parent or teacher in the name of creativity.** Parents should communicate their concerns to the other parent or the teacher, but it must be done respectfully so that the children are not overempowered to avoid home or school expectations.

» **Encourage creative children to be productively engaged in at least one area of creative expression, and help them to find audiences for their performances.** Children that are happily and productively involved in creative areas are less likely to use their energy to fight authority (Rimm, 1996). Whether their choice of creative expression is art, drama, music, or science, a creative outlet frees them of some of their internalized pressures to be nonconformists in other areas.

» **Do not permit children to use their creative outlet as a means of evading academic assignments.** Demanding music practice or impending art show deadlines are reasons for flexibility in academic requirements but not excuses for avoidance of responsibility.

» **Don't label one child in the family "the creative child."** It causes that child to feel pressured to be most creative and causes other siblings to believe that creativity is not possible for them at all.

» **Find appropriate models and mentors in areas of children's creativity.** Creative children, particularly in adolescence, too easily discover inappropriate models that may also be creative underachievers (Rimm, 2008b). Appropriate models should share the child's creative talent area, but must also give messages of responsibility, self-discipline, hard work, and reasonable conformity. Mentors should be achieving, creative people that work both in and out of the box.

» **Find a peer environment that combines creativity and achievement.** Creative children need to feel comfortably accepted by other achieving and creative young people. Gifted resource programs frequently provide a haven for creative underachievers. Many summer opportunities provide excellent creative outlets.

» **Encourage intrinsic motivation while also teaching competition.** Children should learn to enjoy the creative process for the joy and satisfaction of their personal involvement. However, they should not be permitted to entirely avoid the competitive arena (Rimm, 2005). They should experience a balance of winning and losing to build confidence and resilience.

» **Use creative strengths to build up weaknesses.** Children don't have to be equally strong in all areas, but they do have to accomplish, at least minimally, in school-required subjects so that they don't close educational doors for themselves. Artists who don't like math or creative writers who don't like memory work can use their creative strengths as a means of adjusting to their weaknesses. Artistic or unique folders, assignment notebooks, or technology may help the non-mathematician remember to do assignments, particularly if the artist is encouraged to share these artistic creations with peers. Creative children can often find their own solutions to dealing with their weaknesses, and some flexibility and encouragement on the part of teachers will foster creative solutions for creative children.

» **Avoid confrontations, particularly if you can't control the outcomes.** This is not an excuse to avoid firmness and reasonable consequences, but it is a warning to prevent over-reaction, punishments, and the continuous struggles and battles that often plague creative adolescents' environments. Modeling and sharing positive work and play experiences can keep parents, teachers, and children in an alliance.

» **Help creative adolescents to plan a creative future.** Although they are underachievers at this time, it's critical that they understand that most creative careers are open only to achievers. If they're unwilling to compromise and conform to reasonable requirements, they're likely to close doors to future creative opportunities.

There is a precarious balance between creativity and opposition-ality. Creative children often feel so internally pressured to be creative that they define their personal creativity only as nonconformity. If they're unwilling to conform at least minimally, they risk losing the opportunities to develop their unique talents. If parents and teachers don't encourage avoidance of responsibility in the name of creativity, creative children can channel their important talent toward productive contributions, feel better about themselves, and share their creative contributions with society.

REFLECTION QUESTIONS

1. We frequently speak of perfectionism in gifted children. How can perfectionism adversely affect productivity of creatively gifted children?
2. Why does Dr. Rimm encourage parents and teachers to teach creative children how to function in competition?
3. Why is it necessary to teach highly creative children (who often label rigor as "boring") to work both in and out of the box?
4. How can parents who disagree about their children's creativity manage to respect each other and unite in support and encouragement of their children?

5. In what ways can parents communicate to a teacher about their child respectfully if they believe that the teacher doesn't value their child's creativity?

REFERENCES

Rimm, S. B. (1996). The arts are important for your children. *How to Stop Underachievement, 6*(4), 1–5.

Rimm, S. B. (2001). *Marching to the beat of a different drummer.* Retrieved from http://www.sylviarimm.com/article_difdrum.html

Rimm, S. B. (2005). Teaching healthy competition. *Sylvia Rimm on Raising Kids, 16*(3).

Rimm, S. B. (2008a). Learning disabilities. *Sylvia Rimm on Raising Kids, 18*(4).

Rimm, S. B. (2008b). *Why bright kids get poor grades and what you can do about it: A six-step program for parents and teachers* (3rd ed.). Scottsdale, AZ: Great Potential Press.

CHAPTER 23

ADVOCATING FOR YOUR CHILD'S CREATIVITY IN SCHOOLS: YOUR RIGHT, YOUR RESPONSIBILITY

by Richard Shade and Patti Garrett Shade

As your child heads back for another year of schooling, he faces new experiences and challenges: new teachers, a new curriculum, new standards, new procedures, and much more. A disproportionate amount of energy, effort, and emphasis will be placed on academic fundamentals—while creativity languishes. As a parent, you will need to advocate for your child's creativity.

Advocating for creativity is similar, yet slightly different from, other forms of advocacy, such as advocating for more challenging work or for a starting a gifted program in your school district. In advocating for creativity, you are shedding light on the importance of incorporating skills such as imagination, questioning, creative thinking, critical thinking, and problem solving into daily classroom activities.

WHAT DO COLLEGES AND UNIVERSITIES WANT?

The mission of most middle and high schools is to get students into college—to make them "college ready." Although the societal talking point that "everybody needs to go to college" has existed for years, we must seriously consider that there are many reasons not to jump straight into college from high school. Additionally, we must do a better job educating students earlier about different options, such as community colleges, trade schools, and on-the-job training. Being educated in a skill is incredibly valuable, yet often ignored. When we need carpenters, plumbers, electricians, mechanics, and welders, don't we all want gifted and creative individuals? And the best news is that these fields often command very attractive salaries—and a boatload of intrinsic motivation and satisfaction.

But let's say, after considering the options above, college is your son or daughter's choice. Here is the first paradox you will face: the application process. Interestingly, colleges and universities say they are looking for independent and creative thinking students, yet many means used to determine college admission do not really test those qualities. Instead, many colleges look at ACT or SAT scores, GPAs, and the number of AP classes taken. Can you see the irony here?

There are more than 6,000 colleges and universities in the United States. FairTest (https://www.fairtest.org) keeps an up-to-date list of the ones that *do not require* ACT or SAT scores. Currently more than 1,000 colleges have joined the test-optional movement. Instead, they rely on successful academic effort, well-rounded or broad-minded qualities in essays, and participation in extracurricular activities. If the landscape is slowly changing regarding college admission and entrance requirements, wouldn't it be in your child's best interest to be a better prepared creative thinker, critical thinker, communicator, collaborator, and problem solver? This is the message K–12 institutions need to hear from you.

WHAT DO WORKPLACE ENVIRONMENTS WANT?

The truth is, many parents believe that a college education is not really for the knowledge or even the degree, but rather to get a good job! And what businesses want today are people who can think creatively, communicate, collaborate, and problem solve.

The American Management Association (2019) released a Critical Skill Survey stating it desperately needed skilled workers. However, the skills needed have changed:

Proficiency in reading, writing, and arithmetic has traditionally been the entry-level threshold of the job market, but the new workplace requires more from its employees. Employees need to think critically, solve problems, innovate, collaborate, and communicate more effectively—at every level within the organization. (para. 2)

From day one in public school classrooms, students are taught to think reactively and inside the standards box. When a teacher gives students a worksheet, handout, or text, the student must react to it. However, worksheets do not grow dendrites and lead students to becoming passive learners. The real 21st-century world is not passive. Real life requires proactive thinking, creative thinking, and problem solving, and it does not hand you a worksheet. In real life, there is not only one right answer that can be found in the back of the book!

YOUR CHILD'S FUTURE WORK LIFE

Teachers do have a rather challenging job—preparing students for the world of work when no one has any idea what that world will look like. Consider the following predictions for the future world of work (Shade & Shade, 2019):

> » In ten years 40%–50% of the jobs that exist today will not exist! (Do you remember the switchboard operator or the iceman?) Currently many school are actually preparing students for the jobs of the past or present.
> » What courses should your child take to qualify to become a dream designer or a Nano medic?
> » Currently 60%–70% of all businesses are small businesses. The chances are your child will start, own, or work in one.
> » Your child will probably have 10–15 jobs in his or her lifetime! (pp. 78–85)

Given these predictions, to have a chance of being successful, your child will need to have the following skillsets and mindsets of creativity:

> » organizational skills,
> » written communication skills,
> » oral communication skills,
> » problem-solving skills,
> » self-motivation skills,
> » time management skills,
> » administrative skills,
> » collaboration skills,
> » critical thinking skills, and
> » creative thinking skills.

WHAT DO YOU REALLY WANT
FOR YOUR CHILDREN?

You know the answer! What is the number one thing parents want for their children? When asked, they do not reply "good grades," "a good job," or "a good relationship." They do not reply "wealth," "power," or "celebrity." More than anything else—and it dwarfs all of the other answers combined—*parents want their children to be happy.*

Think of your child's creative happiness when he or she was younger. Unfortunately that creative happiness is often put on hold while attending school. We want the school place, home place, and workplace to be where children and adults have frequent opportunities to be creatively engaged in their work—happy.

WHAT CAN YOU DO?

Remember, you are your child's first and best teacher; no teacher knows your child like you do. But, you will have to straddle the fine line of advocacy by trying to both nurture and protect your child's creativity, while complying with the school's rules, guidelines, and principles. So, how can parents respectfully advocate for creativity without compromising the rules?

The first step of advocating for more creativity at school is establishing frequent and purposeful communication with the teacher. In some years this process can be smooth sailing, and in others, the process may seem like rough rushing waters. At the appropriate time, you may wish to talk with your child's teacher to better understand the creative opportunities planned for the upcoming year by respectfully asking questions such as:

>   » Do you teach creative thinking tools to your students?
>   » Do you help children understand that succeeding and failing are a part of learning?
>   » Are there opportunities in the curriculum to create visual and verbal products?
>   » Would you be interested in adding daily activities to challenge your students' creative thinking?
>   » Do students use their strengths and interests to explore and discover their passion areas of learning?

» Does the school participate in any formal creativity competitions, such as Destination Imagination or Future Problem Solving Program International?

Secondly, there are times when parents may need to discuss and advocate for their child's personal levels of creativity. Here are a few suggestions:

» Keep a portfolio and sample products of your child's work. Include work he struggles with and samples of outstanding efforts to share with teachers.

» Keep a journal of your child's creative traits and behaviors (such as intellectual playfulness, ability to make unusual associations, out-of-the-box ideas, off-the-wall humor, persistence). She may do things at home and not exhibit them as easily at school, possibly due to lack of creative opportunity. Date these journal entries and share them at parent-teacher conferences.

» Explore the theory of multiple intelligences with your child so he can discover his strengths and creative passion areas. The question is not "How smart are you?" but rather "How are you smart?" Children with limited exposure may not discover their true passion areas. Provide a broad range of experiences so he may continue to explore his interests and develop his strengths. Perhaps the most heartbreaking scenario ends in adulthood, when he may be stuck in a job that saps or underutilizes his creative energies. For a more detailed explanation of the multiple intelligences theory, check out these websites and search for "multiple intelligences":
  • https://www.verywellmind.com
  • http://www.institute4learning.com

Here are some strategies you can do at home:
» Allow your child the freedom to make mistakes. This encourages her to explore and experiment without fear of punishment. She needs to view mistakes as "good information" that can guide her to the next tweak or improvement or final product.

» Encourage your child to evaluate his creative products honestly. Then ask questions like "What next?" or "What would
happen if . . . ?"

» Reply to your child's questions with "I don't know" when
asked. For example, if she asks, "What color should I use in
my drawing?" it is good to say, "I don't know." Many times
when we quickly provide an answer to a child's question
or our personal opinion, it derails her natural curiosity and
intellectual risk-taking.

As you advocate for your child's creativity, here are some open-
ended questions you might use to find out more about the mindset
of your child's teacher. Choose one or two, and use them as discussion starters for creating a nonthreatening dialog:

» "Would it be possible . . . ?"

» "In what new ways are . . . ?"

» "Have you explored . . . ?"

» "What would happen if . . . ?"

» "Wouldn't it be interesting . . . ?"

» "How could this be changed to . . . ?"

» "Wouldn't it be funny if . . . ?"

» "Can you imagine . . . ?"

» "I wonder . . . ?"

Avoiding getting into an adversarial relationship with your
child's teacher. Parents often approach teachers and say, "My child
is bored in your class" or "My child is not happy in your classroom."
A child may say he is "bored" because the work is too easy, too hard,
or sometimes just not interesting to him! Instead, consider saying,
"Have you ever seen my child struggle with any schoolwork? It seems
like everything is pretty easy for him, and I worry a little about that."
Your child may not be happy because he does not have opportunities to demonstrate his creativity. You might broach the subject of
passion-based or product-based learning (incorporating his interests
and passions into the classroom experience) to see if his interests and
talents can be better addressed.

What you see at home is not always what happens in the classroom and vice versa. A mutual understanding of the "whole picture"

of your child will help you and your child's teacher work together to provide the best learning environment at home and at school.

SUMMARY

You protect your child in many ways: immunizations, warm clothing, holding her hand when she crosses the street with you. But how do you go about protecting her freedom to think and to explore her world creatively? And isn't it a bit intimidating to try to imagine your child's future world? It will be a world in which the assimilation of knowledge and the ability to process new information will not suffice. To face this world with competence, she will need a "toolbox" filled with the tools and skills of creative thinking. These will give her the confidence to face the unknown. They will provide her with the ability to think creatively and critically—to communicate and collaborate—and to work with others in a continuous problem-solving mode.

REFLECTION QUESTIONS

1. Do you believe the demand for creative thinking in the workplace is increasing? Give several examples.
2. When you think of your child's school experience, what activities or academic content do you believe were not worthwhile? Could these have been replaced with creative thinking learning opportunities?
3. What specific things do you believe your child's schools should do to better prepare him or her for real-world work opportunities when he or she leaves school?
4. How might we best educate students in the present for jobs in the future?
5. What jobs do you believe might be reduced, modified, or eliminated by the time your child graduates and enters the workforce?

REFERENCES

American Management Association. (2019). Executives say 21st century needs more skilled workers. Retrieved from https://www.amanet.org/articles/executives-say-21st-century-needs-more-skilled-workers

Shade, P., & Shade, R. (2019). *Setting minds free. Nurturing and protecting your child's creativity.* Denver, CO: RASPO.

CHAPTER 24

FULL STEAM AHEAD!

by Carol Fisher

On the surface, expanding STEM into STEAM—science, technology, engineering, the arts, and math—may seem like a no brainer. After all, who doesn't want his or her child to be well-rounded: to excel in math and science . . . and play in the band, participate in choir, paint, sculpt, dance, or act? However, there is more to STEAM than simply *participating* in the arts. True STEAM means *integrating* the arts into STEM.

In recent years, some educators have been reevaluating their STEM curricula and redesigning curricula to incorporate the arts. Others, such as the Rhode Island School of Design, are championing initiatives in which teachers, researchers, policymakers, and students are spearheading a grassroots movement to integrate art and science research (see https://www.risd.edu/academics/public-engagement/#support-for-steam). Supporters contend that an integrated STEAM curriculum promotes critical thinking and that STEAM is an important pathway to increase U.S. economic competitiveness.

Whether or not your gifted child's school has yet to embrace STEAM, there are many ways parents can expose their children to STEAM principles, both at home and through outside enrichment opportunities.

PATTERNS: A PERFECT PLACE TO START

What is a pattern? Is it the tiles on a floor, the kata in karate class, or an alternating sequence of red and blue blocks? Is it the choreography in a dance class, the spirals on a snail shell, the Fibonacci sequence in music, or the golden ratio in architecture? Is it the rhythm of your favorite song, a bedtime ritual, a checkerboard, or a rainbow? Is it math, is it art, or is it science? It is, of course, all of the above.

Opportunities to explore patterns exist in our everyday environment. Simple objects can be sequenced by asking, "What comes next?" We can look in nature to find many patterns that can be described with mathematics, including symmetries, spirals, tessellations, fractals, and more (Ball, 2016). Cultural artifacts—from African textiles, to the Alhambra in Spain, to mandalas, to quilts—can be examined for their artistic, mathematic, and scientific compositions and basis.

TESSELLATIONS

Tessellations are shapes that can fill a surface without gaps or overlaps. Simple tessellations use triangles, squares, rectangles, or regular hexagons, and they can be created using shapes, geometric dot paper, or graph paper. A variety of shapes can be combined to form more complex tessellations, such as Penrose tilings. M. C. Escher is sometimes referred to as a mathematical artist because of his tessellation-based artwork, in which he explored concepts such as architecture, perspective, and impossible spaces long before the worlds of mathematics and art intersected.

ORIGAMI

Most people think of origami as simply creating animals and flowers folded from a single sheet of paper. However, origami abounds with math. Every fold can be described in mathematical terms. The introduction of modular origami, in which you fold multiples of one (or more) units, allows us to construct anything from the platonic solids to 3-D fractals, in which detailed patterns repeat as they scale in size. Origami and paper models also help visualize advanced science on both microscopic and macro levels, in areas such as electronics, aeronautics, and cell research.

LINE DESIGN

Line design allows us to use straight lines to achieve beautiful parabolas. A simple start is to draw a right angle with equal segments on both lines. This can be done large scale on a floor with square tiles using masking tape, on graph paper, or on plain paper. The secret is to make a straight line connecting the furthermost point (from the vertex) on one line to the innermost point on the other line. Continue to connect points, moving downward and outward point by point. The surprising result is a beautiful curve.

You can expand on this concept by drawing angles of different measurements and analyzing the differences. Angles can be combined to create beautiful art work. These can be drawn on paper or done with string (a technique known as curve stitching) and punched holes or nails. Circles, ellipses, or polygons can be challenging, but are amazing when completed.

The integration of art into math and science is a mindset, a thinking-outside-of-the-box openness, and an acknowledgment that there is creativity in every aspect of math and science if you look for it.

RESOURCES FOR PATTERNS

Bubbles
https://www.exploratorium.edu/ronh/bubbles

Coordinate Art
https://www.superteacherworksheets.com/mystery-graph-picture.html

http://bellevillebulldogs.tripod.com/id21.html

Fractals
https://fractalfoundation.org

Origami
https://gurmeet.net/origami

https://www.origami-resource-center.com/origami-science.html

Parabolic Curves
https://mathcraft.wonderhowto.com/how-to/create-parabolic-curves-using-straight-lines-0131301

https://www.ams.org/publicoutreach/curve-stitching

Penrose Tiles
http://jwilson.coe.uga.edu/emat6680fa05/schultz/penrose/penrose_main.html

Tessellations
http://www.tessellations.org

CREATING STEAM AT HOME

1. **Explore colors.** Young children can learn how red and yellow make orange, while blue and yellow make green. Then, they can begin to learn the science behind color: How are color and light linked? How do rain and sun combine to make a rainbow? More advanced students can learn the four color theorem in mathematics, which tells us that only four colors are needed to color a map with no two adjacent sections sharing a common color. Challenge your child to color a pattern or a map following the four color theorem.
2. **Build and fly a kite.** The construction of the kite requires mathematics, its design is art, and flying is aerodynamic science.
3. **Blow some bubbles.** Bubbles, fascinating and beautiful, incorporate geometry, surface tension, elasticity, chemistry, and light.
4. **Create coordinate art.** Use coordinates, like you use when reading a map or a graph, to create pictures. Coordinates may be positive numbers only or include negative numbers and can range from simple to complex.
5. **Examine the works of famous artists.** Frank Lloyd Wright's architecture uses identifiable shapes, yet defies standard building designs; Alexander Calder, credited as the inventor of the mobile, created models of kinetic energy; and Piet Mondrian's paintings are frequently composed of rectangles.
6. **Get hands-on.** Manipulatives, such as pattern blocks, tangrams, pentominoes, and Cuisenaire rods, provide endless explorations that include art, math, and science.

REFLECTION QUESTIONS

1. What ideas for creating STEAM at home resonated with you? Why?
2. What daily tasks or pastimes could be used as a springboard for discovering various aspects of STEAM?
3. How can you broaden activities outside the home (e.g., dinner at a restaurant, a trip to the zoo, a walk to the park) to incorporate exploration of relationships among science, technology, engineering, art, and math?
4. What creative endeavors that your child currently enjoys could inspire STEAM thinking?
5. How can you realign your thinking (and your child's) to look beyond the obvious and extract meaningful relationships among science, technology, engineering, art, and mathematics?

REFERENCE

Ball, P. (2016). *Patterns in nature: Why the natural world looks the way it does*. Chicago, IL: The University of Chicago Press.

CHAPTER 25

HOW PARENTS CAN NURTURE A LIFELONG LOVE OF THE ARTS

by Kathryn P. Haydon

In *Playing From the Heart*, Peter H. Reynolds (2016), author of *The Dot, Ish,* and *Sky Color,* captures the delight children take in exploring music, art, theater, and other forms of artistic expression. Reynolds's picture book tells the story of young Raj, who enjoys plunking out tunes on his family's piano. As he experiments, he feels like he is "mix[ing] the notes the way he mix[es] his watercolors."

Hearing his son's heartfelt songs, his father signs Raj up for piano lessons to develop his talent. Yet, instead of continuing to fuel his love of the piano, regimented practice has the opposite effect. Raj's interest in the instrument wanes, and he gives it up altogether, not returning to the piano until much later in life.

Sadly, Raj's story is all too familiar.

As parents, how can we more clearly understand what happens to our children's motivation so that we may nurture a lifelong love of the arts?

A shift takes place when intrinsic motivation gives way to extrinsic motivation. Intrinsic motivation is desire kindled within. One who is intrinsically motivated is deeply engaged and enjoys the process—from the heart. Extrinsic motivation is behavior controlled by outside factors, such as a promise of rewards or a fear of punishment.

Harvard Business School professor Theresa Amabile led several decades of research that demonstrates that creativity flourishes under the influence of intrinsic motivation. Intrinsic motivators include "interest, enjoyment, satisfaction, and challenge of the work itself" (Amabile & Kramer, 2011, pp. 55–56). There is, of course, interplay between intrinsic and extrinsic motivation, and Amabile and Kramer documented this as well.

The bottom line for parents is that the task at hand—and the work more generally—must be meaningful to the child in order to sustain intrinsic motivation over time. Purposeful work leads to higher levels of creativity and more joy in one's activities, which results in the ability to persevere.

Intrinsic motivation is, therefore, one of the most important factors to consider when encouraging children to love the arts. So, how can we avoid having to tell yet another story like Raj's of a child who loses interest in the arts after an experience with formal teaching?

KEEPING CURIOSITY ALIVE

Curiosity supports deep creative thinking and expression. Continuous curiosity cultivates a lifelong love of learning. Curiosity also stokes intrinsic motivation (Amabile & Kramer, 2012; Harvey, 2015).

The arts have the potential to create opportunities for self-reflection and self-expression, but gifted kids often lose interest in the arts the same way they lose interest in school: when teachers do not draw out students' own original, exploratory thinking. Many people believe that the mere act of coloring in the lines or following directions to a Pinterest project are creative, but creativity involves problem solving, which is a combination of divergent (generating ideas, imagining, visioning) and convergent (evaluating and choosing the ideas) thinking. If your piano lesson only requires playing songs and memorizing notes, you are not using the full range of creative thinking.

Many teachers operate under the false belief that you must learn skills first in order to be creative. Skills development is certainly part of growth in any art, but this can be done alongside actual creative expression.

Just think of Raj. As a toddler banging on the piano keys, he was getting to know the sounds. Over time, he learned to put them together. This process included the full range of creative thinking, improvisation, and opportunities for self-expression. He may not have been technically advanced, but he was motivated by joy he gained in the process of playing.

Whether a child goes on to be a professional artist or to simply have a lifelong love of the arts, intrinsic motivation is the key to perseverance and to finding a unique voice. So, as a parent, how can you fan this inner flame from an early age to support a lifelong interest in the arts at any level? Here are four tips that will help.

SHARE WHAT YOU LOVE

Your children will respond to your own enthusiasm when you share your love of the arts. To start, create a mind map (a graphical way to represent ideas and concepts) or list of all of the artists and works that inspire you. Keep this list of art forms in mind:

>> Literature—poetry, stories, novels
>> Performance—music, dance, theater
>> Culinary—baking, cooking
>> Media—photography, cinematography
>> Visual—drawing, painting, ceramics, sculpting

Choose one or two art forms to start. Think about fun ways that you can share these works with your kids, such as:

>> Take your kids to see an art show or performance.
>> Virtually enjoy art via the Google Art Project (https://www.google.com/culturalinstitute/about/artproject) or museum and cultural institution websites.
>> Read a children's book together about the artwork or artist.
>> Check out Mike Venezia's *Getting to Know the World's Greatest Artists* series (https://www.mikevenezia.com/artists).
>> Find an online video or article to share.

PROVIDE OPPORTUNITIES FOR YOUR KIDS TO EXPLORE WITHIN THE CONTEXT OF THE ARTS

>> Provide materials such as paint, crayons, and clay. Introduce more advanced tools and ideas as children get older.
>> Provide instruments to truly play, for fun. Consider plastic instruments for younger ages, along with real keyboards, guitars, drums, and others. iPads and electronic apps can provide a partial experience, allowing kids to experiment with mixing music and composing their own pieces.

» Play music in your home. Have family dance or listening parties. You can give your kids paper and crayons or pencil to draw or write what they imagine as they hear the notes.

» Cook with your children. Experiment with new tastes and new combinations. Give them an "Iron Chef challenge" and have them create meals using limited or surprising ingredients.

» When your parents are cleaning out their basement, take home that old typewriter or film camera! These tools are novel and can inspire kids' creativity. You can also give them old mobile phones to take photos or record videos.

» Provide costumes for dress-up, play improvisational games, and encourage your children to stage homespun plays.

LOOK FOR CLASSES THAT VALUE PROCESS OVER PRODUCT

It's important to have teachers who value the learning process over a perfect, finished product. As children grow in their skills and become focused in certain areas, they will likely want to learn the craft more formally. But to nurture a lifelong love of the arts, exploration is key.

Some classes can be too much pressure for a kid who just wants to try something out. Look for classes with a variety of opportunities for self-expression. Observe a class and see if the students are smiling and enjoying the process. Overall, observe your child's interests and ways of learning so that you can match them to teachers and topics.

If your child resists classes or his intrinsic motivation wanes, ask why. Investigate the teaching approach. See if you can get the teacher to incorporate improv, exploration, and idea generation. Be clear about your expectations for the class, explaining that you value process and a love for the topic over rote teaching and perfect products. If the teacher doesn't understand what you're talking about, find another teacher.

TO QUOTE KENNY ROGERS, "KNOW WHEN TO HOLD 'EM, KNOW WHEN TO FOLD 'EM"

Often, interests evolve and change over time, and that's okay. Allow kids to switch instruments or pursue new types of activities. You don't want to raise a quitter, so set out clear expectations about commitments, but don't lock a child into one activity unless there is a clear goal or interest on her part.

As adults, we see a talent and pounce on it with our own adult expectations and ways of teaching. As Peter Reynolds (2016) said, we get serious—often at the high cost of crushing a child's original curiosity and joy. To avoid this outcome and raise a child with a lifelong interest in the arts, remember the importance of intrinsic motivation stoked by curiosity, creative thinking, and self-expression. As you find ways to support this, your child will learn and persevere in the arts with joy.

REFLECTION QUESTIONS

1. What types of art seem to engage my child most (e.g., music, art, photography)?
2. How might I expose my child to more of the arts that she loves, in a way that encourages and doesn't stifle her innate curiosity and joy?
3. Who are the teachers who seem to know just how to engage my child? (These could be informal "teachers," like aunts, uncles, babysitters, and even you.)
4. What are the common best practices among these teachers? Could these practices be the key to my child's engagement?

REFERENCES

Amabile, T., & Kramer, S. (2011). *The progress principle: Using small wins to ignite joy, engagement, and creativity at work*. Boston, MA: Harvard Business Review Press.

Amabile, T., & Kramer, S. (2012). What doesn't motivate creativity can kill it. *Harvard Business Review*. Retrieved from https://hbr.org/2012/04/balancing-the-four-factors-tha-1

Harvey, J. (2015). Is talking about curiosity an entry point to explaining creativity? In M. K. Culpepper & C. Burnett (Eds.), *Big questions in creativity 2015: A collection of first works* (Vol. 3). Buffalo, NY: ICSC Press.

Reynolds, P. H. (2016). *Playing from the heart*. New York, NY: Candlewick.

CHAPTER 26

PARENTING ARTISTICALLY GIFTED CHILDREN: ADVICE FROM THE NAGC ARTS NETWORK

by Hope E. Wilson and John P. Gaa

Many parents are in search of ways to best encourage their gifted children in the arts. As arts programs receive less financial and administrative support from the public school systems, parents are seeking additional resources. This chapter will provide a beginning point for parents to support artistic development for gifted children, based upon the work of the Arts Network of the National Association for Gifted Children (NAGC).

All children benefit from participation in arts programs. Specifically, studies show that the arts support academic and cognitive development and social and emotional development (Wan, Ludwig, & Boyle, 2018). For academically gifted children, the arts not only provide a venue for the development of creative and innovative thinking, but they also facilitate gifted behaviors, such as connection making, task commitment, abstract and symbolic thinking, and analysis. Instruction in the arts has been demonstrated to have connections to the development of understandings across content domains, including STEM fields (Ludwig, Boyle, & Lindsay, 2017; Root-Bernstein & Root-Bernstein, 1999). In addition, for students with specific gifts in the arts, including visual arts, music, theater, dance, and creative writing, instruction in the arts is vital for both the development of talent and the social and emotional support for such students. Finally, for highly creative children, participation in programs for the arts provides an outlet for creative expression as well as the creation of peer groups of other creative children. These experiences can have long-term benefits for highly creative and artistically gifted children.

CHARACTERISTICS OF ARTISTICALLY GIFTED CHILDREN

Parents of young children often wonder how to know if their child has particular gifts in the arts. The first sign of talent in children is often an increased interest in an art form. For example, a child might enjoy concerts, art museum exhibits, or theater productions. Parents can facilitate these interests, if possible, by providing opportunities to attend cultural events showcasing a variety of media. Many cities and towns have theater and musical experiences targeted toward young audiences. In addition, most art museums have family and child galleries and host specific events for young children. Local libraries are another source of cultural experiences for children, hosting events for families and children, along with providing resources for children interested in the arts. Finally, many major art museums and symphonies have an Internet presence that allow families to enjoy their collections from across the globe.

In addition, children may express their interests through the production of art by drawing, painting, singing, acting out stories, or playing musical instruments. By providing access to a variety of developmentally appropriate materials to encourage creative expression, parents can support the child's emerging interests. This may include access to drawing and painting supplies (large paper, crayons, water-based paint), sculpting materials (modeling clay and tools), and music-making instruments (percussion and keyboards), depending on your child's interest. It is important to allow both space and time for your child to explore these materials.

In addition to increased or heightened interest in the arts, another characteristic of many artistically talented children is heightened creativity. Creative children are able to think of many new and novel ideas and to expand upon those ideas. Sometimes creative children express themselves by a lack of adherence to the social norms exhibited by their peers, such as unusual dress or style choices, different out-of-school activities, or language. Additionally, young children often participate in highly imaginative play. These characteristics may make creatively gifted children more vulnerable in social contexts. Thus, participation in programs for the arts with other children who share these characteristics can provide an additional peer network and support for emotional growth. These programs can also act as a safe environment for creative expression.

Another characteristic of children talented in the arts is an increased ability to analyze works of art. In a visual medium, this may include increased attention to color, composition, and design details. For example, a child who insists that her shirt is magenta—not merely pink—may be exhibiting this trait. In music, this may be characterized as heightened consideration of tone, pitch, or quality of auditory input, including not only musical pieces, but also spoken word or environmental sounds. These children may also exhibit increased ability to identify musical pieces or individual instruments within a complete orchestra. In theater and creative writing, children may provide specific insights into the delivery of spoken word, experimenting with inflection and tone or word choice. Gifted writers may choose unusual vocabulary in spoken words. They may be particularly verbose, or alternatively, may be more laconic, as the child may more carefully consider words before speaking or writing. Sometimes these skills naturally develop throughout a child's early years, while at other times these skills are rapidly expanded upon after instruction.

Finally, children who are talented in the arts often express their gifts through the advanced or prolific creation of art. In the visual arts, this may include drawing, painting, sculpting, building, photographing, or creation through digital media. For many children, this includes an ability to create highly representational images with a high degree of precision, and may also include more abstract images that focus on design elements, such as color, composition, texture, and balance. In performance-based arts, such as music, dance, or theater, this technical proficiency may include the ability to match pitch, perform complex musical pieces, or interpret these pieces to reflect personal style. Parents should also keep in mind that all aspects of artistic skill and proficiency take some amount of instruction and practice. Students with innate gifts in the arts must be provided with instruction, experiences, and ample time to develop these gifts into talent.

SUPPORT FOR ARTISTICALLY GIFTED CHILDREN

Parents of gifted children, and particularly those of artistically gifted children, often wonder about the best ways to support their children's artistic development. Perhaps the most important step is to advocate for arts programs at the local, state, and national levels. Parents can become involved in the local school parent organizations and school boards, providing input and support for the continuation and expansion of art and music programs in the schools so that children have the opportunity to further develop their skills and abilities in the arts. As school budgets shrink, parents can find out from local teachers what materials they need and make donations. Parents can also show their support of programs by attending art shows, concerts, and theater productions of local schools. Younger children, as age appropriate, can be encouraged to attend, providing additional cultural experiences.

Parents can also advocate within school systems for arts-integrated instruction. These approaches, in which arts are meaningfully incorporated with other content areas, can enhance the learning of both while also increasing student engagement and critical thinking (Ludwig et al., 2017). Arts integration appeals to gifted children, as they are able to make crosscurricular connections and think critically and deeply about content areas. Current trends in STEM (science, technology, engineering, and math) curriculum are emphasizing STEAM, including the arts as an essential part of innovation in the field.

With the expansion of school choice models, parents have opportunities to encourage their child's artistic growth through a variety of educational opportunities. Some parents may choose a traditional neighborhood school and work within the system to promote high-quality art programs for all children. Other parents may opt for a specialized arts school, which may be a magnet school (run by the local school district), a public charter school (run outside of the school district but funded through public monies), or a private school. These specialized schools may provide advanced arts experiences for students, developing talent on all arts areas to a degree that is not possible in typical public schools. However, these specialized schools are not available in all regions, may not serve academically gifted students particularly well, or may not be as well-rounded as some parents may prefer. Parents of children in typical schools may also opt to supplement the school curriculum with out-of-school arts education through extracurricular activities, private lessons, and participation in youth organizations that promote the arts.

Communities offer a variety of cultural and artistic opportunities. In urban areas, cities have major theaters, symphony orchestras, operas, ballet companies, and art museums. Even in smaller towns and rural areas, local community theaters and art galleries provide opportunities. Community groups, recreational centers, art museums and galleries, and music groups often offer classes and summer programs for children. These often provide an affordable alternative to private schools and lessons for many families, and many offer financial assistance and scholarships to those in need. Local colleges and universities also often provide classes and lessons for children. Additionally, the development of private summer camps that focus on the arts has provided additional opportunities for parents to support their children's artistic capabilities. Many colleges and universities offer summer camps for talented secondary school students as well.

Finally, perhaps one of the most effective and easiest ways to find support for artistically gifted children is to join NAGC's Arts Network (https://www.nagc.org/get-involved/nagc-networks-and-special-interest-groups/networks-arts). The membership of this network includes parents, professionals, teachers, and university faculty who are dedicated to the support of the arts in gifted education. The mission of the group is twofold: to promote the inclusion of arts throughout the curriculum for all students and to promote the advancement of specialized programs for those students with gifts and talents specifically in the arts. Other national organizations that support the arts include:

» Americans for the Arts (https://www.americansforthearts.org), which advocates for the arts in education, communities, and business with a strong legislative agenda;

» The National Endowment for the Arts (https://www.arts.gov), an independent federal agency that supports arts and gives opportunities for participation in the arts;

» National Arts Education Association (https://www.arteducators.org), a national association for visual arts educators; and

» National Association for Music Educators (https://nafme. org).

FINAL THOUGHTS

For parents, the decreasing emphasis on the arts in public education may be discouraging. However, along with NAGC's Arts Network, there are many ways in which parents can encourage artistic and creative development in their children. Arts education and participation in the arts are important for all children and are vital to the development of talent among artistically gifted children. Parents can help to nurture children with talent in the arts through providing opportunities to explore and create in a variety of media.

REFLECTION QUESTIONS

1. How does your child show interest in the arts?
2. Which arts areas seem to hold the most interest for your child?
3. How can you incorporate arts activities into your child's life?
4. What resources are available in your community to enrich the arts in your child's life?
5. How can you work with others to advocate for arts in your community?

REFERENCES

Ludwig, M. J., Boyle, A., & Lindsay, J. (2017). *Review of evidence: Arts integration research through the lens of ESSA*. Washington, DC: The Wallace Foundation, American Institutes for Research.

Root-Bernstein, R. S., & Root-Bernstein, M. (1999). *Sparks of genius: The thirteen thinking tools of the world's most creative people*. Boston, MA: Houghton Mifflin.

Wan, Y., Ludwig, M. J., & Boyle, A. (2018). *Review of evidence: Arts education through the lens of ESSA*. Washington, DC: The Wallace Foundation, American Institutes for Research.

PART V

EDUCATIONAL PROGRAMMING OPTIONS AND STRATEGIES

Not all parents are professional educators, so many must rely on the insight, experience, and wisdom of their child's teachers, counselors, administrators, and other educational professionals. Communication between home and school proves critical. Like any profession, education uses specialized language and jargon that, unintentionally, may interfere with that communication. From differentiation to cluster grouping to IEPs (Individual Education Programs), parents must understand and be able to translate concepts to their child's experience. Likewise, they need to understand the research done on best practices for gifted learners in order to examine what's being done for their child and if the program is an appropriate fit. In short, the more they know, the better they can advocate for their child and partner with their child's school.

This section explores various educational programs, learning options, and strategies that have proven to be effective with gifted learners. Not only are the concepts clearly explained, but also the content is research-based. Answers to questions such as these abound:

> » I've heard so many things about acceleration. Will it really stunt my child socially? What's the truth among all of the rumors?
> » We are moving to a new town and want what's best for our child. What makes a curriculum high-quality? How can I tell?
> » So many varying options exist. What is the best educational fit?
> » What's the difference between online and blended learning? What might work for my child?

» I'm thinking about homeschooling. What do I need to know?

» My child came home with information about Talent Search. Is that really an important thing to do? Isn't he already tested enough?

» So often gifted services disappear in middle school. What could they look like?

» I care so much about my child's social and emotional growth in addition to her cognitive growth. Is there some way to address all of that in school?

Each article in this section, written by an expert in a particular area, addresses one or more of these questions. In order to be an informed advocate for your child, you must understand what is possible, you must know what is fact and what is fiction, and you must be a competent collaborator. These articles empower you to be that informed advocate.

—Tracy Ford Inman

CHAPTER 27

ACADEMIC ACCELERATION: IS IT RIGHT FOR MY CHILD?

by Susan Scheibel

As the parent of a highly able child, your role is crucial in your child's education. Experience and research repeatedly illustrate the need for and value of parent advocates—because you know your child best. Be prepared to take a positive, proactive, and focused role with teachers and administrators in your child's school and district to find the best programming for your child. Academic acceleration should be considered as a differentiation intervention or strategy set in a solid research foundation that allows for fit, challenge, and the development of student potential throughout the education process.

As the parent of a gifted child, you know your child's unique needs best. You know how your child actively responded to your actions and words as a very young infant; communicated, learned, and demonstrated advanced talents at a younger than typical age; and read letters and words from a car seat as you traveled around town. You know your child is sensitive, caring, and fair-minded. You may even have heard family and/or friends comment on how your child seems to grasp so much so quickly. Truly you know your child best, and you are your child's best advocate. One significant strategy to consider is academic acceleration.

Academic acceleration is an individual, educational intervention that allows a learner to progress through the educational system at a faster rate or younger age than typical learners based on appropriate level of challenge. Many types of academic acceleration strategies address academic needs, provide academic challenge, and allow students to complete traditional schooling tailored to each child's academic and social and emotional readiness (Assouline, Colangelo, & VanTassel-Baska, 2015).

ACCELERATION STRATEGIES

Academic acceleration can be by grade or by subject. The following types of acceleration strategies should be woven together over time to serve the needs of a student and family (National Association for Gifted Children, n.d.; Southern & Jones, 2015).

- » *Early admission to kindergarten* is allowed depending on the school district or state. A child may enter kindergarten prior to the minimum age for entrance.
- » *Early admission to first grade* can result from skipping kindergarten or accelerating a child through kindergarten and into first grade.
- » *Grade-skipping* permits a child to skip a grade or grades at the beginning of or during the school year.
- » *Continuous progress* refers to students who complete and master content and then are given further work at an accelerated pace in comparison to their classmates.
- » *Self-paced instruction* is a type of continuous progress allowing the student, Individualized Education Plan, or Advanced Learning Plan control over pacing decisions.
- » *Subject-matter acceleration/partial acceleration*, or content-based acceleration, provides students placement in higher level classes, or with more advanced curriculum, in one or more content areas for part of the day, after school, or during the summer.
- » *Combined classes* consist of two grades. For example, a second-/third-grade split class can offer younger students the opportunity to interact with older peers and be exposed to advanced content.
- » *Curriculum compacting* considers students' proficiency in the basic curriculum and allows them to exchange instructional time for other learning experiences.
- » *Telescoping curriculum* covers the same amount of materials or activities in less time, thereby allowing more time for enrichment activities and projects that better suit the interests, needs, and readiness levels of gifted students.
- » *Mentoring* allows a community member to share his or her expertise with a student who has similar interests in a particular field or career.

» *Extracurricular programs/talent search programs* encompass a variety of programming options that result in advanced instruction with possible credit toward graduation.

» *Correspondence courses* allow students to participate in instruction inside or outside of school. These courses are typically delivered online.

» *Concurrent/dual enrollment* typically involves high school students taking college courses, often for college credit. The term can also be applied to middle-grades students taking high school courses and earning credit toward high school graduation.

» *Advanced Placement (AP),* designed by the College Board, allows high schools to offer courses that meet criteria established by institutions of higher education. College credit may be earned with the successful completion of an AP exam in specific content areas. (Check with individual colleges and universities regarding their policies on AP courses.)

» *International Baccalaureate* allows authorized schools to offer a specialized education program with IB courses and credit.

» *Acceleration/honors high school or residential high school on a college campus,* designed for gifted learners, has students attend a selective day or residential advanced high school program—often with access to college-level work, mentors, and professors.

» *Credit by examination* permits a student to receive credit for a course by completing a test of mastery or an activity.

» *Early entrance into middle school, high school, or college* provides opportunities for credit and achievement in advanced levels of learning at least one year above the norm.

» *Early graduation from high school or college* includes graduation from high school or college in less than 3 1/2 years. This is achieved through additional coursework, dual enrollment, or Advanced Placement courses.

» *Acceleration in college* is employed with dual enrollment or credit by examination. A university professor or instructor can also determine advanced instruction.

RESEARCH TO GUIDE YOUR DECISIONS AND ADVOCACY

Decades of research demonstrate the need for and benefits of gifted education strategies and programs. These include the use of acceleration, enrichment, curriculum enhancement, and differentiated curriculum and instruction, which have all been shown to increase the achievement of high-ability learners. Despite the large corpus of research supporting acceleration practices, there still remains reluctance to institute these practices. Borland stated:

> Acceleration is one of the most curious phenomena in the field of education. I can think of no other issue in which there is such a gulf between what research has revealed and what practitioners believe. The research on acceleration is so uniformly positive, the benefits of appropriate acceleration so unequivocal, that it is difficult to see how an educator can oppose it. (as cited in Colangelo, Assouline, & Gross, 2004, p. 16)

Rogers (1999) offered evidence that supports acceleration, specifically in science and mathematics:

» Gifted students are significantly more likely to retain science and mathematics content accurately when taught 2–3 times faster than the typical class pace.

» Gifted students are significantly more likely to forget or mislearn science and mathematics content when they must drill and review it more than 2–3 times.

A Nation Empowered (Assouline et al., 2015) further synthesized decades of research and practice on the topic of academic acceleration:

» Acceleration works.

» Well-researched methods exist for evaluating and guiding the accelerated student, along with teachers, administrators, counselors, and parents, through the process.

» Acceleration can be provided in a variety of ways and tailored to the student.

» Acceleration supports the social and emotional development of students.

» Acceleration provides for continuous development of students' abilities.

» Acceleration is an inexpensive educational option.

» Resources for acceleration decision making are available.

With a keen focus on the socioaffective impact of acceleration supports, Neihart (2007) recommended the following best practices in support of highly able learners:

» Acceleration should be routine for highly gifted children. All highly gifted children should be evaluated for grade-skipping, in particular.

» Acceleration options should be available for capable students. No school district or school administrator should have a policy that prohibits accelerative options for students, including grade-skipping.

» All school districts should have written policies and procedures in place to ensure that acceleration options are available in all schools to guide parents and teachers in the steps to follow for referral and evaluation of students.

» Students who are being considered for acceleration should be screened for social readiness, emotional maturity, and motivation for acceleration. A tool, such as the Iowa Acceleration Scale, may help to select candidates for acceleration.

» When possible, students who are grade-skipping or making an early entrance to college should do so as part of a cohort. There appear to be benefits to cohort acceleration that are more difficult to replicate when students go it alone.

ADVOCATING FOR YOUR CHILD

Your role as an educational advocate is to foster the academic and social-emotional development of your child using available resources for academic acceleration. The great news is that although the road may not be smooth, there are a range of tools, guides, individuals, educators, and programs to help along the way. Your task is to find the right information, people, and programs to parent your high-potential child.

Although you cannot control the educational system or the minds of teachers or administrators, you can be guided by more than 30 years of solid research, best practice, and amazingly passionate individuals in the field of gifted and talented education. Begin the process today by thoughtfully considering these guiding points:

» You know your unique child. Observe and listen.

» Advocate clearly for your child based on each year's needs and as necessary.

» Empower your child to believe, self-advocate, and share her needs and feelings.

» Every learner has the right to learn something new and be challenged.

» Get involved in the school to build knowledge, trust, contacts, and credibility.

» Do your homework. Educate yourself about gifted education, gifted learners, and best practice.

» Research school districts, policies, online programs, Talent Search opportunities, schools, and teachers to find the best fit for your child.

» Present trusted and well-researched information and be prepared when you meet with teachers, administrators, and policy makers.

» Talk and communicate about acceleration and support others. Pay it forward.

» Intervene when you know there's a problem. Think and problem solve outside the box each year and as necessary.

» Create safe environments for your child. Empower, but do not enable.

It is never too early nor too late to support your child's educational growth. Although early intervention is preferred, begin right now to do what is best for your child. Make a commitment to listen to your heart, your gut, your child, and other parents to become an active, informed decision maker in the educational process for your child's growth and well-being. Start today.

REFLECTIVE QUESTIONS

1. Is your child interested and motivated for advancement?
2. Have your child's abilities been assessed with multiple criteria to show that your child is ready for an advanced, fast-paced curriculum?
3. Based on your child's assessment data, what type(s) of acceleration might best address your child?
4. Who will systemically monitor and support your child longitudinally? Is there an Advanced Learning Plan K–12 system?

REFERENCES

Assouline, S. G., Colangelo, N., & VanTassel-Baska, J. (2015). *A nation empowered: Evidence trumps the excuses holding back America's brightest students* (Vol. 1). Iowa City: University of Iowa, The Connie Belin & Jacqueline N. Blank International Center for Gifted Education and Talent Development.

Colangelo, N., Assouline, S. G., & Gross, M. U. M. (2004). *A nation deceived: How schools hold back America's brightest students* (Vol. 1). Iowa City: The University of Iowa, The Connie Belin & Jacqueline N. Blank International Center for Gifted Education and Talent Development.

National Association for Gifted Children. (n.d.). *Glossary of terms.* Retrieved from https://www.nagc.org/resources-publications/resources/glossary-terms

Neihart, M. (2007). The socioaffective impact of acceleration and ability grouping: Recommendations for best practice. *Gifted Child Quarterly, 51,* 330–341.

Rogers, K. B. (1999). Research synthesis on gifted provisions: Update of a best-evidence synthesis of research on accelerative options for gifted students. In N. Colangelo, S. G. Assouline, & D. L. Ambroson (Eds.), *Talent development: The proceedings from the 1991 Henry B. and Jocelyn Wallace National Research Symposium on Talent Development* (pp. 406–409). New York, NY: Trillium Press.

Southern, T., & Jones, E. D. (2015). Types of acceleration: Dimensions and issues. In S. G. Assouline, N. Colangelo, J. VanTassel-Baska, & A. Lupkowski-Shoplik (Eds.), *A nation empowered: Evidence trumps the excuses holding back America's brightest students* (Vol. 2, pp. 1–18). Iowa City: University of Iowa, The Connie Belin & Jacqueline N. Blank International Center for Gifted Education and Talent Development.

CHAPTER 28

ADVOCATING FOR GRADE-BASED ACCELERATION

by Keri M. Guilbault

Acceleration is one of the most widely researched, effective interventions for advanced learners, yet it is not often discussed as a desirable option for gifted learners in schools. Acceleration allows carefully selected advanced learners to "progress through an educational program at rates faster or at ages younger than conventional" (Pressey, 1949, p. 2). Acceleration does not just refer to grade-skipping; in fact, there are 20 forms of acceleration outlined in the report *A Nation Empowered: Evidence Trumps the Excuses Holding Back America's Brightest Students* (Vol. 1; Assouline, Colangelo, & VanTassel-Baska, 2015). You may find yourself at a loss for how to begin the acceleration process for your own child or how to decide which form of acceleration is needed and when to accelerate. As your child's advocate, you can work effectively with your school system to secure an appropriate academic placement that matches your child's ability level, interests, and readiness to learn.

A Nation Empowered outlines 20 different forms of academic acceleration, including subject-based acceleration options and grade-based acceleration strategies that shorten the number of years a child spends in the K–12 school system. Parents often struggle with the decision to accelerate their child and may worry about social and emotional issues, although research indicates positive effects on the social and emotional adjustment of carefully selected accelerants (Rogers, 2015). Once you have read the research on acceleration, have considered the pros and cons, have discussed acceleration with your child, and are ready to approach the school, the following steps can help ensure careful consideration and successful adjustment.

KNOW YOUR STATE AND
LOCAL DISTRICT POLICIES

Some states and local school systems have formal acceleration policies already in place. As of 2015, 15 states had an acceleration policy that specifically permitted acceleration (National Association for Gifted Children & the Council of State Directors of Programs for the Gifted, 2015). These policies may include guidelines for early entrance to kindergarten or first grade, earning high school or college credit for courses taken at an earlier age, subject acceleration, or grade-skipping. Become well-informed of any written policies before you approach the school. You can locate your state policies at the NAGC website or by contacting your state gifted association.

BE FAMILIAR WITH THE RESEARCH

When requesting that your child be considered as a candidate for grade-based acceleration, you may meet resistance from teachers or administrators. One of the main reasons often provided for not accelerating a gifted student is the belief that it may cause social or emotional harm (Assouline et al., 2015). As your child's advocate, you can help to dispel this myth by sharing some of the research on this topic:

» There is no evidence that acceleration has a negative effect on a student's social-emotional development.
» Gifted children tend to be socially and emotionally more mature than their age-mates.
» For bright students, acceleration has long-term beneficial effects, both academically and socially.
» Acceleration can provide access to classmates whose interests and stages of friendship are more closely in sync with your child.
» Doing nothing is not the same as doing no harm.

FOLLOW THE CHAIN OF COMMAND

Once you've reviewed the research and are ready to approach the school, remember that the typical protocol is to request a meeting with your child's classroom teacher first. Be specific but polite in your request. Explain that you are interested in exploring learning options for your child that will match her ability and offer an equal opportunity for academic and personal growth. (Be careful not to use the "b" word: *bored.*)

The classroom teacher may have recent academic achievement data that can provide evidence of ability that is above grade-level expectations. Your child's teacher may even be able to address some acceleration needs in the regular classroom first, especially if the school has a gifted education specialist who can provide support. If this is not sufficient, then ask that the gifted education specialist (or a school counselor) screen your child for acceleration. Additional assessments may be required at this stage.

If there is resistance, be polite but persistent and request a meeting with the appropriate school administrator. Be sure to gather a portfolio of evidence to bring to your meeting, including independent work samples, achievement test scores, any outside testing (such as individual IQ testing or above-level testing from participation in talent search programs), awards received, and any other samples that showcase your child's areas of strength and above-grade ability. The team that makes acceleration decisions will want to know that your child is working at least 2 years above grade level in multiple content areas so that, once accelerated, he will remain at the top of the class. Multiple pieces of evidence documenting above-grade-level ability across content areas can help support your request.

DEVELOP A PLAN

If your school does not have formal acceleration policies or procedures, you might suggest that they use an evaluation tool, such as the Iowa Acceleration Scale (IAS; Assouline, Colangelo, Lupkowski-Shoplik, Lipscomb, & Forstadt, 2009). This research-based tool is designed to help schools make an objective decision by looking at the whole child. Information will be collected regarding your child's current academic achievement, ability, and motivation, as well as social factors, such as maturity and peer and teacher relationships.

The following are some suggestions for creating your child's acceleration plan:

»   Request a copy of all meeting notes, including the Summary and Planning Sheet of the IAS for your records.

»   Include a plan to identify and address any potential academic gaps prior to the transition.

»   Ask that the receiving teacher locate a peer to help with your child's transition to the new class, especially if acceleration takes place after the school year has begun and friendships have formed.

»   Schedule a follow-up conference approximately 30 days after the initial acceleration to review and discuss your child's academic and social-emotional adjustment with all of the educators involved.

»   Ask that your child's acceleration plan include counseling or study skills support during the transition if needed.

»   Be aware that there will be a temporary period of adjustment. Give your child time.

»   If you don't agree with the school committee's decision, ask about the appeals process. If one does not exist, you can typically continue up the chain of command to an assistant superintendent, director, or supervisor at the school district office.

Acceleration is one of the most effective and research-based interventions for gifted learners (Assouline et al., 2015). Acceleration can be an inexpensive and cost-effective way for schools to meet the academic and affective needs of highly able learners who learn at a faster rate. As a parent of a highly able child, your voice is important when it comes to actively advocating for an appropriate educational placement. Don't hesitate to ask questions and speak up for your child's needs.

REFLECTION QUESTIONS

1. Which type of acceleration is right for your child?
2. How will you know if your child is making progress commensurate with ability after she has been accelerated?
3. What should you do if grade-based acceleration is recommended, but your child is not interested?

4. How should you or your child respond when neighbors and friends ask why your child was accelerated?
5. What are some ways to identify and address gaps in knowledge before or during the acceleration transition?

REFERENCES

Assouline, S., Colangelo, N., Lupkowski-Shoplik, A., Lipscomb, J., & Forstadt, L. (2009). *Iowa Acceleration Scale: A guide for whole-grade acceleration K–8* (3rd ed.). Tucson, AZ: Great Potential Press.

Assouline, S. G., Colangelo, N., & VanTassel-Baska, J. (2015). *A nation empowered: Evidence trumps the excuses holding back America's brightest students* (Vol. 1). Iowa City: University of Iowa, The Connie Belin & Jacqueline N. Blank International Center for Gifted Education and Talent Development.

National Association for Gifted Children, & the Council of State Directors of Programs for the Gifted. (2015). *State of the states in gifted education: National policy and practice data 2014–2015.* Washington, DC: Authors.

Pressey, S. L. (1949). *Educational acceleration: Appraisals and basic problems* (Ohio State University Studies, Bureau of Educational Research Monograph No. 31). Columbus: Ohio State University Press.

Rogers, K. B. (2015). The academic, socialization, and psychological effects of acceleration: Research synthesis. In S. G. Assouline, N. Colangelo, J. VanTassel-Baska, & A. L. Lupkowski-Shoplik (Eds.), *A nation empowered: Evidence trumps the excuses holding back America's brightest students* (Vol. 2, pp. 19–30). Iowa City: University of Iowa, Connie Belin & Jacqueline N. Blank International Center for Gifted Education and Talent Development.

CHAPTER 29

SUPPORTING SOCIAL AND EMOTIONAL LEARNING FOR GIFTED LEARNERS WITH THE COMMON CORE STATE STANDARDS

by Sheri Nowak Stewart and Lori Comallie-Caplan

In addition to increased intellectual capacity, gifted children often have sensitivities and intensities, interests, personality traits, and moral and ethical challenges that are different from those of their age peers. Cognitive complexity, emotional sensitivity, heightened imagination, and magnified sensations combine to create "a different quality of experiencing: vivid, absorbing, penetrating, encompassing, complex, commanding—a way of being quiveringly alive" (Piechowski, 1992, p. 181). The gifted not only think differently from their peers, but they also feel differently. This amplification of depth, degree, and intensity in a gifted child's emotional life can have both positive and negative aspects. Coping mechanisms such as unhealthy perfectionism, self-criticism, poor self-concept, or the development of depression, eating disorders, and antisocial behavior may manifest if social-emotional learning is missing from the curriculum. However, when the instructional curriculum is integrated with social and emotional learning to meet their needs, gifted children may develop healthy coping styles and achieve greater overall academic success.

WHAT IS SOCIAL AND EMOTIONAL LEARNING?

The Collaborative for Academic, Social, and Emotional Learning (CASEL) organization advocates evidence-based practices for social and emotional learning (SEL) in the school community. SEL is comprised of five core competencies that help students develop life effectiveness and contribute to positive learning environments (CASEL, 2012):

> » **Self-awareness**—labeling emotions, analyzing triggers, and realizing their impact on others;
> » **Self-management**—setting and working on goals, and overcoming obstacles to attaining these goals;
> » **Social awareness**—identifying and predicting verbal, physical, and situational cues in relation to others' feelings;
> » **Relationship skills**—describing approaches to making and keeping friends, learning to cooperate, and evaluating communication skills; and
> » **Responsible decision making**—identifying problems, evaluating strategies and actions, and understanding repercussions of decision making.

These SEL core competencies also align with the NAGC-CEC Teacher Preparation Standards in Gifted Education: "Standard 2: Learning Environments—Beginning gifted education professionals create safe, inclusive, and culturally responsive learning environments so that individuals with gifts and talents become effective learners and develop social and emotional well-being" (National Association for Gifted Children & The Association for the Gifted, Council for Exceptional Children, 2013). Mastery of SEL skills helps gifted children succeed both in school and as lifelong learners. However, parents sometimes are left wondering how gifted children can learn these skills at school, where academics are often the sole focus.

HOW DO THE COMMON CORE STATE STANDARDS SUPPORT SEL COMPETENCIES?

By 2018, only eight states had adopted K–12 SEL competencies, and 16 states had guidance in the form of SEL goals or benchmarks integrated within academic standards. In addition, eight additional states were working on plans that would result in policy and guidance to support SEL (CASEL, 2018). These SEL competencies do not have to be taught in isolation. The Common Core State Standards (CCSS) can support the cultivation of SEL skills. Examples of the embedded skills can be found in language arts, science, social studies, and even physical education:

» An example of embedded instruction for the *self-awareness* competency is found in the identification of a character's feeling in a story.

» The *self-management* competency can be taught to middle school students when they set and analyze goals for a science fair project.

» The *social awareness* competency can be taught at the high school level through empathy within the context of the Civil Rights Movement using archival and digital media.

» The *relationship skills* competency can be taught in physical education through cooperation in team games or team-building activities in outdoor education.

» *Responsible decision making* occurs in CCSS speaking and listening activities when high school students work with peers in civic and democratic discussions.

Thus, numerous examples exist within the CCSS that allude to the same five core SEL competencies. Teachers' implementation of the CCSS can promote both academic and social and emotional learning for gifted students.

HOW CAN PARENTS SUPPORT SEL COMPETENCIES THROUGH THE CCSS?

The most natural way to support academic and social and emotional learning through the CCSS at home is through language arts. Discuss with your child what topics, events, or activities he likes. Then seek out stories, poems, articles, or other literature about these topics. Provide time and a place for your child to read independently and then make time for conversations about what she has read. Ask questions that relate to the SEL competencies:

» **Self-awareness:** Tell me the words or phrases in this story (or poem) that invoked feelings or appealed to your senses. How did these words or phrases make you feel?

» **Self-management:** How did the outcome of this story influence you and your future decision making? Did you learn anything that would help you overcome future barriers or challenges?

» **Social awareness:** Describe the characters in this story (e.g., their traits, motivations, or feelings). How did their actions contribute to the sequence of events?

» **Relationship skills:** Describe how you initially felt about the main character. How did your attitude change over the course of the story?

» **Responsible decision making:** Describe how characters in a story respond to major events and challenges. Evaluate the strategies and actions of the characters. Do you think they fully understood the potential consequences of their choices?

PARENTS PARTNERING WITH SCHOOLS

When parents and schools join together in supporting children's holistic and cognitive needs, children will reap the rewards in improved social skills, individual goal attainment, and academic success. Although schools prioritize assessment of cognitive knowledge and skills, parents can support the integration of SEL in the schools as the CCSS provide a natural integration of the two. The five SEL core competencies provide an evidence-based framework that is consistent philosophically and in practice with the CCSS. Parents who understand this relationship can advocate for the implementation of SEL competencies to meet the exceptional needs of gifted children in the schools.

REFLECTION QUESTIONS

1. How can a social and emotional learning curriculum impact a gifted student's educational experience?

2. In what ways can parents be involved in their child's social and emotional learning?
3. What are the key components of an effective social and emotional learning curriculum?

REFERENCES

Collaborative for Academic, Social, and Emotional Learning. (2012). *2013 CASEL guide: Effective social and emotional learning programs: Preschool and elementary school edition.* Retrieved from https://casel.org/wp-content/uploads/2016/01/2013-casel-guide-1.pdf

Collaborative for Academic, Social, and Emotional Learning. (2018). *2018 state scorecard scan: More states are supporting social and emotional learning.* Retrieved from https://casel.org/wp-content/uploads/2018/02/2018-State-Scan-FINAL.pdf

National Association for Gifted Children, & The Association for the Gifted, Council for Exceptional Children. (2013). *NAGC-CEC teacher preparation standards in gifted education.* Retrieved from https://www.nagc.org/sites/default/files/standards/NAGC-%20 CEC%20CAEP%20standards%20%282013%20final%29.pdf

Piechowski, M. M. (1992). Giftedness for all seasons: Inner peace in a time of war. In N. Colangelo, S. G. Assouline, & D. L. Ambroson (Eds.), *Talent development: Proceedings of the Henry B. and Jocelyn Wallace National Research Symposium on Talent Development* (pp. 180–203). Unionville, NY: Trillium Press.

CHAPTER 30

FACTORS TO CONSIDER IN CHOOSING A MIDDLE SCHOOL: IS ACADEMIC GROWTH ONE OF THEM?

by Linda E. Pfeiffer

Few things strike fear in the hearts of parents like sending their child off to middle school. Parents of gifted learners fear for their child's safety—both emotional and physical—and academic well-being. Sleepless nights of worry can be the norm for parents during the entire first year of their child's middle level experience.

So, what exactly can parents do to relieve the anxiety that this transition creates for us and our children? Although safety is important, we also want our children to leave middle school ready for high school, having made the growth that will allow them to be most successful in high school and beyond. We can educate ourselves and make the best possible choice in middle level education, trust our schools, our teachers, and our children, and then stay involved! Hopefully what is presented here will help you in making the best possible choice.

As parents we feel pretty confident in identifying the factors that will determine if our children are physically safe in school, but do we know what to look for in schools that produce high academic growth results? Like many things that are worth the effort, there is a process. Four research-based, relevant factors are involved (Pfeiffer, 2013):

- » programming,
- » leadership,
- » school culture, and
- » school size.

Before we can look at these elements, however, we must first determine which schools have the highest growth-performance metrics. Examples of scores to look for include Smarter Balanced Assessment, Partnership for Assessment of Readiness for College and Careers (PARCC), or even criterion-referenced tests, such as Measures of Academic Progress (MAP)—tests used by many states or districts to show academic change for cohort groups annually.

Be sure you are tracking down growth scores—not achievement scores—for the schools you are considering. Although achievement levels can be influenced by things such as socioeconomic factors, which are mostly static, growth is more dynamic and is more accountable to the performance of the school and its staff (McCoach, Rambo, & Welsh, 2013). Growth information is generally available through several outlets. Places to investigate include:

» the school(s) you are considering,
» the gifted and talented department within the school district, and
» the state's department of education.

Typically, student data are aggregated or reported as a whole—either by state, district, school, grade, or class. Look for *dis*aggregated data, which means that subpopulations are reported separately to provide a more accurate view of growth—in gifted or English language learners (ELLs), for example (Technical Education Research Centers, 2014; Tomlinson, 2014). Investigating scores for the identification of high growth for the general population as well as for gifted learners may provide insight to a more systemic belief in the ability for all children to experience high academic growth.

Identify those schools with the highest academic growth scores in your desired neighborhood or community, or, if those growth scores are not available to you, you can look for the characteristics mentioned previously: programming, leadership, culture, and school size.

PROGRAMMING

First of all, high-growth schools don't just use buzz words; they actually use the tools that get results. For example, differentiation is viewed as more than providing students with the choice to build a diorama or draw a poster to demonstrate learning. Differentiation for gifted learners in high-growth schools contains content, process, and product modification. Schools with process modifications allow students to create independent learning contracts, to conduct in-depth investigations through inquiry and problem-based learning, or to experience curriculum at rates matched with their abilities (Winebrenner & Brulles, 2018). Other programming strategies in schools demonstrating high student growth include the following:

» Students have opportunities to spend additional time in core classes, with interventions for both high-ability and struggling learners, if needed.

» Flexible grouping designed for the individual learner's needs is present.

» Individual differences are recognized in students, and schedules are built to honor student strengths and weaknesses. (Many gifted learners have academic strength in specific core areas and aren't gifted in all areas.)

» Passionate teachers are viewed as content experts, understand the needs of all, and recognize that one size does not fit every child.

» Teachers have autonomy to teach what they know, without having specific curricula to follow each day. (This can still be done in a standards-based setting.)

Feel free to ask questions of administrators, such as these:

» Is there a flexible curricula for all students?

» Do teachers have autonomy to create lessons?

» Is ability or cluster grouping implemented to aid student collaborative efforts?

» Does differentiation include content, process, and product? If so, what does each look like?

» Do teachers collaborate to strengthen their teaching practices?

LEADERSHIP

School leadership also plays a significant role in the success of high-growth schools. How? Principals are specific in their hiring, acting as coaches who are building the team that will take them to the championships. They know the qualities to look for that indicate whether teachers are likely to support each other (and the students) to the best of their ability. These leaders are willing to help teachers to be their best.

These leaders are rarely in their offices because they are frequently in classrooms and hallways, interacting with staff and students. They take personal interest in their staff and students, recognizing when other factors may be affecting their teaching or learning. They support teachers, but hold them to high standards—just as teachers hold their students to high standards for academics *and* behavior. Principals seek teachers as leaders to help them grow professionally, require collaboration to build strong content and grade-level alignment, and respect that teachers are experts in their fields, giving them the freedom to design curriculum with critical and creative thinking, not just simple recall. Be present in your research and consider the following:

» Ask to walk through the building during the school day. Are students and staff smiling? Are students and staff respectful in their dress and demeanor?

» Do you hear and see affirmations of belief in students and in their potential for success?

» Are students engaged and enthusiastic?

» Are teachers serving as "sage on the stage" or "guide from the side"? Remember, you want students to be leading their learning!

» What are the roles and expectations of families and community members in supporting the school? Are there active parent groups?

CULTURE

A clear expression of happiness is visible on the faces of children, teachers, and administrators in high-growth schools. Principals recognize the strength of the community, including families and businesses, and place high value on including families in the fabric of the school. Just as collaboration is required among teachers, parents are expected to be part of the school's decision-making process, participate in family nights, and attend parent-teacher conferences. The community supports the belief that all students will be academically successful via daily affirmations of each child's ability to achieve and grow. Children are told that the adults in their life believe in them and in their ability to succeed, and child is taught to understand that academic success will come with hard work, not just ability.

SCHOOL SIZE

Smaller, more intimate middle school environments, with an average of 375 students, seem to have greater growth metrics among their student populations. Smaller school size allows teachers and principals to know every child and family. The school community is caring and compassionate toward each child and family because everyone works in partnership for the betterment of the child. Over time, a pervasive sense of trust is built. The school is as much a part of the community as the community is part of the school.

CHOOSING A SCHOOL

It makes sense that parents want their children to be aligned with schools that boast high numbers of advanced learners. However, my research also suggests that the quantity of advanced learners should not necessarily be the most important consideration when deciding which school a child should attend. As hard as it might be, I encourage parents to look beyond a school's reputation for high achievement and to consider other factors.

For gifted and talented learners to have their academic needs met, I would argue it is more important for the school to demonstrate high student growth. Characteristics such as programming options, culture, leadership, and size are important factors to consider when selecting a school that will nurture all students' potential. Although no school may ever be perfect, we can always work to stack the deck in our favor as much as possible. A final request: Include your children in this decision. Explain what you believe are factors for them to consider and provide them with the results of your research. Remember you were their first teacher, and you have been a huge part of making them who they are today.

REFLECTION QUESTIONS

1. What is the difference between achievement and growth when looking at testing data?
2. Is it possible to have high academic growth without the presence of all four factors? For example, what if small schools are being closed in your neighborhood—can high academic growth still happen?
3. Are there alternative ways for your gifted child to experience high growth if the schools in your area do not reflect high growth data?

REFERENCES

McCoach, D. B., Rambo, K. E., & Welsh, M. (2013). Assessing the growth of gifted students. *Gifted Child Quarterly, 57,* 56–67.

Pfeiffer, L. E. (2013). *The pursuit of high academic growth for gifted middle level learners* (Doctoral dissertation). Retrieved from https://pdfs.semanticscholar.org/6b44/999e6752194865ba633 773b55235395a9a95.pdf

Technical Education Research Centers. (2014). *Disaggregate your data to make the invisible visible.* Retrieved from http://www. usingdatasolutions.org/disaggregate.html

Tomlinson, C. A. (2014). *The differentiated classroom: Responding to the needs of all learners* (2nd ed.). Alexandria, VA: ASCD.

Winebrenner, S., & Brulles, D. (2018). *Teaching gifted kids in today's classrooms: Strategies and techniques every teacher can use* (4th ed.). Minneapolis, MN: Free Spirit.

CHAPTER 31

FINDING YOUR VOICE: TALENT DEVELOPMENT CENTERS AND THE ACADEMIC TALENT SEARCH

by Amy S. Rushneck

THE STORIES WE SHARE

Perhaps one of these stories sounds familiar: Your child is being referred for behavior issues because he is "acting up" or "horsing around" in class, she is "constantly disrupting class by asking too many questions," or he "refuses to participate when we know he has the answers." Perhaps your student is suddenly failing mathematics when you know she loves the subject and has always found it quite easy. Maybe your child is successful in everything he attempts—first chair trumpet, honor roll every semester in every subject, class president, starting quarterback, and lead in the musical—and he navigates all of these social circles with enthusiastic popularity—but you find him weeping in bed at night or lashing out in anger at home. Perhaps you have grown to understand that all of these scenarios mark an unidentified or underidentified gifted youth; an underachieving kid who is struggling to make the social worlds of school, community, and being smart all work together; or a kid who is burning the wick at both ends and then lighting the middle to see if the wax will melt, just out of curiosity.

These are the types of stories families bring to Talent Development Centers nearly every day: e-mails from parents desperate to just "get the school to believe that their child is bored," calls from grandmothers worried that their grandchildren cannot live in their neighborhood and be smart without being in danger, or letters from counselors just wanting to help kids who are ahead of proficiency standards. If you're nodding along as you read, then it is time to think about how to participate in programming at your local or regional Talent Development Center. Talent Development Centers are just one of many tools every family, teacher, and gifted advocate should have in their toolbox.

FREQUENTLY ASKED QUESTIONS

To understand the importance of Talent Development Centers, it is essential to also understand the Academic Talent Search Program. Talent Search participants in grades 3–9 who obtain scores comparable to college-bound high school seniors generally continue a pattern of high achievement in high school and college, take more advanced and accelerated courses, earn more awards and honors, and have higher educational aspirations (Barnett & Durden, 1993; Benbow & Arjmand, 1990; Lee, Matthews, & Olszewski-Kubilius, 2008; Olszewski-Kubilius & Grant, 1996; Robertson, Smeets, Lubinski, & Benbow, 2010). The following three questions are those we encounter most frequently from those new to Academic Talent Search:

I JUST FOUND OUT MY STUDENT QUALIFIED FOR TALENT SEARCH, BUT WHAT IS IT?

Academic Talent Search is an opportunity for younger students to take off-level testing typically not available until college entrance. These tests (PSAT 8/9, ACT, SAT) offer a higher ceiling than standardized state or other national grade-level tests on which these talented kids are already achieving in the top 5%. Although Talent Search scores offer only one snapshot of students' abilities, they do help bright kids evaluate their academic strengths in order to advocate for their educational needs, to access higher level or accelerated academic programming, or to design individualized educational plans.

WHY WOULD WE DO THIS? AREN'T WE TESTING KIDS TOO MUCH ALREADY?

This is a very reasonable concern for new families frustrated with information gleaned from at-level testing. However, Talent Search really is not about the test or score. It *is* about the benefits students receive from participation, and even the wariest families come back after several years of participating, grateful for the opportunity their student had to practice these tests. It opens doors for new programs and opportunities they would not have otherwise been aware of, and families are happy that they have the necessary tools to be heard and have their students be visible in their schooling environments. Yes, we are testing a lot, but at least these scores can authentically mean something.

Many of our kids are asked to just "float." The assumption is that they can be given additional assignments when they finish early, can tutor another student who is struggling, or can just do something else while everyone catches up, and they'll be fine. We are interested in more than fine. We are interested in what's next. What new level could students achieve if they actually were allowed to move ahead? What new level of inquiry might be achieved if students were allowed to ask questions that "shouldn't" be asked until the next school year? What new level of skill sets might be accomplished if students were challenged appropriately? The Academic Talent Search is a passport of sorts to beginning these conversations at home. Plus, kids report that they like it when they can go into a testing site and watch those high schoolers get nervous!

Unfortunately, in today's educational world, we still often need documentation in the form of a score report to demonstrate readiness for these opportunities. This is especially critical for those students who may be developing asynchronously—that is, their academic achievement is very high, while their social skills are lagging in development. As a nationally recognized program with nationally understood testing rigor, Academic Talent Search provides a means to advocacy in healthy, supported ways for families; a means for accessing courses, programs, schools, or scholarship opportunities that require this documentation; and a means for building the self-confidence and comfort that ultimately are necessary for students to be successful on these tests when they, as our students often state, take them "for real."

WHAT ARE THE ACTUAL BENEFITS? CAN'T I JUST DO THIS WITHOUT A TALENT CENTER?

» Grade-level testing generally does not reveal the upper limits of student abilities. Participants gain early experience taking an off-level college entrance test, reporting increased comfort with standardized testing and significant score gains that can make the difference when applying to college. The more times students participate, the steadier the increases in success.

» Students receive access to a summer opportunities guide that lists special programs across the country for high-ability students. In a survey conducted by Northwestern's Center for Talent Development, educators "overwhelmingly confirmed the value of Talent Search in helping their students find program options not available through their schools" (Olszewski-Kubilius & Lee, 2005, p. 233).

» With permission, schools receive Talent Search scores that teachers and counselors can use to accommodate student course choices or curriculum modifications.

» Scholarship opportunities become available, and many qualification requirements are met for higher level or accelerated programming, grade-level adjustments, or schools for gifted. Talent Search is an outstanding resume builder, especially when hundreds of thousands of other very bright students are participating annually.

» Students are invited to participate in Talent Development Summer Programs (or other format models, such as distance education) designed to provide an optimal match and allow students to develop a socioemotional network of peers in a living/learning community. Many students age through these programs with a lifelong community.

» Top-scoring participants are invited to a State Recognition Ceremony, if one is offered in the area.

» During the spring, participants receive interpretive materials that provide information needed to interpret test scores in relationship to other grade-level Talent Search participants across each region. This information can be the most critical advocacy tool many families use to work with their schools.

» Young students may not otherwise be able to take these tests. Contrary to concerns expressed primarily by educators, when young students participate through Talent Search, they do not "fail" in their scoring. Percentages of students who score at the low end of these tests are about the same for the Talent Search and high school populations (Wilder & Casserly, 1988).

» Scores are archived by Talent Development Centers and do not report or transcript unless families choose to release these scores, meaning students cannot be penalized in college admissions processes for scores intended for academic information purposes rather than acceptance. The goal is a positive student experience, regardless of the final test score.

FINDING YOUR VOICE—WHAT THIS MEANS FOR OUR KIDS

Most important is the original intent of Talent Searches—what do we do with this information, or "what's next?" The most salient piece of information to arm yourself with as a parent or educator is this: Students need to do something they love that will be uncomfortably challenging in an environment of support and friendship—with an emphasis on all three of these elements. For Talent Development Centers, this means an invitation to participate in accelerated summer programs specifically designed for rigor in both academic pace and content, as well as socioemotional growth in a community of peers. Gifted students report that these summer programs are very important to them (Enersen, 1993):

> The satisfaction of challenging course work taught by caring, expert teachers and the opportunity to live on a university campus [are] significant, [while] making friends and gaining confidence in their own abilities and participating in a variety of activities were equally vital. (p. 169)

Significant research supports talent development programs as supplemental summer opportunities, in-school accelerated models, university-based course or weekend offerings, residential cohort schooling options, distance learning, or personalized student services, such as grade or subject-area acceleration (Corwith & Olszewski-Kubilius, 2012; Lupkowski-Shoplik, Benbow, Assouline, & Brody, 2003; Robinson, Shore, Enersen, 2007; VanTassel-Baska, 2007). Talent Search is more than just taking a test and finding educational resources; it is really the beginning of finding a new sense of family—of shared stories, shared lives and experiences, and shared conversation about possibilities. For many of our students, it means finally being given a voice.

REFLECTION QUESTIONS

1. What challenges are there for gifted students to be "seen" in traditional school environments, and why are these present?
2. How might Talent Development Centers work cohesively with schools and school districts to deconstruct these visibility issues?
3. What role do families play in helping school communities better understand the unique needs of this population?
4. How might students from populations not proportionally represented in gifted services be more visible and better heard?

REFERENCES

Barnett, L. B., & Durden, W. G. (1993). Education patterns of academically talented youth. *Gifted Child Quarterly, 37,* 161–168.

Benbow, C. P., & Arjmand, O. (1990). Predictors of high academic achievement in mathematics and science by mathematically talented students: A longitudinal study. *Journal of Educational Psychology, 82,* 430–441.

Corwith, S., & Olszewski-Kubilius, P. (2012). Talent search. In T. L. Cross & J. R. Cross (Eds.), *Handbook for counselors serving students with gifts and talents* (pp. 543–554). Waco, TX: Prufrock Press.

Enersen, D. (1993). Summer residential programs: Academics and beyond. *Gifted Child Quarterly, 37,* 169–176.

Lee, S. Y., Matthews, M. S., & Olszewski-Kubilius, P. (2008). A national picture of talent search and talent search educational programs. *Gifted Child Quarterly, 52,* 55–69.

Lupkowski-Shoplik, A., Benbow, C., Assouline, S., & Brody, L. (2003). Talent searches: Meeting the needs of academically talented youth. In N. Colangelo & G. A. Davis (Eds.), *Handbook of gifted education* (3rd ed., pp. 204–218). Boston, MA: Pearson.

Olszewski-Kubilius, P., & Grant, B. (1996). Academically talented women and mathematics: The role of special programs and support from others in acceleration, achievement and aspiration. In K. D. Noble & R. F. Subotnik (Eds.), *Remarkable women: Perspectives on female talent development* (pp. 281–294). Cresskill, NJ: Hampton Press.

Olszewski-Kubilius, P., & Lee, S. Y. (2005). How schools use talent search scores for gifted adolescents. *Roeper Review, 27,* 233–241.

Robertson, K. F., Smeets, S., Lubinski, D., & Benbow, C. P. (2010). Beyond the threshold hypothesis: Even among the gifted and top math/science graduate students, cognitive abilities, vocational interests, and lifestyle preferences matter for career choice, performance, and persistence. *Current Directions in Psychological Science, 19,* 346–351.

Robinson, A., Shore, B. M., & Enersen, D. (2007). *Best practices in gifted education: An evidence-based guide.* Waco, TX: Prufrock Press.

VanTassel-Baska, J. (Ed). (2007). *Serving gifted learners beyond the traditional classroom: A guide to alternative programs and services.* Waco, TX: Prufrock Press.

Wilder, G., & Casserly, P. L. (1988). *Young SAT takers: Two surveys. Survey 1: Young SAT takers and their parents. College Board Report No.88-1.* New York, NY: College Entrance Examination Board.

CHAPTER 32

HIGH-QUALITY CURRICULUM: A LESSON IN COLLABORATION

by Jennifer G. Beasley

The National Association for Gifted Children (NAGC) Curriculum Studies Network focuses on promoting and creating high-quality curriculum to meet the needs of academically advanced learners. This network of researchers, administrators, and practitioners undertakes projects that (a) develop standards for curriculum development, (b) develop a working relationship and mutual projects with other national curriculum groups, (c) provide a clearinghouse of appropriate curriculum materials for gifted students, and (d) promote research and development in curriculum for gifted students. One of our favorite ways to promote high-quality curriculum for students is through our annual Curriculum Studies Award. Each year teachers from across the nation submit curriculum units they have designed to a team of experts. From these submissions, outstanding curricula for math, social studies, science, and language arts are recognized. Many of these units become published and are used in classrooms across the country. This network is proud of the collaboration promoted among educators, but in order for high-quality curriculum to continue to be the standard in our field, we realize the valuable role parents play in the process as well.

Why is promoting high-quality curriculum so important? With the continued emphasis on standards-based curriculum, first in the form of Common Core State Standards and now with new state standards, it is still important to recognize that we need to meet the unique needs and interests of students. The connection between high-quality curriculum and the students' needs can be strengthened in collaboration with parents.

RECOGNIZING HIGH-QUALITY CURRICULUM

It is hard to evaluate what students are learning in school by just looking at what they bring home in their backpacks each day. How do parents recognize high-quality curriculum? A great place to start thinking about quality curriculum is NAGC's (2010) Gifted Programming Standards. The NAGC Standards were developed to assist school districts in examining the quality of their programming for gifted learners. When defining exemplary curriculum and instruction, the standards suggest:

> » curriculum adapted, modified, or replacing the standard curriculum to meet the needs of both students with gifts and talents as well as those with special needs, such as twice-exceptional, highly gifted, and English language learners;
> » balanced assessments that can assess level(s) of learning through both preassessment and formative assessment;
> » curricula that are conceptually challenging and in-depth, and provide complex content;
> » opportunities for curricular acceleration in gifted learners' areas of strength and interest; and
> » differentiated curriculum modified to provide learning experiences to match students' gifts and talents and to respond to diversity.

Parents can examine each of these standards in more detail as well as related resources and guiding questions about the school curriculum on NAGC's website.

District and state websites are another good source of information about school curriculum. Many school districts as well as virtual (online) schools have an area devoted to information about curriculum for gifted and talented programs. Often these resources are focused just on the elementary grades, but there are exceptions. In the case of a virtual school, take time to find out whether the curriculum can be modified for advanced learners.

CONNECTING WHAT WE TEACH
TO WHO WE TEACH

One of the most powerful ways that parents can collaborate with the school in the area of curriculum is helping the school understand their child's unique needs and interests. In order for schools to truly differentiate to meet the needs of a child, they need to get to know the child. Parents and guardians who know their child best can help with this. Parents can take the following steps to begin collaborating with the school:

» Talk with your child's teachers regularly about your child's progress and what you can do to help her improve. Give teachers information on how your child learns best.

» Volunteer to help with school activities and find other ways to connect with the life of the school in order to learn about the school community.

» Encourage your child to complete challenging work. Work that is "just the right fit" for your child should be challenging and rigorous for her.

» Provide feedback to the teacher on your child's work—not just the issues that might come up, but the successes, too. This can help the teacher monitor and adjust to better meet your child's needs.

» Dedicate at least 15 minutes each day to talking with your child and reading with him. This gives you some special time with your child during which he may express interests and passions that you can share with your school.

» Help your child with her homework. The time you spend understanding the challenges and successes that your child has with schoolwork can be valuable information that you can share with the teacher.

» Help your child develop a growth mindset. Anything worth learning requires hard work; give your child feedback that focuses on the hard work she is doing, not just the letter grade at the end of the assignment.

COLLABORATING FOR SUCCESS

When teachers craft their lessons, they begin with the end in mind. They ask themselves: "Where do I want students to be at the end of this lesson or learning experience?" This question helps teachers make decisions along the way for how to best meet the unique needs and interests of their students. They can make those necessary changes, knowing that, in the end, all students will arrive at the destination—the learning goal. Parents can ask themselves a similar question: "Where do I want my child to be at the end of this experience?" By collaborating with the school and providing the needed information to help the teacher get to know the strengths, passions, and needs of your child, together you both can help your child arrive at the destination of being a lifelong learner prepared for what lies ahead.

REFLECTION QUESTIONS

1. How does curriculum for gifted children differ from other curriculum?
2. What is the biggest obstacle when it comes to learning more about gifted curriculum? How can this obstacle be overcome?
3. What is one way you could help your child's teacher get to know your child better?
4. This chapter mentioned many resources for learning more about gifted curriculum. Which resource do you think will help you most?

REFERENCES

National Association for Gifted Children. (2010). *NAGC Pre-K–Grade 12 Gifted Programming Standards: A blueprint for quality gifted education programs.* Washington, DC: Author.

CHAPTER 33

GIFTED HOMESCHOOLING: OUR JOURNEY WITH A SQUARE PEG: A MOTHER'S PERSPECTIVE

by Gwen Olmstead

Our journey to gifted homeschooling was filled with our own folly and a slow learning curve. By sharing some of our struggles and insights, I hope others will benefit or find solace in knowing they are not alone when their square peg children don't fit into round holes. Sure, if you hammer a square peg long enough, it will fit into a round hole—but aren't there more effective construction methods?

WHY HOMESCHOOL?

A question most frequently asked of homeschooling families is "Why do you homeschool?" Everyone has different stories and reasons, but, ultimately, families choose homeschooling with the hopes of providing a learning experience more suited to their children's needs.

For us, our gifted son was unchallenged in his traditional school setting. This led to excessive talking, doodling on schoolwork while waiting for others to finish, and losing recess privileges for these behaviors. In third grade, he ultimately came home from school feeling like a "bad kid" and "hating school."

Our efforts to advocate for challenge and differentiation involved the teacher, the principal, and the school board. All three avenues were a dead end for us. Repeatedly, meetings ended with the administration's stated inability to change the school program and their suggestions for us to supplement our son's education with evening and summer coursework. We decided this was not an option for us, as we feel gifted children shouldn't be expected to spend additional time working to make up for deficits in their regular school day.

Over time, the answer became clear. We asked ourselves, "If we were going to provide our son some of his education, why shouldn't we provide all of it?" So, after a lot of research, soul-searching, scheduling, and family conferences, we decided to homeschool. And, eventually, all three of our children, in their varying ages and abilities, were withdrawn from public school and brought home for their education.

KNOW THE LAWS

It is essential you know your state's laws regarding homeschooling before making any decisions. As parents, you are responsible for abiding by the homeschooling laws. You might have to do the research yourself, as we found that most people are not familiar with the laws, including the local school district. We also discovered that policies differ by state. Some states require testing and/or documentation of student progress, while other states simply require written notice of withdrawal. Some states require schools to provide curriculum to homeschooling families, while others do not. Websites by the Home School Legal Defense Association (https://hslda.org/content) and A2Z Home's Cool (https://a2zhomeschooling.com) provide overviews on state-by-state laws. However, before proceeding, don't simply rely on website information. Always confirm current homeschooling requirements with your state department of education and your state's homeschooling association.

POSSIBLE QUESTIONS YOU MIGHT HAVE

WHAT ABOUT SOCIALIZATION?

The most frequent concern we heard was "What about socialization?" We have found homeschooling to be as socially isolating as we choose it to be. One plus is that homeschool has provided more opportunity—and more free time—to join as many activities as we see fit. Taking courses at local community colleges, homeschool cooperatives, community centers, and libraries allows gifted learners to excel in areas of personal interest, regardless of grade. As a home-schooling family, we are busier than ever as we've discovered the many amazing opportunities available to our children. Connect with as many homeschooling groups as possible. They are out there. Perhaps there isn't a formalized group yet, but you can create one by network-ing with others. Online groups are also a form of socialization. Be sure to check out Gifted Homeschoolers Forum (https://ghflearners.org). Expect to spend plenty of time driving. Learn to car-school; it's much more fun for everyone than the license plate game!

Some gifted learners are socially advanced well beyond their years and may feel isolated with their age peers in traditional school settings. Through homeschooling, my 8-year-old son was able to participate in the Model United Nations program with a group of middle school-aged homeschoolers and flourished in this setting because he was surrounded by academic and socioemotional peers instead of age peers.

Know your local resources and let them know you. Be sure your local libraries, museums, conservatories, artists' guilds, and state and local parks know you are a homeschooling family. Often, they pro-vide services for homeschool families at off-peak times. Additionally, they can help connect you to other homeschooling families.

PARENT AS TEACHER?

"Can I do this?" Yes, you can. Even though I have a Ph.D. in curriculum and instruction and am a certified English teacher, I still had no idea how to teach my youngest child to read or to conceptu-ally understand subtraction. No teacher is ready to "cover" all grades and all subjects. The beauty of homeschooling is that you learn with your child.

Parents develop question-making and answer-seeking skills. It's gratifying to see the love of learning thrive as your child becomes the seeker of interesting versus required knowledge. These days, a com-bination of online courses and outside activities is available for nearly every child's interest and level, which should ease parent concerns about the teaching process.

WHICH METHOD IS BEST?

There are countless methods of homeschooling, and there's no right or wrong approach. The needs of the child as well as the needs of the family (both time and money) will help guide curriculum and method decisions. Your homeschool might look and feel like a traditional school (often referred to as "school at home") or be free-spirited, like alternative education proponent John Holt's unschooling movement (Holt & Farenga, 2009). Throughout his life, Holt advocated that children should "learn without teaching"—by doing, by wondering, and by figuring things out on their own—without well-intentioned adults forcing a particular subject at a particular time. We've found that most families end up somewhere in the middle, with a bit of structured curriculum and a bit of student-directed learning. You will find your own unique path, too.

END OF THE ROAD?

Both local school district and home situation options can change at any time, so we reevaluate our homeschooling needs for each child prior to each academic year. Ultimately, though, we've decided to homeschool until our "square peg children" and the "round hole classroom setting" can constructively build together. We know parents who homeschool anywhere from part of an academic year (to resolve a short-term situation) to several years. Many people successfully homeschool through high school; many colleges actively seek home-educated children. Continue open conversations with your school leaders. There may be opportunities to create a blended format for your child, by mixing and matching public or private school, online, community college, and tutoring options. Any of these can help the transition back to traditional school, should that be in the future.

LOOKING BACK

Looking back, I've had as much of an education on the homeschooling journey as my children. I see now that it took me entirely too long to let go of the clock when we started homeschooling. Rather than struggling with my son for an hour to complete an assignment because "Mom said it was time to do it now," I could wait until he was focused and ready to learn, and that same concept was mastered in minutes.

When purchasing curriculum, choose wisely. It's very easy to get carried away when planning ahead. Also, be ready to ditch materials if they aren't working for you or your child. The money wasted on those materials is immaterial compared to the time wasted with frustration. Library book sales are your new best friends, along with free gallery guides and materials at museums. Through these resources, we have taken the dread out of "the dreaded worksheet." My children and I learned together that just because it was a photocopied paper, it didn't have to mean rote memorization of excessive repetition. We were in control of what was on the paper. Initially, I wouldn't use the same sources, for fear of boredom from repetition. But even in my classroom of three students, I needed to recognize that one child needed the routine of the same source. What better place to individualize and differentiate instruction than our tiny school?

I can laugh out loud when I remember myself believing the house would be cleaner because we would be home all day and would have more time to clean. But I can also appreciate that life's education has taught my children how to clean just about everything around the house.

I now know that as the primary teacher, my relationship with my children has changed and deepened—and it's almost unfair to Dad. Because Dad's job requires that he work long hours and travel, we have made extra effort for the children to also see him as a teacher in his own right and not the recess playmate (although that is also important).

Lastly, be ready to be spoiled by never having to wait in line or fret over when to schedule a doctor's appointment. Off-peak errands and field trips are wonderfully addictive. In turn, be ready for the inevitable question: "Why aren't you in school today?"

REFLECTION QUESTIONS

1. What roles do you envision each family member taking during your family's homeschool journey? Are there people around you who would be willing and able to share their knowledge?

2. What sort of community resources do you have to include in your curriculum? Are there parks, museums, libraries, or special programs that may offer homeschool programs?

3. What barriers do you foresee in the homeschool process, whether school or community officials or even those in your homeschooling family and community?
4. What fears do you have as you ponder the idea of being responsible for educating a gifted mind?

REFERENCE

Holt, J., & Farenga, P. (2009). *Teach your own: The John Holt book of homeschooling*. Cambridge, MA: Perseus Books.

CHAPTER 34

NAVIGATING EDUCATIONAL CHOICES: FINDING THE BEST FIT FOR YOUR GIFTED CHILD

by Ellen Honeck, Anne Johnson, and Megan O'Reilly Palevich

Once your child is identified as gifted and talented, the next question you may ask is "Which educational environment is the best fit for my child?" Answers to that question are as individual as the family and the child being served. And, because the quality and variety of programs and services vary significantly throughout the country, available educational environments differ by geographic location. A gifted program available in New York City, for example, might not be available in Kickapoo, KS.

Many programming options are available for gifted learners across the country and world. Computers and the Internet have created opportunities for gifted students available beyond the local school program or the classroom. Finding the right educational environment can be challenging and overwhelming. Our goal is to provide you guidance to navigate this process.

UNDERSTANDING YOUR CHILD AND FAMILY

Before starting your program and/or school research, reflect on your child's unique needs and what qualities your family seeks in an educational community. If a program seems wonderful but is in conflict with your personal beliefs, it won't be a good match. Ask yourself the following questions:

>   » What educational settings, programs, or services did you participate in as a child or young adult? What were the posi-

tives and negatives? Are there new and developing programs or services that you might be willing to consider?

» Do you want your child to have the same programs and services you had, or something different? Are you willing to commit to something different?

» Are you committed to a public educational setting, or would you consider an alternative setting, such as an online, private, independent, or faith-based school or homeschooling?

» How important are standardized test scores and/or school rankings?

» Reflect honestly on your child's individual needs:
  • Is your child working above age peers? At age level? Does he need an accelerated program of study?
  • In what areas does your child demonstrate a talent or exceptional area of strength: academics, arts, technology, or athletics?
  • Is your child twice-exceptional? Does she have a need for specialized programming to support her learning differences?
  • Does your child work well in a small or large environment? Is he mostly independent, or does he prefer the collaborative and social nature of learning with peers?
  • Does your child struggle with transitions?
  • Are peer relationships important to your child?

» What are your goals for your child and her educational setting? If she is old enough, what goals does she have for herself?

» What part do you want the educational community to play in the area of spiritual and/or character development?

» What kind of social and emotional support/curriculum/program would be beneficial to your child?

SETTING GOALS

In *Re-Forming Gifted Education*, Rogers (2002) offered four guidelines in setting educational goals and in evaluating whether a program meets those goals:

» Does it provide for academic progress?
» Does it remediate academic weakness?
» Does it enhance psychological adjustment?
» Does it provide for socialization?

Rogers reminded parents that it's important to be honest with yourself about expectations and to realize that you may be looking for a best fit—not necessarily a perfect fit—for your child and family.

TYPES OF SCHOOLS, PROGRAMS, AND OPTIONS

School structures vary according to their goals and the students they serve. Various types of schools include charter, magnet, private, gifted, homeschooling, and online or blended learning environments.

Charter. These tuition-free public schools are open to all children with no special entrance requirements. Often there is a unique school culture or focus (e.g., science, technology, engineering, and math [STEM]; arts; project-based learning), and although the school receives public funds, it operates autonomously in exchange for accountability of results.

Magnet. Magnet schools are free public elementary or secondary schools that focus on a specific subject, vocation, or curriculum (such as STEM, International Baccalaureate [IB], or world languages). A lottery system generally determines entrance (with no entrance criteria), and diversity is an important element.

Private. Private schools may be faith-based or independent and are typically based on a particular philosophy or focus (e.g., Montessori, Waldorf, project-based, highly gifted, arts, trade, STEM). They charge tuition, yet many offer financial aid. Applicants must meet entrance requirements specific to the school.

Gifted schools. Gifted schools, private or public, provide an immersive experience in which the entire population of the school is gifted, offering gifted students an opportunity to interact with like-minded peers across all grade levels. Applicants must meet specific entrance requirements.

Homeschooling. Homeschooling is the process of educating school-aged children at home rather than at a school. Homeschooling parents can use a variety of methods to teach their children and focus

:as that their children find interesting and excel in the most.

:s can tailor their lessons to fit their child's abilities, maturity, and interest, while meeting homeschool curriculum standards for their state.

Online schools. Public or private online schools remove the confines of a physical classroom, and students access learning experiences via the use of technology. With online learning, students participate in a formal course or program delivered remotely via the Internet, so students have control over when and where they learn, and how fast they progress through the material. An increasing number of students are participating in distance education programs in which they learn at any time, across geographic boundaries, and at their own pace. Distance learning can be a good option for gifted students who attend schools with few advanced courses and gifted programs, cannot obtain early access to advanced courses, want to take additional advanced courses but cannot fit them into their school schedules, are not thriving in a typical school setting, or are homeschooled (Olszewski-Kubilius & Corwith, 2010).

More and more online learning K–12 options are available to gifted learners in different flavors:

» full-time, private gifted online schools (e.g., Laurel Springs School);

» full-time, public online schools in select states (e.g., Connections Academy);

» online personalized learning programs in select curriculum areas, such as math, science, and English (e.g., https://cty. jhu.edu/online/index.html); and

» session-based honors, Advanced Placement, or enrichment courses through gifted and talented centers (e.g., Northwestern University Center for Talent Development's Gifted LearningLinks or Johns Hopkins Center for Talented Youth).

Blended learning. A blended learning environment combines a traditional brick-and-mortar classroom experience with online instruction, often through a student's home school district. The amount of face-to-face time is dependent on each program and provides an opportunity for peer interactions and socialization.

Christensen, Staker, and Horn (2013) defined blended learning as a formal education program in which a student learns:

» at least in part through online learning, with some element of student control over time, place, path, and/or pace;

» at least in part in a supervised brick-and-mortar location away from home; and

» with connected modalities along his learning path within a course or subject to provide an integrated learning experience (p. 7).

With blended learning, students learn in part through online learning and in part through direct classroom instruction. They have some control over where and when the work is done as well as the path and pace of learning. Home and school learning are connected to provide a seamless experience (Christensen et al., 2013). This method delivers content along with voice and choice for the student within a learning management system (which is software used to deliver, track, and report).

In addition to reviewing the types of school options available, consider the programs within each school. Some schools address the needs of gifted learners through the push-in/pull-out program method; others may choose to cluster group, ability group, or even have self-contained classes. It's important to understand the educational lingo in order to effectively speak with school and program administrators in your quest to find the best educational fit for your child.

THE EVALUATION PROCESS

Gather information. Start your information-gathering process via the Internet. Visit school and program websites to obtain the most accurate information. Look for the following items:

» statement of mission, philosophy, and goals;

» accreditation;

» quality curriculum;

» approach of curriculum offered (such as project-based or textbook-based), including approved courses (e.g., College Board, University of California A-G, NCAA);

» focus on gifted learners or statement about gifted education services;
» quality of faculty and staff (e.g., How long they have been in the field of education? What types of professional development do they experience? Is the faculty trained in gifted education?);
» how the program is implemented, including if the schedule is fixed or flexible; and
» proven test scores and track record.

Visit schools and/or programs. Speak to individuals involved with the program and, if it's a physical environment, visit the school or program to get a better sense of the actual environment. Some things to do when visiting:
» ask questions;
» for a brick-and-mortar school, look at the environment (children's work on wall, students engaged in the classrooms);
» for online or blended settings, ask to see a sample of the course(s);
» talk with faculty, students, and parents (as available); and
» determine admissions requirements, processes, and fees (if any).

Identify your choices. After researching the options and visiting the programs, you'll need to identify your top choices. When considering the options, you should note the following:
» Is it a fit for your child and family?
» Does your child meet the admissions requirements?
» Do you understand the financial obligations? Volunteer commitments?
» Is the commute time or transportation feasible?
» Do you have the right tools needed (e.g., computer, work space, reliable Internet)?

Go for it! Remember that your child's priorities and needs will change throughout her academic career—this doesn't have to be a school for life! A school that is appropriate for your young student may not be a good fit in later elementary school. When things no longer feel right, learning needs aren't being met, or your child exhibits a change in behavior or attitude toward school, it might be time to look again for a different environment.

CONCLUSION

Finding a school or program for your child can be a very stressful process. Four walls no longer determine a student's educational path. Leveraging new models for learning provides transparency in education for parents and entrusts students to be the architects of their own learning. However, resources abound, and many parents who have been on this journey are willing to help. The most important thing is to jump in: Reflect on your goals and get the process started.

REFLECTION QUESTIONS

1. As you reflect on your own educational experiences, identify the elements that you would like for your child and those that you do not want for your child.
2. Which programming option feels right for your child? Why is this your preference?
3. Would you be willing to consider a choice that is unfamiliar to you and your family but might be the best fit?
4. Are there other adults who interact with your child who could provide valuable insight into the process and answer questions?
5. Talk to your child about educational options. Try a summer course in one of the programs. Ask your child which model he prefers.

REFERENCES

Christensen, C. M., Staker, H., & Horn, M. B. (2013). *Is K–12 blended learning disruptive?: An introduction to the theory of hybrids.* Retrieved from https://www.christenseninstitute.org/publications/hybrids

Olszewski-Kubilius, P., & Corwith, S. (2010). Distance education: Where it started and where it stands for gifted children and their educators. *Gifted Child Today, 34*(3), 17–22, 65–66.

Rogers, K. B. (2002). *Re-forming gifted education: Matching the program to the child.* Scottsdale, AZ: Great Potential Press.

PART VI

NURTURING GIFTED CHILDREN AT HOME

Research suggests that parents and caregivers are perhaps the most influential persons in a gifted child's life. Why? Parents are a child's first teachers. Parents of gifted children often notice skills, interests, passions, and gifts in their children long before professionals do. They also set the tone with respect to the family's values—including attitudes regarding the importance of nurturing high abilities, giftedness, and talent development.

It's also essential for parents to realize that giftedness does not just exist when their children are at school. Gifted children are gifted 24 hours a day, 7 days a week, 365 days a year. Their insatiable inquisitiveness, appetite for challenge, and talents in specific domains usually require enrichment at home and in the community. One could argue that what happens outside school walls is just as or even more important than what happens at school. Parents are in a unique position to know their child best and take steps to fuel their child's talents inside and outside the home.

The following chapters offer parents strategies for supporting their gifted children outside of school—ranging from math, science, and reading to social media, summer camp, sports, and spending time outdoors. Because each gifted child has her own learning style, beliefs, behaviors, interests, passions, and needs, there's no one solution that works for every child. Parents need to find the right combination of activities that appeal to their individual child. However, we do know that:

> » children who are involved in their own learning, both inside and outside of school, develop positive attitudes toward their abilities;

» summer programs and enrichment activities develop talent, instill creativity, spark innovation, build friendships, and provide lasting learning gains;

» parents are critical in fostering inquisitiveness, critical thinking, and problem solving in their gifted children by creating fun, yet enriching, learning opportunities outside of school in STEM, reading, or specific interest areas;

» although some gifted children do not gravitate toward physical activity or playing outdoors, finding the right sport to match a gifted child's personality and physical profile helps build strong muscle tone, increase psychosocial skills, improve memory, and lower stress; and

» nature and the outdoors offer a colorful palette from which families can creatively find ways to stoke their child's interests, while offering social and emotional benefit.

After reading the chapters on the following pages, you'll gain new insights, ideas, and inspirations on how you can help your gifted child reach his potential. Most of all, it's important for your child to know that "home is where the heart is" and that you, as his parent, caregiver, grandparent, or extended family member, support his talents and interests lovingly and wholeheartedly.

—Kathleen Nilles

CHAPTER 35

BEYOND SCHOOL WALLS: WHAT PARENTS CAN DO TO WIDEN THE HORIZONS OF THEIR GIFTED LEARNERS

by Joan Franklin Smutny

Parents of gifted children play a powerful role in expanding their children's world and helping them discover what they love. When gifted children have impassioned, open-minded, and creative family members, they soon discover what they love and who they are as people.

For gifted learners, curiosity, passion, and interest are absolute essentials. Gifted children have a questing spirit; they live for discovery. You may even notice that when children find interesting problems to think about, they look different. There is palpable excitement, eagerness, a burning need to know, and a lively curiosity you can see in their eyes.

Parents often ask: "What can I do that will make a difference?" I encourage parents to begin by looking at themselves and their homes as a rich resource for their gifted children.

YOU AND YOUR HOME

Adults often say their fondest childhood memories are those of when their parents swept them along in some new adventure or explored a new curiosity. Moments when they felt excited, awed, fascinated, and even humored by shared experiences vividly stand out. Experiences when they learned new skills and knowledge—or the value of patience, skill, and problem solving—meant the most.

For some children, including English language learners (ELLs), home is a doorway back to a familiar world—adorned with spicy cooking smells, richly colored fabrics, wall hangings, and instruments from their native countries.

EVERYDAY PROBLEM-SOLVING AT HOME

Author and teacher Harry Roman (2013) pointed out that parents don't have to create elaborate schemes for challenging their gifted children: "As parents, we must strive to involve our children in everyday things because not only will we teach them something useful and how to solve real problems . . . we will teach them how to be patient, caring, and memorable parents." Simple ways parents can challenge their high-ability children at home include:

» **Redesigning their room.** Have children participate in designing their rooms or other spaces where they work. They can create a 3-D model of their room to develop their ideas, which integrates measurement, visual thinking, architecture, structural engineering, and estimation of costs.

» **Designing the backyard.** Have children measure areas of backyard space and divide it into sections according to activity (e.g., play, gardening, bird feeding, shed, and outdoor furniture). Create a plan and break it down into small steps.

» **Becoming chefs for a day or week.** Help children plan a menu for a meal. They learn the fundamentals of food chemistry, and how to combine flavors and food ingredients. They can also create a restaurant-style menu by collecting samples and designing their own.

» **Exploring vacations.** Vacations offer endless opportunities for children to exercise their minds. Let them plan parts of the trip, research accommodations, calculate travel costs, and determine not-to-miss sites on the way. This teaches planning, how to break big goals down into smaller steps, and map reading (promotes visual thinking).

» **Saving energy.** Have children investigate ways to make the home more energy efficient, from blocking out air from drafty windows to installing energy efficient appliances to reducing the use of lights. They can explore solar applications for their home. Where might they work? What changes would have to be made to prepare for solar panels? Topics include engineering and conservation.

» **Reducing waste.** Hold a family meeting about reducing waste. Create an understanding of the problems of waste through investigations. What happens to the recycling materials in your town, city, or rural area? Where do materials go from there, and how does the recycling process work? Plan visits to recycling centers. This can be an eye-opening experience as children begin to appreciate the scope of the problem. Explore methods of recycling and garbage disposal, and speculate about reducing waste in the future.

NATURAL WORLD

Families who enjoy the outdoors can make a regular practice of activities around bird and plant study. Ideas include:

» **Nature as your palette.** Take walks every day and gather bits of the natural world—acorns, sticks, and leaves. Look up the names of the different trees, flowers, and birds encountered. When returning home, collections and observations can become material for something children create—a painting (gluing what they've collected onto construction paper), a science display, or a sculpture.

» **Gardening and plant life.** Teach about the plants in your garden and offer each of your children a section to create their own gardens. Have them research types of plants most suitable for your climate and environment, discuss plants, look at garden magazines, create designs, and experiment. Visit botanical gardens, neighborhood nurseries, and ecology centers to learn about native grasses and what it takes to have native grasses on your land. Through this process, children learn about local ecology, the chemical components of different soils, and what different plant types need to thrive.

» **Volunteering.** Most children are born enthusiasts of animals and nature. By volunteering with their children—caring for animals at a shelter or wildlife rehab center, removing invasive plants at a nature preserve, or participating in a yearly bird count—parents help children understand the complex needs of plants and animals. Gifted children are often eager to learn about the biology of different animals and the ecological system of local forests and water systems.

THE READING LIFE

Parents need to make literacy a part of their home. They can read everything in their environment with their children—be it retail circulars, the names of train stations, or traffic signs. Set aside times each week to read different kinds of texts—short stories, cartoons, poems, raps, and memoirs.

Most children have access to public libraries that provide books, magazines, DVDs, and Internet access if they lack this in their homes. At library events, children become aware of reading as a social experience: something to be shared and even performed. They learn that words come alive on the page when they speak, interpret, and embody them. Having a close relationship with the local library is especially vital for gifted English language learners, whatever their proficiency level may be.

Consider these daily or weekly reading practices to further your child's creative potential:

» **Storytelling.** Have children record family stories heard in either your home or a relative's home. Have them write about events they remember. Activities may include sketching and writing each part of the story, dramatizing the story, choosing a special word describing the person or story, writing the word (in both English and native tongue if applicable), and creating a short poem.

» **Specialized professions.** Inspire children to learn words in specialized fields, such as auto mechanics, ornithology, and botany.

» **Collages.** Help children use collage as a medium for exploring language and meaning, especially by incorporating foreign and English text and images from different magazines. Both ELLs and non-ELLs can select their country of origin, write words on the collage that express their personal feelings and thoughts about their home country, and write a letter to their country and the people they miss.

» **Journaling.** Get notebooks for children to use as private journals. At regular times each week, encourage them write or draw about things they saw, heard, and did. Inspire more creative approaches. Children can write upside down, or draw outside while sitting on a rock. They can draw on colored tissue paper. They can draw little creatures around the words they write. The journals are *theirs* alone.

MUSIC AND ART

According to writer, teacher, and publisher Maurice Fisher (2013), "Gifted students must learn to squeeze as much music and art into their lives as possible to counter the many useless and insipid experiences they will encounter throughout life" (p. 62). For greater learning exposure, parents should take advantage of opportunities in their immediate community and nearby, such as:

» **Performing arts concerts.** A well-rounded exposure to the arts is highly important for gifted children as it develops their sensitivity and openness to their own and others' cultures. Explore all types of music—classical, contemporary, jazz, blues, folk, roots, rock, and rap. Dance options include ballet, jazz, tap, modern, mime, and many cultural forms from around the world. Incorporate classical plays and operas, musicals, improvisation, and international traditions into the mix. If money is tight, there are free and low-budget performances off the beaten path. Open air concerts in the warmer months are the norm in many areas.

» **Studios or afterschool programs.** Studios and afterschool workshops offer classes in the arts and other subjects. For ELLs, volunteers who speak their language (often parents) can assist the teacher or act as translators. For gifted children from other countries, an art studio or computer lab can be a quiet place where they can imagine and invent.

» **Art museums.** Most art museums have activity areas for children of all ages. Parents should prepare for the trip by exploring the options with their children first. If the trip involves specific exhibits, parents can help children learn about the artists and art movements in advance, including pointillism, surrealism, and abstract impressionism. At home after the trip, children can create their own art project in a particular style, compose a poem, or write about a figure in a painting.

» **Community centers.** Community centers often provide a wide range of classes and workshops at a reasonable price. Reflecting the needs and interests of local populations, they may, for example, offer advanced computer classes, visual and performing arts workshops, Maker events, as well as bilingual support, cultural celebrations, and much more. If children are already skilled in a particular area, parents might negotiate with the teacher to see if they can try a higher level. Parents can participate by volunteering or by sharing resources and materials.

PROTECTING FROM THE PRESSURE TO CONFORM

As parents, we have the important job of helping our children navigate the world and learn how to integrate into society. At the same time, children depend on us to defend what is unique and special about them.

Most importantly, a nurturing home allows the individuality of gifted children to emerge naturally. By supporting the creative needs and interests of the family, the home becomes a more vibrant place and everyone feels it. Regardless of their experiences at school, gifted children need a treasured place where they feel safe and can thrive as living, breathing learners.

No message could be more important than conveying to your children that it's normal and right to pursue what they love. No message better safeguards their dreams and aspirations from the conforming forces of society.

REFLECTION QUESTIONS

1. How do you see your home as a nurturing environment for your children's needs and interests?

2. Are there ways that your children can learn new skills and be creative while participating in daily life activities, such as cooking, home or yard design, building, gardening, caring for animals, repairing, composting, and so forth?

3. What resources in your community could expand your children's interests and expose them to professionals in the fields they most love (e.g., workshops with musicians, scientists, writers, artists, computer scientists, etc.)?

4. What websites, online mentoring programs, competitions, or projects exist for gifted students in different fields?

REFERENCES

Fisher, M. D. (2013). Educating gifted students effectively in the home: Ten themes and variations. *Illinois Association for Gifted Children Journal*, 62–71.

Roman, H. (2013). Creative problem solving in the home of the gifted and talented. *Illinois Association for Gifted Children Journal*, 72–78.

CHAPTER 36

RECOGNIZING AND NURTURING MATH TALENT IN YOUR CHILD

by M. Katherine Gavin, Janine M. Firmender, and Tutita M. Casa

While walking to the gate at the airport, Jenna is always dawdling but notices the most unusual things. She talks about the patterns she sees and asks the infamous question "Why?" over and over: "Why did they use cylinders to create the lighting mobiles? Why did they decide on hexagons in the carpeting pattern?" She is so curious.

George loves to go to the supermarket. He likes to look at the price of different items to find the best buy. He easily figures out the cost of a single item when there are sales advertised. His number sense and estimation skills are amazing.

How can parents nurture their children's interest in and talent for mathematics? There are many opportunities at home and outside of school in which you and your child can experience the joy in doing mathematics.

RECOGNIZING MATH TALENT IN YOUR CHILD

In *Preparing the Next Generation of STEM Innovators: Identifying and Developing Our Nation's Human Capital*, the National Science Board (2010) emphasized that "the U.S. education system too frequently fails to identify and develop our most talented and motivated students who will become the next generation of innovators" (p. 5). As parents, you have perhaps the best opportunity to spot math talent and talent potential in your children.

What is math talent? Ten different educators will most likely provide 10 different answers. One reason mathematical talent is difficult to describe involves the different ways children manifest math talent. Vadim Krutetskii (1968/1976), a Russian psychologist who did seminal work in the field of math talent, observed children in the process of doing mathematics. He found children were of three different types: (a) those who reasoned abstractly and had an algebraic cast of mind, (b) those who had strong spatial skills with a geometric cast of mind, and (c) those who had a combination of both.

So often children with mathematical talent are identified as those who know their times tables early and can compute any of their math facts quickly without errors. But it is important to know that Krutetskii (1968/1976), along with more recent researchers and math educators (Davidson & Sternberg, 1984; Seeley, 2015; Sowell, Bergwell, Zeigler, & Cartwright, 1990), have found that speed in computation is secondary to mathematical insight. A different approach to identifying this talent includes mathematical problem-solving ability and an inquisitive, intuitive mathematical mind.

How does this help you identify talent in your child? At The National Research Center on the Gifted and Talented, researchers used Krutetskii's (1968/1976) characteristics, as well as other behavioral characteristics identified by experts in mathematics, mathematics education, and gifted education to create a research-based scale for educators to rate the behavioral characteristics of mathematically talented students (Renzulli, Siegle, Reis, Gavin, & Sytsma Reed, 2009). These scales have been adapted as an observational tool for parents (see Figure 36.1). Notice that the characteristics focus on mathematical thinking and problem solving. Keep these behaviors in mind as you observe your child in a variety of settings, such as at play, in conversations at the dinner table, and talking with friends.

Your child does *not* have to excel in all of these behaviors. Rather, this is a guide to help you identify areas in which your child has a strong interest and/or seems particularly adept. It is also important to realize that there are many ways to formally identify math talent. If you notice your child has a strong interest in math and displays some of the characteristics in the observation scale, share this with his or her teacher. Educators have additional measures to help give a more comprehensive picture of your child's ability. These include standardized tests, classroom performance, interviews, observations scales, and math performance tasks. The important thing to remember is that identification should be an ongoing process rather than a one-time procedure. There are three important factors to consider

Do you notice that your child . . .

- Enjoys challenging jigsaw puzzles, logic problems, and/or games requiring problem-solving strategies?
- Is eager to solve challenging math problems (e.g., problems for which the solution is not readily apparent)?
- Displays a strong number sense (e.g., makes sense of very large and/ or very small numbers, estimates easily)?
- Has creative and unusual ways of solving math-related problems (including ways you may never have considered)?
- Looks at his or her world from a math perspective (e.g., sees spatial relationships, looks for patterns, recognizes and identifies geometric shapes in objects)?
- Organizes data and information to find math patterns (e.g., likes to create tables or charts)?
- Can switch strategies easily to find the solution to a challenging math problem?
- Frequently solves math problems without any supports, such as math materials or calculators?
- Understands new math concepts more easily than other children?
- Likes to analyze the structure of a math problem (e.g., the way it is set up; how is it similar to or different from other problems)?

Figure 36.1. Observation tool for parents. Adapted from *Scales for Rating the Behavioral Characteristics of Superior Students* (3rd ed.), by J. S. Renzulli et al., 2013, Waco, TX: Prufrock Press. Copyright 2013 by Prufrock Press. Adapted with permission.

during this process (Gavin, 2011): (a) there are different types of math talent, (b) multiple measures should be used to provide a variety of sources of information, and (c) children demonstrate talent at different times and in different ways over the course of their schooling.

NURTURING MATH TALENT IN YOUR CHILD

Young children need to begin developing the habits of mind of professional mathematicians right from the start (Gavin & Casa, 2012; Gavin & Renzulli, 2018; Johnsen & Sheffield, 2013; Johnson, 2011). This is not accomplished by simply moving students into the next grade-level math text, although this can be a good start for some students. The kinds of problems posed to students and the discussions generated around their solution strategies need to be challenging in order to develop student mathematicians who are creative problem solvers. Beyond math class, there are other activities such as math competitions and enrichment clubs, including computer and robotics clubs, that provide challenge and enjoyment within the school environment.

There is also much that can be done outside of school. This does not mean teaching your child more challenging arithmetic, such as multiplying four-digit numbers by three-digit numbers. It also is not about teaching procedures, such as solving algebraic equations. Rather, it is about getting children to think about interesting and challenging problems that encourage them to reason mathematically by, for example, looking for patterns, finding mathematical structure in problems, and determining multiple ways to solve a problem.

MATH ACTIVITIES FOR YOU AND YOUR CHILD

This section provides activities to do at home. The games come from *Unraveling the Mystery of the MoLi Stone* in the Project M³: Mentoring Mathematical Minds award-winning series of units for mathematically talented elementary students (Gavin, Chapin, Dailey, & Sheffield, 2015). In these activities, children go far beyond computation and think deeply about place value, addition, subtraction, and probability. The activities also are fun, and children love to play them over and over, learning something new each time.

To play "Card Game Capers," you will need a total of 10 cards. Each card displays one digit, 0–9. The object of the game is to write the greatest two-digit number after three cards are drawn, one at a time. It's not as easy as it sounds! Here are a few twists:

» You cannot look at the cards.
» Three digit cards will be drawn one at a time, and you must record where you plan to place the digit: either in the tens place, the ones place, or in the discard spot *before* you draw the next card. You cannot make a change after you write it down.
» The digit cards will not be placed back in the deck once they are picked.

For example, say the first digit drawn is a 6. You might think it will be the greatest digit selected, so you put it in the tens place.

Figure 36.2. Card game capers example.

Your child feels that there is a good chance that a greater digit will be drawn and records it in the ones place. In this case (shown in Figure 36.2), she beats you. However, the greatest possible combination would have included the 9 that was drawn last.

At first, your child may think that this game has to do with luck. In fact, to be successful with this game, you need to not only understand place value (e.g., the 6 in the tens place is worth more than the 6 in the ones place), but also probability. That is, after you draw a 6, you have three out of nine ways to pick a digit that is greater (7, 8, and 9) and six out of nine ways (0, 1, 2, 3, 4, and 5) to pick a digit that is lesser. As seen from the pictured example, this is not always guaranteed! As one of our students stated, "It depends on how much of a risk-taker you are as well." As play continues, discuss digit placement and what the differences are in their values.

Also try the "Think Beyond" activity as an extension in which players make the greatest three-digit number using four digit cards with a discard option. Additionally, you can challenge yourselves to try to create the least two- or three-digit number. What strategies might you use that are the same or different? A further extension challenges children to figure out how many two-digit numbers are possible to create if the tens digit cannot be zero and the same digit cannot be repeated when writing the number. There are many solution paths to the answer besides writing down all of the numbers!

"Some Sum" and "Some Difference" are games that build off of "Card Game Capers" (see Figure 36.3). You again will use the same 10 digit cards and draw four cards, one at a time without replacing them to make two two-digit numbers. The object of the games, respectively, is to make either the greatest or least sum or difference between the numbers. Children will learn that you can get the same sum with different addends (e.g., 94 + 63 = 93 + 64). However, this

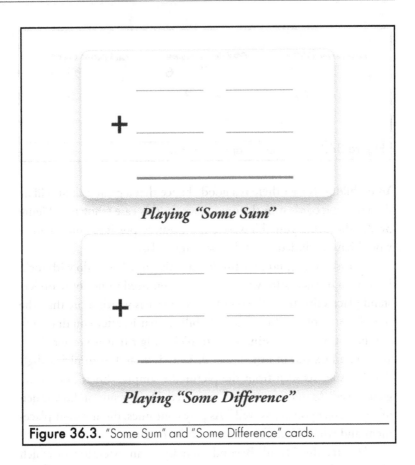

Playing "Some Sum"

Playing "Some Difference"

Figure 36.3. "Some Sum" and "Some Difference" cards.

does not work for subtraction (e.g., 94 – 63 ≠ 93 – 64). Additional strategies are needed when playing "Some Difference" when trying to get the greatest difference (when the numbers have to be as far away as possible) and least difference (when the numbers have to be as close to each other as possible).

ADDITIONAL ACTIVITIES

Did you know that by participating in team sports, such as basketball and soccer, your child is developing spatial sense as well as learning how to solve problems? Players need to have a sense of where all of the other players are on the court or field and where they themselves need to be to advance the ball. They need to think quickly regarding adjustment of positions and plays based on the strategy of the opposing team. Encourage your child to try these and other sports.

Visiting science centers and math museums is another enjoyable way to experience mathematics. Make sure you and your child take advantage of the activities. There are often problems to solve and experiments to explore, and you need to take the time to do them together and discuss them. Look for afterschool, Saturday, and summer math enrichment programs. Often these programs provide scholarships, so do not be deterred by the cost at the outset.

Finally, there are many excellent websites with challenging, interesting problems and games. However, a word of caution is necessary. There are also many websites that are not challenging and offer repetitive practice and boring drill. Clearly, these are not appropriate. Look instead for ones in which your child needs to grapple with the mathematics by problem solving.

CONCLUDING THOUGHTS

Think of yourself as a talent scout. Encourage your child's interest in mathematics. Provide experiences at home to fuel the spark. Play strategy games like Yahtzee and Battleship, construct jigsaw puzzles, create origami animals, and do Sudoku puzzles together. Find patterns in nature as you walk in the park or along the beach. Most of all, have fun with math. If children develop a love for mathematics, they will likely continue to pursue it. And we definitely need a new generation of mathematicians in this increasingly technological world. You can play an important part in this process.

RESOURCES

» Davidson Institute (https://www.davidsongifted.org): Type in "mathematics" in their search engine. This website has extensive listings of organizations, competitions, curriculum, games, problem-solving websites, printed materials, summer and online programs, and other links to develop math talent.

» Figure This! Math Challenges for Families (https://figure this.nctm.org): Sponsored by the National Council for Teachers of Mathematics, this site provides real-world math challenges across all mathematical areas for children and families to investigate together.

» Project M³: Mentoring Mathematical Minds (http://www.projectm3.org) and Project M²: Mentoring Young Mathematicians (http://www.projectm2.org): These 23 research-based NAGC award-winning math units (grades K–6) focus on advanced content across a variety of topics for mathematically talented elementary students. Each of the project websites also has a list of resources including websites for parents and children.

REFLECTION QUESTIONS

1. What type of mathematical concepts, such as number relationships and spatial ideas, does your child take an interest in and make sense of on his or her own?

2. How might you promote your child's love for math in your family's daily life?

3. In what ways do you encourage your child to ask mathematical questions or pose new math problems at home?

4. How can you encourage your child to look at mathematics from different perspectives or think about math in new and creative ways in your daily lives?

REFERENCES

Davidson, J. E., & Sternberg, R. J. (1984). The role of insight in intellectual giftedness. *Gifted Child Quarterly, 28,* 58–64.

Gavin, M. K. (2011). Identifying and nurturing math talent. In F. A. Karnes & K. R. Stephens (Series Eds.), *The practical strategies series in gifted education.* Waco, TX: Prufrock Press.

Gavin, M. K., & Casa, T. M. (2012). Nurturing young student mathematicians. *Gifted Education International, 29,* 140–153.

Gavin, M. K., Chapin, S. H., Dailey, J., & Sheffield, L. J. (2015). *Project M³: Unraveling* the *mystery of the MoLi Stone: Exploring place value and numeration.* Dubuque, IA: Kendall Hunt.

Gavin, M. K., & Renzulli, J. S. (2018). *Using the schoolwide enrichment model in mathematics: A how-to guide for developing student mathematicians.* Waco, TX: Prufrock Press.

Johnsen, S. K., & Sheffield, L. J. (2013). *Using the Common Core State Standards for Mathematics with gifted and advanced learners.* Waco, TX: Prufrock Press.

Johnson, D. T. (2011). Adapting mathematics curricula for high-ability learners. In J. VanTassel-Baska & C. A. Little (Eds.), *Content-based curriculum for high-ability learners* (2nd ed., pp. 187–216). Waco, TX: Prufrock Press.

Krutetskii, V. A. (1976). *The psychology of mathematical abilities in schoolchildren* (J. Teller, Trans.). Chicago, IL: University of Chicago Press. (Original work published 1968)

National Science Board. (2010). *Preparing the next generation of STEM innovators: Identifying and developing our nation's human capital* (NSB-10-33). Arlington, VA: National Science Foundation.

Renzulli, J. S., Siegle, D., Reis, S. M., Gavin, M. K., & Sytsma Reed, R. E. (2009). An investigation of the reliability and factor structure of four new scales for rating the behavioral characteristics of superior students. *Journal of Advanced Academics, 21,* 84–108.

Renzulli, J. S., Smith, L. H., White, A. J., Callahan, C. M., Hartman, R. K., Westberg, K. L., . . . Sytsma Reed, R. E. (2013). *Scales for rating the behavioral characteristics of superior students* (3rd ed.). Waco, TX: Prufrock Press.

Seeley, C. (2015). *Faster isn't smarter: Messages about math, teaching, and learning in the 21st century* (2nd ed.). Sausalito, CA: Math Solutions.

Sowell, E. J., Bergwell, L., Zeigler, A. J., & Cartwright, R. M. (1990). Identification and description of mathematically gifted students: A review of empirical research. *Gifted Child Quarterly, 34,* 147–154.

CHAPTER 37

SUMMER ENRICHMENT OR JUST HANGING OUT?: WHAT PARENTS SHOULD KNOW ABOUT EXTENDED LEARNING OPPORTUNITIES

by J. Denise Drain and Melissa R. Hasan

As parents, we often worry about our overscheduled children. How much is too much? Should they have time off during their breaks from school? Should they attend academic, music, or sport camps; hang out with friends; vacation on Grandpa's farm; or go to the beach? Of course, children and adolescents need time alone to just be themselves, but how many of us have heard, "I'm bored. I don't have anything to do," after a week of downtime?

Research has shown that summer learning based in family and community activities increases students' school achievement (Alexander, Entwisle, & Olson, 2007). Students who participate in summer learning activities—whether camp-based, community-based, or family-based—score higher on their fall achievement tests than students who are left to their own devices during their free time. This research suggests that the achievement gap is substantially linked to unequal learning opportunities in children's home and community environments, especially during summer months.

Although learning gains during the school year for students who participate in out-of-school activities is nearly equal for those who do not, students who do not participate in learning activities during a typical summer vacation often lose more than 2 months of reading achievement (Alexander et al., 2007). The authors also found that *all* students lost more than 2 months grade-level equivalency in math over the summer, even those participating in learning activities. Finally, a few studies (Atteberry & McEachin, 2016; Augustine et al., 2018) found that as much as two-thirds of test score differences could be traced to summer learning differences during elementary school and that these differences continued into high school and even college.

Note that studies do not suggest we should put our children into the traditional school setting year-round (Beckett et al., 2009). Activities during school vacations should include games, field trips, enrichment, and *fun*. These activities should connect to academics while not necessarily resembling a typical classroom setting. Successful out-of-school learning experiences combine new ideas, places, relationships, hands-on opportunities, application of knowledge, and encouragement for students (Quinn, 2002; Sunmonu, Larson, Van Horn, Cooper-Martin, & Nielsen, 2002). Many of the summer programs available for gifted students combine content acquisition with creative and critical thinking processes and authentic encounters. They may also provide significant social experiences with an academic peer group not available in the students' school environment. Students often come away from these programs having made lifelong friends who share their deepest interests.

Summer programs should build on children's interests and expertise. They may give children and adolescents an opportunity to develop expertise in areas such as sports, visual and performing arts, music, and academics. Being engaged in their own learning increases motivation and helps children to develop goals and positive attitudes toward their abilities (Miller, 2007). Programs specifically designed for gifted students require sustained attention, flexibility, and persistence—all of which are important executive functions that gifted students may not utilize throughout the regular academic year (Hasan, 2013). Time spent doing high-interest work with other gifted students also offers opportunities for greater intellectual challenge and stimulation, as well as peer support for academic excellence (Olszewski-Kubilius, 2007).

A child's social competence may also be developed through participation in summer programs of sufficient length (2 weeks for residential, 3 weeks for commuter; Olszewski-Kubilius, 2007). Social competence and emotional well-being are intertwined with cognitive abilities and have been shown to provide a strong foundation for cognitive learning. Summer programs provide students with opportunities to meet and work with peers who have many of the same interests and abilities. Through interactions with these peers, social competence is developed.

Although traditional summer school learning has been shown to provide small gains especially in math, those gains seem to disappear by the end of the next school year (Alexander, Entwisle, & Olson, 2012). For gifted students, there are programs available that delve deeply into math concepts in order to promote *understanding* as opposed to *memorization*. These programs, which are vastly different from traditional school math programs, may be enrichment or acceleration programs. In enrichment classes, students may be introduced to advanced topics, such as calculus, at early ages in a manner that moves students from concrete perceptions to abstract understandings. Acceleration programs allow students to master a module of mathematics that typically is completed over the course of a school year.

Studies also suggest summer academic camps that are carefully designed and implemented can make a difference in preventing summer learning loss and promoting lasting learning gains (Augustine et al., 2018; Miller, 2007). Several universities have specialized camps for gifted students—some are commuter camps, some are residential camps, and some are a blend of the two. Nonprofit organizations and for-profit organizations provide camps as well, although some have scant research to validate the effectiveness of their programs.

In order to be successful, VanTassel-Baska (2007) suggested three nonnegotiables that programs for the gifted must include. First, personnel must be a trained team of leaders with an understanding of the subject matter and the characteristics and needs of gifted children and/or adolescents. Second, a high-quality differentiated curriculum should be based on best practices in gifted education as well as the interests of the students. Third, the program should include an evaluation system of the students' growth and the program overall.

SUMMER OPPORTUNITIES

Summer activities can vary widely by location, type, focus, and duration (see Figure 37.1 for a sampling of gifted programs). Many

Program	Site and Contact Information	Description of Program*	Ages or Grades
Camp Summit Residential Summer Program for Gifted, Talented, and Creative	Marin, CA, and Northbay, MD; http://www.campsummitforthegifted.com	Two locations of Camp Summit provide the perfect setting for gifted, talented, and creative youth to gather together for a very special summer camp.	Ages 9–14
Center for Talent Development	Northwestern University, Evanston, IL; https://www.ctd.northwestern.edu/program_type/summer-programs	CTD offers both residential and commuter summer programming.	Pre-K–grade 12
Center for Talented Youth	Johns Hopkins University; locations in California, Maryland, New York, Pennsylvania, Rhode Island, Virginia, New Jersey, Connecticut, Washington, and Hong Kong; https://cty.jhu.edu/summer	CTY offers eligible students the opportunity to engage in challenging academic work in the company of peers who share their exceptional abilities and love of learning.	Commuter: Grades 2–6 Residential: Grades 5–12
Concordia Language Villages	Various sites in Minnesota; http://www.concordialanguagevillages.org/newsite	Summer Villages are a powerful combination of world language immersion, new cultural experiences, and summer camp fun.	Commuter: Ages 6–14 Residential: Ages 7–18
Embry-Riddle Aeronautical University	Prescott, AZ; https://prescott.erau.edu/degrees/summer-camps	Summer programs introduce the technology of today to the aviators and astronauts of tomorrow. Topics include aviation, aeronautics, cybersecurity, and robotics.	Commuter: Ages 7–12 Residential: Ages 12–18
Gifted Education Resource Institute (GERI) Summer Programs	Purdue University, West Lafayette, IN; https://www.education.purdue.edu/geri	GERI engages gifted, creative, and talented students to stimulate their imagination and expand their abilities.	Commuter: Grades K–6 Residential: Grades 5–12
iD Tech	150 locations around the world, including coed and all-girl options; https://www.idtech.com	iD Tech offers STEM education featuring cutting edge courses, in-demand skills, and innovation; includes course on design, coding, game development, and robotics.	Ages 7–19
Interlochen Arts Camp	Northwest Michigan; https://camp.interlochen.org/summer-arts-programs	Features course on creative writing, dance, motion picture arts, music, theatre arts, and visual arts.	Grades 3–12

Figure 37.1. Summer programs for the gifted and talented. Note. This list is a sampling of programs available and is not intended to be exhaustive.

Program	Site and Contact Information	Description of Program *	Ages or Grades
Satori Summer Camp	Eastern Washington University, Cheney, WA; https://www.satoricamp.org	Satori is an opportunity for academically and intellectually talented students to experience their first taste of college with others who share their enthusiasm for learning.	Ages 12–18
Summer Enrichment Program, William & Mary School of Education	Williamsburg, VA; https://education.wm.edu/centers/cfge/precollegiate/index.php	This program offers commuter programs for high-ability students. Courses are offered by William & Mary and various locations in Richmond, VA.	Grades K–10
Summer Institute for the Gifted	Commuter and residential programs in various states; https://www.giftedstudy.org	Unique programming combines academics with social, cultural, and recreational opportunities. Courses are led by qualified instructors representing an array of professional backgrounds.	Commuter: Ages 5–12 Residential: Ages 8–17
Talent Identification Program (TIP)	Duke University; sites in North Carolina, Kansas, Texas, Georgia, Louisiana, and Florida; https://tip.duke.edu	1- to 3-week sessions are intense and demanding; students are challenged to think critically about themselves and their world.	Grades 7–10
The Summer Program for Verbally and Mathematically Precocious Youth (VAMPY)	Western Kentucky University, Bowling Green, KY; https://www.wku.edu/gifted	VAMPY offers summer camps with STEM courses in astronomy, computer science, environmental science, forensic chemistry, genetics, mathematics, and physics. Humanities courses include writing, humanities, and presidential politics.	Commuter: Grades 1–5 Residential: Grades 6–8
The THINK Summer Institute	University of Nevada, Reno; https://www.davidsongifted.org/Think-summer	In this 3-week residential program for profoundly gifted children, participants can earn up to seven transferable college credits.	Ages 13–16
Vanderbilt University Program for Talented Youth	Vanderbilt University, Nashville, TN; https://pty.vanderbilt.edu/students	Students engage in accelerated coursework taught by Vanderbilt faculty and scholars. The residential camp requires qualifying ACT or SAT scores.	Commuter: Grades 1–6 Residential: Grades 7–12

* Program descriptions adapted from program promotional materials.

Figure 37.1. Continued.

private studios offer day camps for dance, gymnastics, music appreciation, or art. These are often in the week-to-week format, in which students may or may not have the same peers each week. Some colleges and universities offer 1–2-week sports camps that tend to be residential. Museums and zoos also offer day camp opportunities. Although none of these offerings specifically target the gifted, they may provide the gifted learner with positive peer interaction and an opportunity to develop expertise in less traditionally academic realms. Hands-on science and technology camps are also cropping up nationwide (such as Camp Invention and Mad Science), although these generally group students by age and grade level rather than ability.

Parents are fortunate that today there are many more camps and opportunities designed especially for gifted students (see NAGC's Gifted and Talented Resources Directory at http://giftedandtalented resourcesdirectory.com). These programs have the added benefit of allowing children and adolescents to meet others with their same interests and ability level. So, whether you decide to have your child attend a camp or create your own "summer intensive," gifted children and adolescents need opportunity to engage in intellectual challenge, to develop friendships with intellectual peers, to support and nurture intense interests, and to explore other fields and cultivate new interests.

REFLECTION QUESTIONS

1. If you were to design your child's summer experience, which areas would you want to emphasize?
2. What are some ways you could include STEM or math experiences during your child's summer vacation to minimize loss of mathematical concepts and skills?
3. What summer programs are available in your area? How do they support gifted, talented, and/or creative students?
4. Given that gifted children have varied interests and are eager to partake in numerous activities, how do you determine how much may be "too much" for your child? Is it important to keep your child "on the go," or are there benefits to scheduling downtime in the summer?

REFERENCES

Alexander, K. L., Entwisle, D. R., & Olson, L. S. (2007). Lasting consequences of the summer learning gap. *American Sociological Review, 72,* 167–180.

Alexander, K. L., Entwisle, D. R., & Olson, L. S. (2012). Schools, achievement, and inequality: A seasonal perspective. In G. D. Borman & M. Boulay (Eds.), *Summer learning: Research, policy, and programs* (pp. 25–51). New York, NY: Routledge.

Atteberry, A., & McEachin, A. (2016). School's out: Summer learning loss across grade levels and school contexts in the U.S. today. In K. Alexander, S. Pitcock, & M. Boulay (Eds.), *The summer slide: What we know and can do about summer learning loss* (pp. 35–54). New York, NY: Teachers College Press.

Augustine, C. H., McCombs, J. S., Pane, J. F., Schwartz, H. L., Schweig, J., McEachin, A., Siler-Evans, K. (2018). *Learning from summer: Effects of voluntary summer learning programs on low-income urban youth.* Santa Monica, CA: RAND.

Beckett, M., Borman, G., Capizzano, J., Parsley, D., Ross, S., Schirm, A., & Taylor, J. (2009). *Structuring out-of-school time to improve student achievement* (NCEE #2009-012). Washington, DC: National Center for Education Evaluation and Regional Assistance, Institute of Education Sciences, U.S. Department of Education.

Hasan, M. (2013). Bend or break: Your IQ is not your identity. *Parenting for High Potential, 2*(5), 4–6.

Miller, B. M. (2007). *The learning season: The untapped power of summer to advance student achievement.* Quincy, MA: Nellie Mae Education Foundation.

Olszewski-Kubilius, P. (2007). The role of summer programs in developing the talents of gifted students. In J. L. VanTassel-Baska (Ed.), *Serving gifted learners beyond the traditional classroom: A guide to alternative programs and services* (pp. 13–32). Waco, TX: Prufrock Press.

Quinn, J. (2002). Youth work's vitamin E. *Youth Today.* Retrieved from https://youthtoday.org/2002/05/youth-works-vitamin-e

Sunmonu, K., Larson, J., Van Horn, Y., Cooper-Martin, E., & Nielsen, J. (2002). *Evaluation of the extended learning opportunities summer program.* Rockville, MD: Office of Shared Accountability, Montgomery County Public Schools.

VanTassel-Baska, J. L. (2007). Alternative programs and services: A creative response to the unmet needs of gifted students. In J. L. VanTassel-Baska (Ed.), *Serving gifted learners beyond the traditional classroom: A guide to alternative programs and services* (pp. 241–256). Waco, TX: Prufrock Press.

CHAPTER 38

SPORTS THAT WORK FOR GIFTED CHILDREN

by Scott Lutostanski

Finding an enjoyable, exciting, and engaging activity for gifted students can be a challenging balancing act. On the one hand, as a parent, you're eager to get your child to become active and involved. On the other hand, children may face some setbacks as they try to find the right fit, with many gifted children grappling with poor fine and gross motor abilities.

Although a high percentage of gifted children are very talented athletes, other gifted children develop asynchronously, with a superior intellect developed well ahead of their social and emotional skills and their physical maturity (Neihart, Pfeiffer, & Cross, 2016). For these children, sports and other physical activities may not come as easily. The impact of asynchronous development on the motor cortex, coupled with social and emotional obstacles, can discourage some gifted children from finding athletic and social outlets.

Of course, physical activity is vital to the overall health and well-being of children, and exercise is needed to build muscle tone, maintain a healthy body weight, and strengthen the cardiovascular system. Additionally, exercise can have psychological and mental health benefits: Research suggests that movement and physical activity can improve children's memory while also lowering stress (Ford, 2011). This is particularly true for gifted students. Research shows that participating in sports can enhance academically talented teenagers' physical capabilities, physical appearance, emotional stability, self-concept or general sense of self, and same-sex peer relationships (Rinn & Wininger, 2007).

Yet, finding a sport that meets the needs—and helps overcome the deficits—of the gifted student can often feel like threading a needle.

WHAT ARE THE CHALLENGES?

PHYSICAL

Asynchronous or unbalanced development can manifest itself in gifted kids as a lack of muscle tone, balance, or coordination. This translates to an awkward, or even clumsy, child who may struggle with any physical task, especially sports that require a high demand of coordination—like baseball, golf, tennis, basketball, or soccer. Additionally, gifted children may process visual or auditory information at a much slower pace. This can impact their ability to participate in a sport that relies on ample flexible processing and problem-solving skills. These developmental differences can be present from a very young age and are even more common in boys than girls (Blackburn & Erickson, 1986). Hitting a backhand over the net while in a full sprint involves a high level of coordination, and nailing an iron shot from 150 yards out puts tremendous demands on the player's fine and gross motor movements. The sheer physical nature of many athletics can be taxing for many gifted children—especially given that academic and cognitive tasks come so easily to them.

SOCIAL

Flexible thinking and language processing are two areas in which these children struggle (Palmer, 2012). Team sports require a lot of communication among teammates, players, and coaches. Being on a team means adhering to rules, following drills, participating in practices, and listening to authority figures. A gifted child may have a hard time meeting the demands of the social rules, interactions, and hierarchies that engaging in a team sport requires. Sports like soccer and basketball involve skills like passing, moving, and coordinating plays; such team-based skills require constant verbal and nonverbal communication throughout the game as well as during practices. This can lead to system overload for a gifted and talented student.

EMOTIONAL

Underdeveloped emotional regulation may present challenges for some students when it comes to athletics (Palmer, 2012). In sports, such as those in school, this often may result in meltdowns, tantrums, rule-breaking, and getting into trouble. Sports require sharing, working well with others, graciously losing, persisting through challenges, accepting penalties, and publicly displaying ability. This combination of social pressure and high motor skill demand can overload children's emotional regulation skills. Ultimately, this can lead to more social struggles, further discouraging gifted children from persisting in sports.

PUTTING IT ALL TOGETHER: CHOOSING A SPORT

In many cases, these three components can interact in a cyclical process that will compound, rather than cure, the student's struggles. Imagine a 12-year-old playing Little League Baseball. Placed out in right field, the child repeatedly misreads the play and throws to the wrong base each time the ball is hit toward him. When he comes to the plate, he often strikes out due to his underdeveloped gross motor skills, causing him to cry, scream, and throw his helmet. By the time the game wraps up, all of the other players are upset with their teammate, leaving him to sit on the bench alone. So, what might be a better fit for this child than Little League Baseball? Some factors to consider are outline in Figure 38.1.

You must be thoughtful about what your child will be able to manage—*and* have fun participating in. The following list includes sports that gifted children are most often successful in, based on their physical, social, and emotional needs.

INDIVIDUAL SPORTS

Fencing and martial arts: Much like chess, fencing is a tactical sport requiring a high level of technique and strategy. Working with a coach can help promote self-evaluation, reflection, and metacognition, and training involves footwork, endurance, and mental focus. Like fencing, karate relies heavily on physical endurance, but it adds in elements of respect, relaxation, and discipline. Karate is done individually but within a group setting, a fact especially beneficial for younger children. It relies on very little one-on-one competition and provides consistent short-term rewards in the form of the belt color system. Neither fencing nor martial arts has a lot of publicity surrounding it.

Factors to Consider	Questions to Ask Yourself
Physical Ability	How much athleticism and coordination is needed? What is your child's ability level?
Social Ability	What is the level of social interaction? How much communication is involved in participating? How developed are your child's communication skills?
Emotional Ability	How does your child cope? Is he or she able to handle success, failure, and challenge? Are there scenarios (e.g., losing, following rules) that your child struggles with in particular?
Individual, Individual Team, or Team Sport	Is your child better suited to work alone or individually? Will being with teammates be beneficial or too challenging?
Setting	Are there a lot of spectators? Is it a popular sport that has a high level of competition? Are there tryouts? Does everyone make the team?

Figure 38.1. How to find the right sport for your gifted child.

INDIVIDUAL TEAM SPORTS

Wrestling, gymnastics, cross country, and swimming: Although team sports, these sports all involve individual competition, and they require endurance, practice, and athleticism—and considerable coaching and training. Additionally, wrestling and gymnastics are poor fits for children who lag in development in strength and agility, while cross country and swimming may not be good fits for some children based on their balance and endurance. These four sports keep children physically fit, allow them to socialize, and let them compete against only themselves. Additionally, these sports usually don't make cuts at the high school level, so anyone can be on the team.

TEAM SPORTS

Soccer, hockey, basketball: These sports are great for the student who is socially adept, providing camaraderie, teamwork, and socializing with other students. Although on the high end of athletic ability and hand-eye coordination, soccer, hockey, and basketball often provide children the most well-rounded experiences. The child participates in a more public forum, in which teammates directly rely on them. As a result, there is also a bigger potential for failure or social ostracization if a child cannot keep up. For young children, team sports are an excellent way to connect with others and make friends; however, competitiveness in these sports increases quickly as students get older. This can make it tough for any child to keep up, but can also be particularly challenging for a gifted student who may be frustrated if her ability level is not on pace with that of her peers.

The position a child plays on the team can also impact his or her experience. For instance, a child who struggles socially but craves a team experience may play goalie, which provides a social buffer and requires a lower level of on-the-field teamwork.

Although finding the right sport for a gifted child can sometimes seem like a hopeless chase, there are plenty of options out there waiting to be discovered. Parents must be very thoughtful when analyzing the team environment, competition level, social demand, and physical ability that exist within a given sport. There are plenty of sports that can provide the right fit and will allow children to have fun, be active, and interact with others. All it takes is a little bit of research into various options, and some dedicated thought about how to align a child's strengths and weaknesses with the demands of the sport.

HOW TO FIND RESOURCES

» **Hire a private trainer.** If you don't know your child's need and developmental profile, then it's best to start with someone who is a private trainer who can work with children to meet them where they're at and help them in their desired sport.

» **Talk with a coach.** If you're going to have your child participate in a sport (and he or she has developmental challenges with growth, etc.), start by meeting with a coach who can advise on the best plan for your child.

» **Work with a counselor.** Allow your gifted child to receive support and gain self-awareness so your child can better understand the role of sports in his or her life.

REFLECTION QUESTIONS

1. Take an inventory of your awareness of your child's physiological development as a gifted child. Based on his or her physical development, which types of sports or physical activity is best suited to your child's profile?
2. What types of scaffolding will you need for your gifted child with developmental issues to become a participant in sports?
3. Do you understand your child's gross motor issues as they pertain to playing certain sports?
4. What are your own values about the role sports play in a child's life? What about the role sports play in a gifted child's life when he or she is developing asynchronously?

REFERENCES

Blackburn, A. C., & Erickson, D. B. (1986). Predictable crises of the gifted student. *Journal of Counseling & Development, 64,* 552–555.

Ford, D. M. (2011). *An action research inquiry into the relationship among aerobic activities, memory, and stress with students identified as gifted* (Doctoral dissertation). Retrieved from ProQuest Dissertations Publishing.

Neihart, M., Pfeiffer, S. I., & Cross, T. L. (2016). *The social and emotional development of gifted children: What do we know?* (2nd ed.). Waco, TX: Prufrock Press.

Palmer, D. (2012). Gifted kids with learning problems. *Psychology Today.* Retrieved from https://www.psychologytoday.com/us/blog/gifted-kids/201112/gifted-kids-learning-problems

Rinn, A. N., & Wininger, S. R. (2007). Sports participation among academically gifted adolescents: Relationship to the multidimensional self-concept. *Journal for the Education of the Gifted, 31,* 35–56.

CHAPTER 39

GETTING GIFTED KIDS OUTDOORS: TIPS FOR A SUMMER OF PLAY

by Leigh Ann Fish and Patti Ensel Bailie

For many, childhood memories are of outdoor play: "baking" mud pies, building forts, climbing trees, playing tag at the park, and constructing sand castles at the beach. Children today spend only half as much time playing outside as their parents did 30 years ago (Clements, 2004). Childhood is moving indoors, yet research shows that a lack of outdoor play can have serious consequences for children.

There are several factors that are influencing this phenomenon. With more cars on the road and speed limits increasing, many parents are reluctant to allow their children to play, walk, or ride bikes on streets or near roadways (Gill, 2007). Green spaces are also disappearing at an alarming rate, limiting the number of available parks. At the same time, many parents' fear of injury or "stranger danger" means many children don't take advantage of the limited green space available. Finally, kids may opt for screen time over play time, and increased participation in organized sports and other extracurriculars means kids don't have as much time for play outdoors.

Kids who don't have a lot of unstructured outdoor play are at risk for a range of negative outcomes (Louv, 2008):

- » greater risk for unhealthy lifestyles and childhood obesity,
- » fewer sensory-rich experiences,
- » higher likelihood of diagnoses of ADHD-type symptoms,
- » lower academic performance in school,
- » less empathy for plants and animals,
- » more apathetic/destructive attitude toward others,

> » lower self-confidence,
> » less independence, and
> » diminished creativity.

The good news is that many of these can be reversed or restored by spending time outdoors! The benefits of outdoor experiences, although important for all children, can help nurture gifted children in many ways.

IMPROVED SOCIAL SKILLS

Some gifted children crave time alone; others may want to engage with peers but find it difficult. Their advanced vocabularies and intellectual curiosity, when coupled with asynchronous social skills and heightened emotional sensitivity, can lead to rejection if others perceive gifted children as annoying, bossy, contrary, intense, serious, self-absorbed, negative, sarcastic, or boastful (Lovecky, 1995). Being in nature can provide space for being alone, but it may also advance interactions with others and build resilience in social situations by allowing children to practice social skills.

Provide opportunities for children to work together. Social skills, such as communicating clearly, asking for help, encouraging others, disagreeing politely, actively listening, sharing resources, staying on task, waiting patiently, and resolving conflicts, are practiced authentically as children build forts or collect tadpoles.

Sharing the natural world can foster prosocial behaviors and increased empathy. Children learn to look after each other when hiking on woodland trails. Learning to care for plants and animals may lead to greater sensitivity and care toward others.

ENHANCED EMOTIONAL WELL-BEING

Gifted children's emotional intensity can fuel passion for learning and motivation to achieve, but it can also create anxiety, self-criticism, and doubt. Being outdoors in nature can offer a break from anxiety, providing a quiet space in which to relax and calm down.

It can also boost self-confidence as children learn to persevere and overcome obstacles.

Make time for being outdoors on a regular basis. Provide quiet time in a natural area outdoors, such as near a lake or in the woods. Help children find ways of expressing their intense emotions through stories, poems, art, music, journal entries, or physical activities—all of which can be done in nature!

MORE RISK-TAKING, RESILIENCE, AND GRIT

Taking risks in academic or intellectual areas may be more comfortable for some gifted children than physical, social, emotional, or creative risk-taking, which may come less easily or less naturally. Older gifted children, in particular, may have adopted risk avoidance behaviors, preferring tasks with clear, unambiguous steps or choosing to stick with what they can already do well. But children can't develop resiliency or grit when tasks are too easy. Spending time outdoors can be the perfect way to practice taking risks, to try and fail and try again, and to put forward effort in overcoming obstacles. Doing so may contribute to a growth mindset rather than a fixed one.

Give children autonomy to take risks outdoors. Exploring natural areas with trees to hang on and boulders to climb allows children to build confidence. If they don't succeed, help them view success differently by giving praise for effort rather than accomplishments.

BETTER PHYSICAL HEALTH

When gifted children are asynchronous in their development, their intellect can outpace their physical maturity, leading them to struggle with fine and gross motor abilities (Lutostanski, 2018). Outdoor physical activity can improve memory, enhance muscle tone, strengthen the heart and circulatory system, build strong bones, and help maintain a healthy body weight. Children who regularly play outdoors have been shown to eat and sleep better; outdoor play has been linked to improved eye health, healthier immune systems, and higher levels of vitamin D (Kernan & Devine, 2010; National Environmental Education Foundation, 2011).

Climbing trees, balancing on logs, and hiking on trails can aid physical development on a large scale. Fine motor development can be supported by taking apart flower heads, pine cones, or seed pods to examine how they function.

Cross-lateral movement (crossing the body's midline) such as digging with a shovel, raking leaves, and sweeping with an insect net enables the two sides of the brain to communicate, strengthening nerve cell pathways.

GREATER CURIOSITY, CREATIVITY, AND IMAGINATION

Creativity should be nurtured in all children. Playing in nature-rich environments provides variety and challenge, requiring thoughtful decision making to navigate. Whereas manufactured toys promote more predictable play, open-ended, natural materials encourage children to be inventive, imaginative, and resourceful.

Encourage children to use sticks or rocks in unique and inventive ways, such as making fairy houses, building forts, or creating works of art.

Feed children's curiosity by encouraging them to ask questions and investigate things in the natural world of interest to them. Model this process for them by asking questions you wonder about and follow up by seeking answers.

REDUCTION IN ADHD-TYPE SYMPTOMS

Many gifted children show high levels of intellectual, emotional, physical, sensory, or imaginational intensity, called overexcitabilities. Some researchers suspect overexcitabilities play a role in the misdiagnosis of ADHD in gifted children, especially those with psychomotor (physical) overexcitability. Recent studies suggest that there is a reduction in symptoms of ADHD when children play in natural areas (Taylor & Kuo, 2011).

Nature can provide a release for pent-up energy and tension in safe, gratifying ways. Choose outdoor sites like parks, prairies, or wooded areas where children can run, climb, and explore.

GETTING STARTED

As a family, where do you start? Families should consider a variety of opportunities for spending time outdoors with their children, in both structured and unstructured play. Firsthand, multisensory encounters with nature don't have to be wilderness experiences. Even time spent on a patch of ground, in the corner of a yard, or "on the fringes" can work. If you don't have a backyard, find a local park to explore.

One of the most important things you can do is model the desire to be outdoors, get your hands dirty, and share your enjoyment of the natural world. Prioritizing time in nature makes sense on a total development level for all children—so much so that some advocates are now calling regular time in nature a right that should not be denied (Kernan & Devine, 2010). We believe the benefits for gifted children are no exception.

REFLECTION QUESTIONS

1. How does your child feel about and react to being outdoors?
2. What are some of the barriers or obstacles keeping your family from getting outside? What has helped your family be successful getting outside?
3. What are some of your child's interests or passions that could translate to the outdoors?
4. What green spaces or natural settings do you have near your home or within your community?
5. Does your child's school or community have any programs that support nature-based education (Audubon, 4H, Scouts, etc.)? If not, have you considered starting a nature club with like-minded families?

REFERENCES

Clements, R. (2004). An investigation of the state of outdoor play. *Contemporary Issues in Early Childhood, 5,* 68–80.

Gill, T. (2007). *No fear: Growing up in a risk averse society.* London, England: Calouste.

Kernan, M., & Devine, D. (2010). Being confined within? Constructions of the good childhood and outdoor play in early childhood education and care settings in Ireland. *Children & Society, 24,* 371–385.

Louv, R. (2008). *Last child in the woods: Saving our children from nature-deficit disorder.* Chapel Hill, NC: Algonquin Books.

Lovecky, D. V. (1995). Highly gifted children and peer relationships. *Counseling and Guidance Newsletter, 5*(3), 2, 6–7. Washington, DC: National Association for Gifted Children.

Lutostanski, S. (2018). Sports that work for gifted children. *Parenting for High Potential, 7*(1), 9–11, 15.

National Environmental Education Foundation. (2011). *Fact sheet: Children's health and nature.* Retrieved from https://www.neef usa.org/resource/childrens-health-and-nature-fact-sheet

Taylor, A. F., & Kuo, F. E. (2011). Could exposure to everyday green spaces help treat ADHD? Evidence from children's play settings. *Applied Psychology: Health and Well-Being, 3,* 281–303.

CHAPTER 40

CReaTE EXCELLENCE: USING A TEACHER FRAMEWORK TO MAXIMIZE STEM LEARNING WITH YOUR CHILD

by Janet Tassell, Margaret Maxwell, and Rebecca Stobaugh

Your daughter Aubrie appears to have many signs of being gifted in science, technology, engineering, and mathematics (STEM) disciplines. In fact, you have already contacted the local school district to have her assessed for the gifted and talented program next year. That said, with the amount of free time you have with her during holidays and weekends, and with the high degree of interest that she has in STEM, you would like to help develop her ability and encourage her interest in STEM concepts. Your hope is that she will have a comprehensive concept of what constitutes STEM beyond what the media and school have provided.

Gifted children crave meaning through learning experiences, and they are naturally inquisitive (Hays, 2018). Often, even classrooms for the gifted and talented are full of worksheet curriculum materials that are sterile in connections to what is currently happening in the real world and/or do not allow for sense-making (Wood, Merkel, & Uerkwitz, 1996). When considering this scenario, a possible solution may come to mind—one in which parents long for children to have the opportunity to construct their own understanding with experiences comprising challenging questions and real-world tasks.

This chapter provides a teaching framework that parents can adapt for use with gifted children to help facilitate STEM knowledge and skills.

THE CReaTE FRAMEWORK

The CReaTE Framework, adapted from an evolving lesson plan, can promote learning in a nontraditional, yet comprehensive way (Maxwell, Stobaugh, & Tassell, 2016, 2017; see also https://create-excellence.com). The components of CReaTE are: Cognitive complexity, Real-world learning, Technology integration, and Engagement (see Figure 40.1). One approach that parents can borrow from the world of education is to make learning scenarios student-centered rather than teacher-centered. (*Note.* In this chapter, the term *teacher* is used to globally represent any individual in a mentoring position.) Parents can shift the onus of learning to the student, or child, rather than simply functioning in a didactic manner to tell learners information.

COGNITIVE COMPLEXITY

The cognitive complexity component within the CReaTE Framework is based on Bloom's revised cognitive taxonomy and is hierarchically organized (Anderson & Krathwohl, 2001). At the basic level of the framework, the cognitive complexity component, learners are engaged in remembering, understanding, and applying learning experiences. The higher levels embrace the top three cognitive levels (analyze, evaluate, and create). At these levels, the learners, rather than the teachers, are identifying the questions, tasks, or areas of interest. Gifted learners should maximize their time in the upper cognitive levels.

Furthermore, gifted learners should be encouraged to generate projects and topics at the create level while thinking like an expert focused on an open-ended, global learning emphasis. Teachers should avoid the quiz-bowl or *Jeopardy!* type of questions because these emphasize low-level knowledge and factual recall. Instead, learners should experience challenging questions that inspire them to deeply investigate and develop perseverance and resiliency in searching for solutions.

REAL-WORLD LEARNING

Real-world or authentic learning occurs when learners interact with—and potentially have an impact on—the real world with the goal of solving a problem. Learners involved in authentic learning may be motivated to persevere despite initial disorientation or frus-

CReaTE Levels	Cognitive Complexity	Real World	Technology Integration	Engagement (Teacher-Directed → Student-Directed)
Investigating	Students interact with content at an *analyze, evaluate,* or *create* level.	Learning simulates the real world.	Technology is an add-on or alternative—not essential, and students use technology to *analyze, evaluate,* or *create* thinking tasks.	Students choose tasks, and tasks are differentiated by content, process, and/or product.
Integrating	Students generate questions/projects with content at *analyze, evaluate,* or *create* level.	Learning emphasizes impact to the classroom, school, or community, and learning is integrated across subject areas.	Students' technology use is embedded in content and essential to project completion, promotes collaboration (students) and partnership (teacher), and helps them solve authentic problems at the *analyze, evaluate,* or *create* levels.	Students partner with teacher to define the content, process, and/or product, students use inquiry-based approach, and students collaborate with other students.
Specializing	Students generate questions/projects with content at *create* level, demonstrate complex thinking (like a content expert), and emphasize open-ended, global learning.	Learning has a positive impact on a national or global issue or problem, and students collaborate with experts in a field or discipline.	Student-directed technology use is seamlessly integrated in content at the *create* level, incorporates several technologies, and includes collaboration with field experts and/or global organizations to find solutions to an in-depth, real-world problem.	Students initiate their own inquiry-based learning projects and experience, demonstrate thorough immersion and full implementation from topic to solution, and initiate collaborations pertaining to their projects.

Higher Cognitive Complexity

Figure 40.1. CReaTE Framework (Maxwell, Stobaugh, & Tassell, 2016, 2017).

tration, as long as the project embodies what is of practical significance to them (Boss & Krauss, 2014). For example, students may learn letter-writing skills when they want to write a letter to their senator urging him or her to support water conservation near their town. This type of experience helps learners realize that real-world solutions may not always work, may not always please everyone, and will likely have consequences that affect others and other areas. Parents know that when learners make decisions involving the real world, children may be better prepared to make real decisions as an independent adult.

TECHNOLOGY INTEGRATION

Technology integration is the component that has been relatively new to learning experiences, and it is constantly evolving. It also enables learners to communicate and access data (Boss & Krauss, 2014). Technology integration requires that learners must utilize technology to share their learning. At the highest level of the CReaTE Framework, learners design projects that: (a) are seamlessly integrated with content, (b) may include several technologies, and (c) ideally include collaboration with experts in a specific field and/or organization to find solutions to an in-depth, real-world problem.

ENGAGEMENT

The engagement component of the CReaTE Framework indicates the degree to which learners take responsibility or ownership for their own learning by collaborating with their teacher, peers, and/or outside experts, while also managing resources such as teachers, experts in the discipline, and tools/technology (Boss, 2015). Parents can help learners focus their interests and make choices in how they approach the task. They are encouraged to support their children by helping them identify resources and collaborative opportunities. In short, engagement relates to how well or poorly learners are engaged in learning experiences to generate legitimate understanding in STEM disciplines.

CONCLUSION

The CReaTE Framework holds great promise for teachers who have adequate time and resources to focus students' attention on a task over a several-day period. However, another strategy may be to extract components of the model to facilitate learning. As an example, in traveling with gifted children over the summer, parents can use the cognitive complexity component of the CReaTE Framework when learning situations and opportunities arise. An application of the "C" in the CReaTE Framework may have parents design higher order questions on a vacation, such as "Why do you think the waves come in to shore at different sizes and intervals (periodicity), instead of arriving on a perfect interval and at perfectly consistent sizes?" Consider this question relative to the rhetorical question, "Have you noticed how the waves aren't all the same?" The latter (rhetorical) question leaves almost no room for learner input, whereas the former question demands a response from the learner, thus making the learning scenario student-centered.

Until this time, the CReaTE Framework has been only accessible to formally trained teachers in the classroom. However, this chapter illustrates how it can provide a guide for parents and a target for learners hoping to extend their understanding of STEM concepts. Parents no longer need to be bystanders and let valuable learning scenarios go unnoticed. They can use one or more components from the CReaTE Framework to inspire and reinforce their child's self-directed learning. While utilizing this framework, parents can promote a vision for increased Cognitive complexity, Real-world learning, Technology integration, and Engagement.

REFLECTION QUESTIONS

1. Has your child had an experience like Aubrie's in Figure 40.2? How might you approach your child's teacher about the CReaTE Framework?
2. Which components of the CReaTE Framework are embedded in the lessons in your child's classroom?
3. How can the CReaTE Framework help your child's teacher plan lessons that tap into real-world and relevant learning?

Task Scenario: The teacher informs Aubrie's class that the students' desks in her class are being replaced due to being ineffective, unsafe, and old. Groups are assigned to develop the optimal student desk that would meet the needs of the fifth graders.

	Cognitive Complexity	Real-World Learning	Technology Interpretation	Engagement
Student-Directed Task	Aubrie's group identifies what qualities a desk should have to meet the needs of students in their classroom. Students then brainstorm various conceptual designs. Students evaluate which concept is most likely to meet their needs and is cost effective. Using their engineering skills, students make calculations of the size of the desk, cost of materials, etc. They build a prototype. Each group tests and evaluates its prototype, and then groups restructure and improve the original design.	Aubrie's class is told that the desk-constructing groups are in competition for a "school choice" award. The principal will select the best prototype and work with the winning group to investigate school desks that meet similar design qualities. Aubrie realizes that the desks will actually be chosen and purchased for the classroom.	While Aubrie's group is formulating its conceptual design, the students use a free online program, Google SketchUp, to develop their desk design. Their persuasive presentation for the principal is created in Animoto (an online presentation program). The actual process of designing the prototype includes technology integration.	Throughout the design process, Aubrie's team collaborates with the teacher to ensure the group is progressing toward its solution. Students Skype a furniture designer to pose questions about their prototype and get feedback from the designer.

Figure 40.2. Student-directed STEM task example to complement the CReaTE Framework.

4. What are some ways you might collaborate and/or show support for the teacher in expanding your child's learning with the CReaTE Framework?
5. How might you use this framework outside of school to guide you with interactions or planning outings and opportunities for your child?

REFERENCES

Anderson, L., & Krathwohl, D. R. (Eds.). (2001). *A taxonomy for learning, teaching, and assessing: A revision of Bloom's taxonomy of educational objectives* (Complete ed.). New York, NY: Longman.

Boss, S. (2015). *Real-world projects: How do I design relevant and engaging learning experiences?* Alexandria, VA: ASCD.

Boss, S., & Krauss, J. (2014). *Reinventing project-based learning: Your field guide to real-world projects in the digital age* (2nd ed.). Eugene, OR: International Society for Technology in Education.

Hays, C. (2018). *Curiosity and gifted identification: A mixed methods study* (Doctoral dissertation). Retrieved from https://digitalcom mons.du.edu/etd/1435

Maxwell, M., Stobaugh, R., & Tassell, J. L. (2016). *Real-world learning framework for secondary schools: Digital tools and practical strategies for successful implementation.* Bloomington, IN: Solution Tree.

Maxwell, M., Stobaugh, R., & Tassell, J. L. (2017). *Real-world learning framework for elementary schools: Digital tools and practical strategies for successful implementation.* Bloomington, IN: Solution Tree.

Wood, T., Merkel, G., & Uerkwitz, J. (1996). Creating a context for talking about mathematical thinking. *Educação e Matemática, 4,* 39–43.

CHAPTER 41

HOW TO DISCUSS BOOKS WITH YOUR KIDS (EVEN WHEN YOU HAVEN'T READ THEM!)

by Elissa F. Brown and Michele Joerg

Many gifted children are voracious readers who may pick up books you have not had time to read yourself. Parents often struggle with ways to support learning at home that is aligned with their child's schooling, and impediments such as cost, scheduling, and time can further impact a parent's involvement (Rogers, 2002). The use of a questioning model sidesteps these challenges, allowing you to support your child's comprehension and critical thinking skills in your car, at home, on the subway, at the dinner table, or even just on your couch.

Strategic questioning strategies are a powerful tool for developing creative and critical thinkers. Strategic questioning is not the low-level factual, recall, or "read it and repeat it" questions that many children encounter as part of their daily classroom routines (Shaunessy, 2000). Questions that focus on inferencing, generalizing, distinguishing relevant information, or defending a principle or thesis are necessary to stimulate gifted learners' imaginations and foster growth. Moreover, with the advent of the Common Core State Standards, questioning that can support metacognition and deepen a student's understanding of a text is imperative.

Parents can leverage this need for higher level questioning as a way to have meaningful conversations with their children. Questioning can be the conduit between home and school, and it can create an environment that values the process of learning over the "right" answers. The use of a questioning model when discussing books with your child is a targeted approach in which you can be involved with what your child is learning at school by extending, reinforcing, supporting, and encouraging reading. It also has the added value of quality time with your child, which often is in short supply.

One questioning model that parents can easily use in the home was developed by Arthur Costa (2001). His model incorporates everything from factual to creative, and its three levels of questions move children from concrete to conceptual thinking. Although there seems to be a natural hierarchy, questions can be mixed and matched to work on literal skills or abstract reasoning and problem solving—all using literature as the stimulus. Costa's questioning model allows parents to access their child's reading material in a sophisticated way that does not feel contrived. The nature of the questioning is fluid, easy to implement, costs no money, and can be done in a few minutes or as long as you want.

The first and most basic level of questions asks a reader to gather and recall information from the text. These answers can be found explicitly in one or more places in the text. Examples include: *Who are the main characters? When does this story take place?* The second level of questions asks a reader to make sense out of the information that has been gathered. These questions ask the reader to "read between the lines" by comparing and contrasting, determining cause and effect, or analyzing information. Some examples are: *What can you infer about the main character from his or her actions? What surprised you about this topic?* Finally, the third and most complex type of questions asks the reader to answer questions that go beyond the text and may not have a right or wrong answer. Readers must use the information they have gathered and analyzed to make a supported hypothesis about something that cannot be answered directly from the book. Examples of these types of questions include: *What is the overarching theme of this book? How would this book have been different if it had been written 15 years ago?*

USING COSTA'S QUESTIONING MODEL

The questions in Table 41.1 employ Costa's (2001) model under different genres. You can decide (with your child) how to implement these questions. Parents can ask these questions at night before bed-

TABLE 41.1
EXAMPLES OF COSTA'S (2001) QUESTIONING WITH FICTION, NONFICTION, AND BIOGRAPHY AND MEMOIR TEXTS

Fiction	Nonfiction	Biography and Memoir
Level One—Supporting basic comprehension of text (text explicit)		
Who is the author? Have you read other books by this author before?	Who is the author? Have you read other books by this author before?	What prompted you to choose this book and topic?
Summarize what you have read so far.	What is the selection you read mostly about?	Describe the significant events in this person's life.
Retell the important events in the story in order.	What are the most important ideas in the book so far? How do you know?	What contributions to society has this person made?
Level Two—Supporting analyzation of the text (text implicit)		
Describe the setting. Is there a setting in real life that it reminds you of?	What has surprised you about this topic?	Is there a lesson that can be taken away from this person's life? What is it?
Choose a character in your book. Who does he or she remind you of?	What else would you like to learn about this topic?	What personality traits helped this person succeed in his or her field?
Do the "good guy" and the "bad guy" share any similarities? How are they different?	Is this book like any other book you have read? How so? How not?	Do you have anything in common with this person?
Level Three—Supporting conceptual understanding of the text (beyond the text)		
What do you wish the main character would've done differently? How would that have changed the story?	Would this book be different if it had been written 15 years ago? How?	Does this person inspire you? How?
Are all the characters likeable? Why or why not?	What kind of research do you think the author had to do to write this book?	Does this person's life story help you better understand his or her time period? How?
Would you want to live in this story world? Why or why not?	Do the issues raised in this book affect your life? How?	Did reading this book change how you felt about this person? Why or why not?

time, on the way to school, or even as a game at any point. That's the fun. It works with your schedule. Lastly, it is a low-risk, high-rewards way to support your child's learning. This list is not meant to be complete but rather a springboard for quality thinking and discussion.

Questioning is one of the easiest ways to provide differentiated learning experiences and access to your child's thinking. It is an effective way to spend time with your child and learn about a book he or she is reading that you may not have read, and still have a comprehensive conversation about it while also supporting learning in the home. Many teachers and schools emphasize higher order thinking but may not always implement effective questioning as a way to promote critical thinking in high-ability learners. Frequently, due to many constraints, teachers ask questions to prepare students for a state test or as a requirement for class. This is where you, as the parent, play such an important role as a partner in learning. By incorporating Costa's (2001) questioning model, you can guide your child effortlessly into more sophisticated ways of thinking—not only about literature, but about all kinds of things.

REFLECTION QUESTIONS

1. How can you incorporate Costa's questioning model and these leveled questions into your family life?
2. After using some of these questions, what did you learn about your child as a reader? Were there certain types of questions he or she answered exceptionally well? Were there certain types of questions he or she struggled with?
3. What other strategies have proven helpful to enable your child to think deeper and more critically about the books he or she is reading?
4. What surprised you most when using Costa's questioning model with your child?
5. How can you incorporate these various questions into other areas of your interaction with your child?

REFERENCES

Costa, A. L. (2001). *Developing minds: A resource book for teaching thinking* (3rd ed.). Alexandria, VA: Association for Supervision and Curriculum Development.

Rogers, K. B. (2002). *Re-forming gifted education: Matching the program to the child.* Scottsdale, AZ: Great Potential Press.

Shaunessy, E. (2000). Questioning techniques in the gifted classroom. *Gifted Child Today, 23*(5), 14–22.

CHAPTER 42

CENTENNIALS: THE WORLD IS WAITING!

by Angela M. Housand

Today's youth are connected across the street and across the globe in a web of communication like no other generation before. Generation Z, also known as centennials, are considered "mobile natives" and are even more technologically savvy then their millennial predecessors. In 2015, nearly three-quarters of children owned or had access to a smartphone, and a whopping 92% of centennial teens, ages 13–17, reported going online daily (Lenhart, 2015). Thanks to Snapchat, Instagram, Facebook, and myriad other apps, social media has transformed how people communicate and the ways they acquire, create, and share information. No longer is technology merely a tool; it is *the medium* for attaining knowledge, collaborating with peers, exchanging ideas, creating products, and sharing knowledge and insights.

Gifted youth are in an unparalleled position to build influence in a global society. They are highly capable of participating in social networks. Moreover, when students *want* to learn how to do something, a quick YouTube video provides step-by-step instruction to achieve their aims. Use of these virtual networks and information sources by students remains primarily an act of passive consumption rather than active production. If they want to build influence, gifted youth must shift their use of social networks from consuming content to showcasing their talents or attaining recognition of their work. To accomplish this shift, they must identify their interests, know their talents, understand the benefits of engaging in a community of peers, and recognize the power of a give-and-take dynamic. They must see that capability, possibility, exchange, and motivation are required to actively participate in global networks (Inkpen & Tsang, 2005).

CAPABILITY

Active social networkers must be capable of absorbing, applying, and recognizing the value of new information. High-ability youth, who demonstrate outstanding levels of aptitude or competence in a given domain, are well-positioned to see the value of new information and ways to apply it. Characteristics gifted youth demonstrate that suggest they are capable of engaging these opportunities at the highest levels are intense intellectual engagement, openness to new experiences and information, capacity to creatively interpret new information, and rapid application of information to new situations.

Gifted individuals certainly are capable of engaging in social networks, recognizing and interpreting new information, and ultimately applying knowledge in new ways, but should they? Although gifted youth may not have the life experiences of adults, they do have the intellectual capacity to actively engage with adults in meaningful ways that brings value to both parties. This collaboration and interaction opens the door to opportunities previously unavailable. This suggests that allowing gifted children to interact in virtual environments, in developmentally appropriate ways, will ultimately benefit both the children and the communities in which they participate.

Gifted youth can also build a professional web presence that reflects their talents. An easy way to accomplish this is by claiming a unique domain name and creating a website. A unique domain name might simply be a son's or daughter's first and last name (e.g., firstlast.com). The goal is to have control over the children's names so that when they are Googled, they are in control of the content people find. GoDaddy offers affordable domain name registration and web hosting. Some easy-to-use website creators include Weebly, Wix, and Squarespace.

POSSIBILITY

Possibility makes engaging in social networks advantageous, as it provides the opportunity to gain new knowledge and develop new skills. It's possible for gifted youth to participate in social networks by identifying and researching a topic of interest to gain knowledge, skills, and intellectual stimulation. While conducting research about a topic of interest, they should be seeking the "who, what, when, where, and how" of their interest domain. Gifted youth should look for general information, professional conventions, processes or procedures used for productivity, influential thought leaders, and opportunities to contribute in their area of interest.

However, parents shouldn't assume that their children intuitively know how to use the Internet for research purposes. Parents should model these behaviors or enroll their child in a Google Power Search course (http://www.powersearchingwithgoogle.com).

EXCHANGE

Social media provides the opportunity to exchange information at lightning speed while enabling anyone to build social capital or credibility within a network. Building credibility relies on a dynamic, give-and-take process. Individuals share their talents, which provide a benefit to a group or community; in return, the community provides the individual with support, resources, and opportunities for growth. Initially, the *taking* happens through research about a topic of interest. However, gifted youth must also *contribute* to the network community by creating quality content that has value to others in the network. Content can be creative, but also needs to reflect the contributor's advanced knowledge and talents. See Figure 42.1 for rules for creating content.

Younger children might start contributing to a network by participating in the DIY.org community (https://diy.org). Here young people can explore numerous interest areas, learn new skills, and share their own creations in a kid-friendly environment. For adolescents and emerging adults, full access to the Internet is a must, with YouTube being one of the most popular means of sharing content (video products). Other outlets for sharing include:

- » Flickr (photographs),
- » Kaggle (data modeling),
- » Pinterest (interests and ideas),
- » SlideShare (presentations),
- » SoundCloud (music), and
- » Yelp (reviews/critiques).

There are a few rules for creating content that are important for any young person to understand.

- **Less is more.** When contributing online, it's not a matter of quantity as much as quality. Individuals should learn to say less and let their work speak for itself. This requires creators to think and plan prior to contributing to social media and edit their work prior to sharing.
- **Listening is important.** This is particularly true before stating opinions. Nobody appreciates uninformed opinions. Opinions should also be supported with evidence.
- **Be engaging.** Provide only high-quality content (final drafts of written work, edited videos, best images, and stunning artwork) or work that has an emotional component to it (human interest stories, positive effects on community, or solutions to problems that people care about).
- **Contribute consistently.** Adding content regularly to the appropriate online venues will help creators get noticed.

Figure 42.1. Rules for creating content for social networks.

There are also applications for both creating and sharing original content within digital communities:

- » GitHub (coding and software development),
- » Instagram (photographs),
- » Medium (written pieces),
- » Prezi (presentations),
- » Scratch (video game creation), and
- » ThingLink (images and videos).

MOTIVATION

The reason to participate on the Internet can be either prescribed (e.g., school assignments), social, or intrinsically motivated. Often, young people know how to socialize using the Internet, but they may not be skilled at learning on the Internet. The goal is to leverage intrinsic motivation and interest to ensure that the time spent online produces benefits beyond a network of friends to a network of peers and supportive professionals.

Motivation can come from seeking to fulfill curiosity (Housand & Housand, 2012), or it might be tied to identity, aspirations, or the desire to learn something new. Regardless, the content needs to be interesting or personally meaningful if one is to search voluntarily. To ensure that our gifted youth have a goal for seeking information on the Internet, it is helpful to determine those interests in advance. Listen and watch your gifted children to learn:

» How do they *like* to spend their time?

» What books do they read?

» What kinds of things do they ask to know more about?

» When given the opportunity to choose, what types of activities or topics do they choose?

» When do they get excited about learning something new?

For some youth, personal interests are easy to recognize or clearly define. However, when interests are unclear, youth need to be exposed to new opportunities and experiences. The Internet provides a wealth of opportunity for exploration. Parents should consider exploring the Internet alongside their children to investigate interests, model the behaviors they use to find information, and share strategies for staying safe online.

Once gifted youth are aware of their interests and talents, understand the structure of social networks, and recognize areas for contributing to those networks, they can start producing content that has the power to build influence. Whether participating in discussions, writing blogs, creating videos, or sharing products that have been developed, the Internet is rife with opportunity and just waiting for talent!

REFLECTION QUESTIONS

1. What steps might you take to support children in developing healthy cell phone use habits? How might your cell phone use inform your child's understanding of appropriate cell phone use?

2. What is the appropriate age for children to begin accessing the Internet? At what age should youth be free to use the Internet without adult supervision?

3. When conducting research on the Internet, people encounter varying levels of accuracy in the information they find.

How might you support gifted youth in determining the relevance and accuracy of the information they find?

4. What steps might you take to determine your child's interest area? How might you support him or her to explore and expand this interest area?

REFERENCES

Housand, B. C., & Housand, A. M. (2012). The role of technology in gifted students' motivation. *Psychology in the Schools, 49,* 706–715.

Inkpen, A. C., & Tsang, E. W. (2005). Social capital, networks, and knowledge transfer. *The Academy of Management Review, 30,* 146–165.

Lenhart, A. (2015). Teens, social media & technology overview 2015. *Pew Research Center.* Retrieved from https://www.pew internet.org/2015/04/09/teens-social-media-technology-2015

PART VII

ADVOCACY

When it comes to supporting and nurturing gifted children, one important role that parents must assume is that of *advocate*. According to the *Oxford Dictionary*, an advocate is one who pleads a case on someone else's behalf or recommends a specific cause or policy. The word *advocate* originates from the Latin word *advocatus*, which means to "call to one's aid."

In other words, parents—particularly when children are too young to speak for themselves—must become their child's champion, spokesperson, supporter, promoter, and proponent in order to ensure their child receives the appropriate programming and services in order to reach his or her potential. With the absence of a federal mandate, gifted policies and programming are left to the individual state, and often a specific district, to create and implement.

Parent advocates of a gifted child may:

» educate federal and state legislators and policymakers to ensure gifted education policies and funding are established;

» persuade administrators to introduce new or different gifted education policies, programming, and services at the district or school level;

» recognize their child possesses gifted and talented traits, characteristics, and behaviors—and urge school administrators to identify and qualify the child for gifted and talented programming at school or within the district;

» help their child's school to establish extracurricular programs to better serve gifted children;

» collaborate with classroom teachers to ensure their child receives challenging work on a daily basis; and

» teach their gifted child how to self-advocate so the child can ultimately communicate his or her needs independently.

This chapter provides practical, essential strategies for parents in navigating the educational system, communicating effectively with their child's schools and teachers, and understanding how to become a valued partner to their child's school.

As you'll read in the following chapters, advocacy is an art. We must remember that it's often a compromise, and we don't always receive everything on our wish lists. However, if we keep our children's best interests at the forefront—and remain respectful, collaborative, and creative in the process—we will certainly make strides to positively influence and impact our gifted children's futures.

—Kathleen Nilles

CHAPTER 43

ROLES IN GIFTED EDUCATION: A PARENT'S GUIDE

by Ashley Y. Carpenter and Stacy M. Hayden

Being a parent in the "gifted world" is challenging, especially when you don't have all of the information. Whether your child has already been identified and is in a gifted program or you are looking for the school to better meet your child's needs, it's essential to know the various staff who can help you and your child navigate the gifted experience. Each of these individuals has different roles, responsibilities, and levels of training.

Many school staff members do not have training or knowledge of giftedness, gifted children, or gifted education, making your job as an advocate for your child vitally important. In 2014, only one state required preservice classroom teachers to have training in gifted education. For teachers that serve gifted students, only 17 states require they have a certificate or endorsement in gifted education, and often this training does not start until after the teacher is in the position (National Association for Gifted Children [NAGC], & the Council of State Directors for Programs for the Gifted, 2015). As a parent, you can serve as a valuable partner to the school if you know who best to work with and how.

BECOME MORE KNOWLEDGEABLE

First, become familiar with the gifted policy in your area. The federal government does not mandate gifted education on a national level; every state, district, and school may have different policies and/ or programs for gifted children. An excellent resource is your local gifted association, which you can find on NAGC's Gifted By State webpage (https://www.nagc.org/information-publications/gifted-state). If your district has a gifted education program, information such as identification policy and services should be available to you. Search your district's local website for terms such as *gifted, gifted and talented, enrichment, talent development, advanced academics, AIG, G/T,* or *GATE.*

THE PLAYERS

After investigating your local policies on gifted education, it's also important to know who you will be interacting with and who to go to with questions or concerns. Every school and gifted program is different, but staff typically have similar roles.

CLASSROOM TEACHER

A typical classroom teacher has a group of same-age students with varying ability levels. It is his or her job to help every student, regardless of ability levels, master grade-level standards. This expectation of grade-level mastery may be too low for your child, but the classroom teacher likely does not have any formal training in gifted education. Most teacher preparation programs only include a short lecture on gifted students, if that. In addition, gifted education training is not commonplace in many districts.

If you believe the classroom teacher isn't meeting your gifted child's needs, it may not be intentional. The teacher may believe that students' needs are being met by the gifted program, not realizing it is also his or her job to differentiate for gifted students. In schools that do not offer gifted services or identify gifted students, teachers may not be aware that gifted students exist. Many amazing teachers give their all to each and every student but may have never been exposed to information about gifted education.

The classroom teacher is the best resource when your child needs more than what the typical classroom is offering. Classroom teachers will also be the first point of contact if you believe your child should be referred to the gifted program. Take time to build a positive partnership with your child's teacher. Start by meeting with him or her about your concerns and asking for input. Next, discuss your child's strengths and propose gifted strategies that fit the areas of need (see Table 43.1).

GIFTED OR RESOURCE TEACHER

A gifted teacher's responsibility is to provide services to children identified for the local program. Gifted programming looks different in each school. A gifted teacher's responsibilities may include:

» developing and implementing your child's education plan (a few states are required to provide formal Education Plans for gifted, but not many);

» meeting with students (based on services) yearly, monthly, weekly, or daily;

» communicating with the classroom teacher(s);

» providing part-time or full-time gifted instruction;

» developing curriculum and enrichment activities for high-ability students;

» teaching core subjects for high-ability students;

» hosting afterschool clubs;

» coaching academic competition teams; and

» evaluating students referred to the gifted program.

You can typically expect the gifted teacher to have more knowledge of gifted education than a regular classroom teacher. However, the level of training is dependent upon state requirements, the district's professional development offerings, and how long the person has been in this position. It is not uncommon for administrators to recruit teachers to teach gifted students before they are trained.

To work with your child's gifted teacher effectively, it is important to get to know the teacher well and share information or concerns freely. The gifted teacher will likely have more knowledge about available resources and can serve as a bridge between you and the classroom teacher if needed.

GIFTED COORDINATOR

Gifted coordinators typically work at the district office where they ensure the fidelity of the gifted program. This role may be a full-time position or a small portion of his or her overall responsibilities, depending on the size of the district and services offered. The coordinator may be responsible for communicating with the school

TABLE 43.1
GIFTED STRATEGIES TO PROPOSE TO YOUR CHILD'S SCHOOL

Strategy	What Is It?	Examples
Pretesting	A way to find out what your child already knows before the teacher starts teaching; if you suspect your child already knows the material, ask if your child can be pretested.	• Providing a version of the posttest before instruction takes place • Asking an open-ended, big concept question • Asking the essential questions • Asking students to perform a skill • Questioning students verbally • Having students rate themselves on the unit objectives
Curriculum compacting	A strategy that streamlines and eliminates previously mastered curriculum for students who are capable of completing content at a faster pace.	• Name it: Identifying content the student might have mastered • Prove it: Assessing the student on the content • Change it: Replacing the typical activities or content in some way
Acceleration	A strategy that allows the same content to be covered at a faster pace than typical.	• Whole-grade skipping • Early entrance to kindergarten • Subject acceleration • Advanced Placement classes • Dual enrollment
Grouping	A strategy that groups gifted students with their academic peers, making it easier for teachers to provide enrichment and acceleration.	• Ability grouping • Performance grouping • Academic or enrichment cluster grouping • Grouping by specific subjects or talent • Grouping by interest
Enrichment	Activities that go beyond the regular curriculum.	• Diving deeper into the curriculum standard • Researching and presenting a topic of interest • Participating in an academic competition • Designing a science experiment • Proposing an alternative assignment • Undertaking real-world problem solving
Academic competitions	A strategy that can be incorporated as a club, enrichment cluster, curriculum for a gifted class, or an individual enrichment opportunity. Parents can volunteer to coach a team after school or help during the school day.	• Destination Imagination • Future City • Future Problem Solving Program International • Global Math Challenge • Math Olympiads • National History Day • Odyssey of the Mind • Science Olympiad

Note. Table adapted from multiple sourcecs (Guilbault & Lupkowski-Shoplik, 2017; Reis, Renzulli, & Burns, 2016; Renzulli & Reis, 2014).

board, superintendent, and possibly a parent advisory committee. If the coordinator's role is specifically to run the gifted program, it is likely he or she has formal training in gifted education.

It is appropriate to speak directly with the gifted coordinator if you have questions about the district's gifted identification policy or need to appeal a "not eligible" decision. This person can also be helpful as a last resort if speaking with your child's teacher and school administrator has not been successful.

SCHOOL SUPPORT STAFF

School support staff can include guidance counselors, school psychologists, social workers, and special education teachers. These support staff members may be full-time at one school or work at multiple schools in the district. They are often responsible for individual or group testing for admission to a gifted program and determining gifted eligibility. If your child also has a disability, behavioral disorder, or struggles academically, special educators can be good resource. You should contact school support staff with questions about gifted identification, concerns about a possible disability or behavioral disorder, or to request accommodations/504 Plan for your twice-exceptional child.

ADMINISTRATORS

The school administrators, most often the principal or vice principal, are responsible for the safety of all students, meeting state and district requirements, and ensuring the entire school runs efficiently. The administrator may be under immense pressure from the school district to produce satisfactory test scores, especially if the school has had low scores in previous years. The administrators must delegate responsibilities to all staff within the building to be successful. They may hire a gifted teacher or assign a staff member to gifted identification without knowing these processes. Administrators typically lack knowledge of gifted education unless they were gifted teachers in the past or have a gifted child of their own. It is appropriate to go directly to the school administrator if you have already tried to work with your child's classroom and gifted teachers with no success or are concerned about the implementation of the gifted program at your school.

SUPERINTENDENT

The superintendent is the head administrator of the district and, like all school administrators and personnel, is accountable to the school board. Typically, the superintendent will refer all discussions related to a specific child's placement and/or programming back to the school's principal. Superintendents should only be contacted as a last resort, after all avenues have been explored with the professionals listed previously.

YOUR ROLE

Being a parent of a gifted child offers a completely new perspective on education. Although many parents can sit back and trust the process, parents of gifted children need to be prepared to advocate for their child. Talking to other parents of gifted students at your child's school, on the playground, at the grocery store, at church, or even online will provide perspective, information on programming you were unaware of, and a support system.

If you are not happy with your child's current educational experience, start with his or her teacher. There is nothing better for your children than a great relationship with classroom teachers. The best way to work with teachers is to focus on what you want the outcome to be, not push the gifted label. Do you want your child challenged in math, to skip a grade, to be able to test out of a unit he or she already knows? Do you want to help start an academic competition team? By working with the staff members at your child's school, you can help create an environment where gifted children thrive.

REFLECTION QUESTIONS

1. After reviewing Table 43.1, what gifted strategy would you like to see implemented in your child's classroom? How would this support your child's needs?
2. Think of a time when someone asked you to change. How did the way that person approached you make you feel? Is there anything you wish that person did differently? How

can you use that experience to guide conversations with school staff?

3. Think about a time when you worked well with your child's teacher to make something happen? What made that situation successful?

4. Across the country many gifted programs are underfunded. As a parent, how can you volunteer to support gifted students in your district?

REFERENCES

Guilbault, K., & Lupkowski-Shoplik, A. (2017). *Acceleration.* Washington, DC: National Association for Gifted Children.

National Association for Gifted Children, & the Council of State Directors of Programs for the Gifted. (2015). *State of the states in gifted education: National policy and practice data 2014–2015.* Washington, DC: Authors.

Reis, S. M., Renzulli, J. S., & Burns, D. E. (2016). *Curriculum compacting: A guide to differentiating curriculum and instruction through enrichment and acceleration* (2nd ed.). Waco, TX: Prufrock Press.

Renzulli, J. S., & Reis, S. M. (2014). *The schoolwide enrichment model: A how-to guide for talent development* (3rd ed.). Waco, TX: Prufrock Press.

CHAPTER 44

COMMUNICATING EFFECTIVELY WITH YOUR GIFTED CHILD'S SCHOOL

by Joan Franklin Smutny

When gifted children struggle in school, they often have no other advocate than their parents. Parents attending workshops often ask, "What do I do if my child is unhappy in school?" The answer may seem obvious to some, but discussing their child's difficulties in school can be intimidating to most parents. We often hear stories of parents trying to convince a school of their child's unmet needs, and of frustrated attempts to get someone—anyone—to respond to repeated requests for help.

Some of the difficulties parents have communicating with the school can be avoided with the right preparation and planning.

PREPARING TO MEET WITH THE SCHOOL

BEGIN WITH YOUR CHILD

Gifted children need to have a voice in any decisions about their education. Talk to your children about whatever problem they're having in school and try to get them to be as specific as possible. "I'm bored" doesn't really give you enough information. Even in the most stimulating environments there will be times when a class doesn't interest your child. You need to learn more in order to know what kind of boredom this is and whether or not it requires intervention.

TALK TO YOUR CHILDREN ABOUT THE ACTIONS YOU'D LIKE TO TAKE AND DISCUSS THE OPTIONS

What would make school more interesting? If they could change anything in their school, what would they change? When do they feel the most excited about classes? When do they tune out? Interesting information can sometimes surface in discussions like this. A mother once told me that in a casual conversation with her son, he happened to say, "I'd like to do art this summer; I sketched a lot of cartoons in school last year." It turned out that he developed an interest in cartoon art while doodling in his many "time-outs" in class.

COLLECT BACKGROUND INFORMATION

It is important to know what services your district provides for high-ability children before you communicate with the school. You can get this information by contacting your state's department of education. Contact the district office as well, and ask if they have a written policy statement about students with different learning needs, including the gifted. Focus on the underlying philosophy, goals, identification methods, and educational services offered at various grade levels.

If your school has a program in place, you can contact the gifted education coordinator, curriculum coordinator, gifted education teacher, or other parents for more information. In addition, your state gifted association should also know the state's philosophy, guidelines, and goals for gifted education. Visit https://www.nagc.org for links to many state organizations.

GIFTED EDUCATION PRACTICES: KNOW THE LINGO!

What kinds of policies and practices exist in schools? Although it's unlikely that your district will have all of the following options listed, it's helpful to have some general knowledge about what schools may offer gifted students. Some examples include:

» **Identification:** Methods for identifying high ability (including creativity), which may include standardized testing, teacher observations, performance assessments, and so forth.

» **Pull-out programs:** Programs designed to pull advanced students out of their regular classrooms at certain periods of time to work with peers on subjects that challenge and interest them.

» **Acceleration:** The most important strategy for educating gifted learners. It includes any practice that enables students to advance at a faster pace in some or all subjects—commensurate with their ability. In some cases, this may include grade-skipping.

» **Differentiation:** A classroom strategy for individualizing instruction to meet the needs of all students, including high-ability children. Teachers may adjust curriculum to the level of mastery and advanced learning demonstrated by gifted students.

» **Grouping:** Students grouped together according to ability and skill level. Such a strategy has distinct benefits socially, emotionally, and intellectually, as students accelerate and inspire new learning in each other.

» **Learning contracts:** Written agreements between teachers and students that stipulate learning goals, timelines, and rules of behavior for independent projects. Gifted students with specific interests particularly benefit from the opportunity to explore a topic in more depth and create a project that expresses what they've learned.

COMMUNICATING WITH THE TEACHER

ALWAYS BEGIN WITH THE TEACHER

I can't stress this enough. A mother once called me because she had inadvertently offended her child's teacher. In talking to the principal about gifted education, she had discussed her child's problems in the classroom. He, in turn, talked to the teacher who promptly chastised this mother when she tried to pursue the matter further. Although relationships can always be patched up later, it's best to avoid even the appearance of going behind a teacher's back.

KNOW A LITTLE BIT ABOUT THE TEACHER'S ATTITUDE TOWARD GIFTED EDUCATION

In open houses and private conversations, you can gain some insight into curriculum, teaching styles, and philosophy that will help you later on. Many parents I talk to already have a feel for the best way to approach their children's teacher before they go to their first meeting.

PLAN IN ADVANCE WHAT YOU'RE GOING TO SAY

Many parents find it intimidating to meet with their child's teacher. For this reason, it's a good idea to think in advance about what you plan to say. Write down your own observations or thoughts on your child's abilities, and avoid using the term *gifted* for a while. Rather than tell the teacher that you are seeking special services for your "gifted child," you might simply express your concern, for example, that your child consistently finishes her homework in school, or that she seems to be coasting through the year unchallenged. You will accomplish more by avoiding debates with the teacher about whether or not your child is gifted, or whether the school should offer programming for gifted students.

KEEP THE DISCUSSION FOCUSED

Focus on the specifics of your children's characteristics and needs rather than on some hypothetical or philosophical debate about gifted education. Focus on your goals. Examples might include the following: gaining permission for your child to spend more time in the science lab; arranging for your child to be evaluated by the school psychologist; or creating specific agreements on a more differentiated curriculum. Without goals like these, even positive discussions about your child will not necessarily bring tangible change.

BE DIPLOMATIC BUT FIRM

The value of planning ahead is that you have a better chance of finding a balanced and fair approach to the teacher. Your aim should be to avoid communicating in a way that makes the teacher feel criticized or misunderstood. Teachers face extraordinary demands on their time and seldom appreciate it when parents tell them they're not doing enough.

At the same time, your child has legitimate needs that the school should address. It's your job as a parent advocate to take action when this isn't happening.

GETTING THE MOST FROM YOUR TEACHER CONFERENCE

There's a way of expressing concern without negating what the teacher is already doing in the classroom. Here are some useful pointers for getting the most out of your teacher conference:

» Expect the teacher to be reasonable and understanding, no matter what you've heard from other parents or your child. Even unsympathetic teachers respond better to parents who approach them positively than to those who seem already on the defensive.

» Start out by thanking the teacher for giving you this time. Express in your tone and manner that you are a reasonable parent who recognizes the daily demands on a teacher and that you appreciate this opportunity to confer with him.

» Get straight to the point. State the reason why you felt it necessary to meet with the teacher and say it in a diplomatic way. For example, instead of saying, "My son is really bored in your math class," try this: "My son has already learned this material in math, and because he really loves this subject, I wondered if we could discuss other options for him in math."

» Listen carefully to what the teacher says. Objections to certain requests aren't necessarily rejections. Keep pressing for other options. If a teacher says, for example, "I have no time to create a separate set of activities for your child," offer to work as a partner. If the teacher argues that your child has been inattentive, sloppy in her work, or misbehaving, don't automatically interpret this as a criticism. Say something like, "I'm sorry if she's not been following rules, and I'm happy to work with her on that. But could you also allow her to spend more time doing some independent projects when she's finished her work?"

» Work for a consensus. Because your goal is to find a solution for your child, try to find some common ground. Be flexible in areas where you can be flexible, but firm on the points that really matter. If your child is working at a third of his capacity, it is unjust for him to sit in his seat day after day learning almost nothing. But you might be able to be flexible in negotiating how changes are made. For example, the teacher most likely cannot offer an alternative curriculum, but may be able to coordinate with the principal and other teachers about letting your child attend a higher grade in some subjects.

» Before you leave, make sure all of your questions have been answered and that you both know what has been resolved. Repeat back to the teacher what you heard and what you understand has been agreed upon.

» Have a timeline for any follow-up steps. Without some agreement about when certain things will happen, chances are, they won't happen. If the teacher says she'll talk an issue over with a principal, a curriculum coordinator, or anyone else, ask for a general time when this will be done. You should also provide deadlines for your promises as well.

» Thank the teacher for giving you his time and say that you will stay in touch.

GAUGING SUCCESS

A number of parents have felt that their communications with the school went well, only to realize later that no definite course of action was agreed upon. Other parents haven't realized how productive their meeting with a teacher actually was because of a defensive attitude they sensed from the teacher or an initial negative reaction from their child.

Here is a useful list of criteria for creating a successful conference (Smutny, 2001):

» Your child was the main focus, not the opinions or agenda of you or the teacher.

» Both you and the teacher listened to each other and considered each other's point of view.

> » You negotiated for solutions that will meet your child's needs without disregarding the teacher's responsibilities or your knowledge of your child.
> » You came to an understanding even if you had different opinions.
> » You both agreed to work on a solution that will help your child and to continue working together.
> » You both made commitments and scheduled actions. (p. 109)

FOLLOW UP

Even if it all turns out well, there's almost always a need for follow-up and further communication. Lack of communication at this critical point can make your progress uncertain. Examples include the following:

> » The teacher may agree to test your child out of certain material he has already mastered. Be sure this happens.
> » If there's a learning contract for your child that stipulates goals and outcomes, make sure you have a copy.
> » Talk regularly with your child and the teacher to see how your child is doing.
> » Be consistent in supporting whatever learning option you, the teacher, and your child agree to pursue.
> » Don't let the burden of the extra work fall entirely on the teacher. Show that you are willing to do your part and lighten the load in any way you can.

EXPLORING OTHER OPTIONS

Conferences with the teacher don't always work, even when parents have prepared for the meetings and expressed themselves diplomatically. Some teachers oppose gifted education because they think it's elitist or because it will entail more work than they can afford to devote to such a small population. Others have had some negative experiences with a few parents who have made them feel that all parents of gifted children are demanding.

There are also legitimate reasons why a teacher might not be able to do more for your child, including the following:

- » There is a lack of funding for special programs and resources as well as little or no expertise on gifted education in the district.
- » The programs available are not offered for your child's grade.
- » The school holds other priorities for its student population's immediate needs.

If this is the case, you will still need to create some kind of adjustment for your child. If the teacher proves unwilling to work with you, move up the ladder of the school administration. The next person to address may be the gifted coordinator, the curriculum director, the assistant principal, or the principal. If none of these prove receptive, then go to the superintendent.

Explore as many possibilities as you can think of that will help meet your child's immediate need. Can your child be placed in a higher grade for certain subjects in which she has special abilities? Could she spend a morning or day at home once a week to work on projects that interest her? If the teacher is unwilling to provide more advanced content, could the child be paired with a mentor (another teacher, a librarian, a school volunteer) who could work with her after she has completed or tested out of subject matter she already knows?

Find out if there are any parent groups in your area. Contact your state gifted association for this information. Start talking to other parents and find out if others feel as you do. Parent groups can provide valuable information about local schools and resources as well as moral support for you and your family.

Look into gifted programs outside the school. These may be sponsored by a local university or institute. State gifted associations often have information on programs and other services for high-ability children.

In addition to whatever other support services you can find, try to supplement your child's education at home. Spend time with him exploring subjects he loves; seek out materials that will challenge his imagination and critical thinking. Consider locating a mentor for your child in an area of particular interest at universities, visual and performing arts studios, and personal contacts. Think of new and different ways you can enrich your child's life.

This is a challenging time for gifted children in our schools. A drastic decline in funding for gifted education has meant that their parents have to work doubly hard to convince districts to respond to the needs of highly able learners. At present, there is no federal mandate to provide services for them.

Yet parents have an advantage today. The explosion of information on the Internet and the ease with which parents can research topics that concern their children have made it easier for them to strategize how to approach their district and to network with other parents. Websites on gifted children and gifted education, blogs, webinars, online lectures, and other sources bolster parents' advocacy in significant ways.

SOME FINAL THOUGHTS

If I could give parents only one piece of advice, it would be this: *Never underestimate your power.* Determined parents have made gifted education what it is today. You can bring substantive changes to your children's education, even if the changes seem small or incremental at first. Also, the process of advocating for your children will teach them the value of determination and creative problem solving—skills all children need to negotiate the obstacles to their continued progress and achievement.

REFLECTION QUESTIONS

1. What are the main challenges your children have faced in their school and that you have faced while advocating for them?
2. What actions on your part have given your children more opportunity to learn at a pace and level appropriate for their ability, knowledge, and skill?
3. What human and material resources exist in the school and district that could assist you in your advocacy?

4. What successes have you had creating relationships with teachers, other parents, and school personnel who could help your children receive the services they need?
5. How are you enriching your children's education outside of school and building their confidence and resiliency?

REFERENCE

Smutny, J. F. (2001). *Stand up for your gifted child: How to make the most of kids' strengths at school and at home.* Minneapolis, MN: Free Spirit.

CHAPTER 45

HOW TO START THE SCHOOL YEAR ON A POSITIVE NOTE WITH YOUR GIFTED CHILD'S TEACHER

by Dina Brulles and Karen L. Brown

The new school year is on the horizon, and already you are feeling somewhat anxious and apprehensive. You know that transitions are a challenge for your gifted child, whether it's a new school, a new grade level, a new teacher, or all of the above. You want to make sure your child's new teacher understands that your gifted child has learning needs that differ from others. You feel that establishing a close and respectful partnership with your child's teacher early in the year can ease stress and set a structure for a successful year of learning.

In anticipation of meeting your child's new teacher, think about the questions you want to ask, starting with the obvious: "Are you aware that my child is gifted? What is your experience teaching gifted children? How do you plan on challenging my child this year?" At the same time, you don't want to come across as one of "those" parents! What's a parent to do?

In this chapter we offer advice on building a positive working relationship with the person who will be guiding your child's school time for the next 9 months or so. The advice stems from our experiences as parents of gifted children, former gifted teachers, teacher trainers, and school administrators who work every day with gifted children, their parents, and their teachers. With that introduction, know that there is no single method for developing a mutually supportive relationship with your child's teacher. The only imperative is to approach the relationship with trust, respect, and enthusiasm for a productive and enjoyable learning experience for your child.

Here are five key strategies for helping you form a strong relationship with your gifted child's teacher:

1. **Share information about how your child thinks, feels, learns best, and any specifics that will help the teacher understand and support your child's learning needs at school.** Respect the process the teacher has structured for seeking information from all of her students' families. Bear in mind that the first weeks of school are hectic for teachers. Providing a quick look into your child's world goes a long way in helping your new teacher connect with your child. Many teachers send surveys, questionnaires, learner profiles, and so forth, at the start of the school year. Use this tool to inform the teacher about your child.

   If your child's teacher does not send home a parent survey or questionnaire to all parents in the class, consider sending her some information directly. Remember that the teacher is working to learn the ins and outs of every student in the classroom; keep your initial information specific and concise. This introduction allows the teacher to get to know your child in an easy and nonconfrontational manner. If you have medical information to share, be sure to include the school nurse in your communication. Consider preparing an index card for that initial connection (see Figure 45.1).

2. **Approach the partnership with respect.** Know that your child's teacher wants to be there. Teachers enter the field because they enjoy helping children learn. As parents, this is what we want! Sadly, most teachers enter the classroom with little to no previous experience with gifted children and little, if any, understanding in how to recognize and respond to gifted learners, as only a few states require this training in teacher preparation programs. Unless a teacher sought out the training or is a parent of a gifted child, it is likely that you (the parent) may have more background and understanding of gifted children than the teacher. After introducing your child to the teacher, ask her if she would be open to you sharing information, such as an occasional article or event about a topic in gifted education that you feel is relevant to the education of your child in

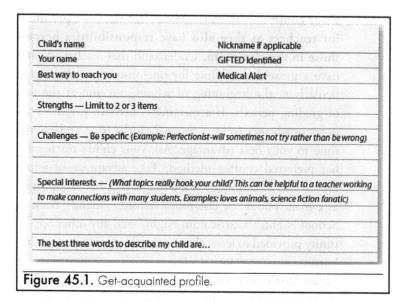

Child's name	Nickname if applicable
Your name	GIFTED Identified
Best way to reach you	Medical Alert

Strengths — Limit to 2 or 3 items

Challenges — Be specific (*Example: Perfectionist-will sometimes not try rather than be wrong*)

Special Interests — (*What topics really hook your child? This can be helpful to a teacher working to make connections with many students. Examples: loves animals, science fiction fanatic*)

The best three words to describe my child are...

Figure 45.1. Get-acquainted profile.

her classroom. In brief, appreciate that even if the teacher has little experience working with gifted children, she is there to know and teach all of her students.

3. **Appreciate teachers' attempts to meet the needs of all of their students.** As a parent of a gifted child, you want your child's teacher to know that you respect the range of learners she has and believe that every student in the class is equally important. This approach will help you share your expectations that all children in the classroom deserve to make academic progress every day, including the advanced learners. Offer support in whatever way you can. Often teachers feel frustrated that their schools have limited resources or services for their advanced learners. Teachers can rarely impact the programs offered in their schools or district. They do, however, greatly influence what occurs in their classrooms. This understanding means that whether your school is cluster grouping, has pull-out gifted services, or relies solely on the classroom teacher, it is the classroom teacher who has the largest impact on your child's education. Knowing she has the support of her gifted students' parents helps build a collaborative and respectful relationship between the family and school.

4. **Clear communication is critical, but time is a premium for teachers as they also have responsibilities beyond those in the classroom.** Understand that teachers do not have a great deal of time for one-on-one meetings, particularly at the beginning of school year and at the end of grading periods. If a meeting is needed, prepare your notes in advance to keep focused on the issue and use the time to your best advantage. Ask your child's teacher for her preferred contact method. Take advantage of whatever means of communication the teacher has set up, such as e-mail, phone, or classroom website. Attend "Back to School Night," "Curriculum Night," and any other opportunity provided to learn about the structures in your child's learning environment.

5. **Please don't fuel a fire! Be very careful not to spread misinformation.** Far too often parents become distressed or anxious based on inaccurate information passed along by other well-intentioned parents. Examples of information that may be inaccurately perceived and passed along include changes in the identification process, programming, funding, and/or services offered to gifted children. If you question the validity of news you hear, go to the source that should be sharing that information, such as the teacher, the school principal, or the school or district's gifted coordinator. As stated above, clear communication is critical and can support—even build—your school's gifted services when approached in a positive and proactive manner.

The best advice we can offer is to have confidence that your child's teacher is there because she enjoys nurturing her children's minds. She truly wants to give her best to all of her students. At times during the school year she may reach out to you to share information, ask questions, or seek input. Be supportive, be kind, and appreciate her efforts; she is the strongest influence on your child's learning this school year, and she shares your wishes for a productive school year.

REFLECTION QUESTIONS

1. What is your primary goal for the teacher conference?
2. What do you want the teacher to know about your child and how your child learns?
3. How can you best support your child's learning at home?
4. What do you see as the biggest challenge your child will face this year?
5. What do you see as your child's greatest strength based on the information shared?

CHAPTER 46

PARENTS NEED SUPPORT, TOO!: HOW TO START AND SUSTAIN A PARENT GROUP

by Kathleen Nilles

Cry is exactly what my husband and I did upon learning that our then 5-year-old son was gifted. After fully exhausting a box of tissues and dusting ourselves off, we mobilized and embarked on a weekend-long crash course to digest everything we could about giftedness. We scoured information from the library, websites, local affiliates, and the National Association for Gifted Children (NAGC). Then, when we finally came up for air, we were eager to speak with others in the same boat. We needed support, guidance, and reassurance, but who could we talk to? Who would understand?

Parenting a gifted child can sometimes be a lonely journey. Relatives may be empathetic. Friends may listen politely. Neighbors may not understand at all. It's tough to find those who actually "get it"—those who experience the same joys and frustrations of raising a gifted child every day. That's why parent groups can be an important way for parents and caregivers to receive support, information, tools, and tips for navigating the world of giftedness.

Parent groups come in all shapes and sizes. They range from the informal—a few like-minded friends sharing stories over coffee—to the more formal, with a mission, purpose, and actionable goals. Some groups are just for adults; others provide friendship and connections for families and kids with playgroups, picnics, field trips, and other entertaining activities.

There are district-based Parent Teacher Association gifted subgroups, homeschooler meetings, gifted social media networks, and special interest groups for virtually every hobby, passion, or religious affiliation. Meetups are also becoming popular, with more than 220,000 meetup groups in 181 countries, connecting more than 20 million people. (Go to https://www.meetup.com and search with key words, such as "gifted" or "homeschool gifted" to find groups in your local area.)

There are formal support groups, too. Supporting the Emotional Needs of the Gifted (SENG) has an extensive SENG Model Parent Group (SMPG) system, which brings together 10–20 interested parents of gifted and talented children to discuss topics such as motivation; discipline; peer, sibling, and parent relations; stress management; communications; and depression (see https://www.sengifted.org/smpg). The groups meet locally for 8–10 weeks, led by trained facilitators in a nonjudgmental atmosphere.

Other groups are formed with an advocacy goal in mind. In fact, if it weren't for the advocacy of parents, gifted education would not be where it is today. Many of the gifted programs and services that exist in schools are the results of small groups of parents who banded together and campaigned for gifted education (Smutny, 2003).

STEPS TO SETTING UP A PARENT GROUP

Although it may seem daunting at first, it's not hard to set up a support group if you have a few interested parents who share a common interest or goal. You'll be quickly on your way if you follow six main steps.

CLARIFY YOUR PURPOSE

Parent groups vary across the country, partly because each state operates its educational system and budget process differently. Although one group can serve multiple functions, the main purpose of your group will help determine how it can best be organized. Parent groups commonly address the following needs:

» **Celebrating giftedness.** Parents and those involved with the day-to-day support of gifted children can discuss the wonders and pleasures of listening to, talking with, and dealing with extraordinary children.

» **Teaching parents, educators, and the public about giftedness.** Parent group meetings outline how best to support gifted children, not only for the children's sake, but for the greater good of the world.

» **Providing social and cultural interaction.** Family fun nights, cultural outings, athletic games, and other social events help attach members emotionally to each other.

» **Developing effective advocates.** As a support group grows in membership and/or state influence, parent group members can become local, state, and national advocates for the rights and needs of gifted youth in our society.

REVIEW YOUR OBJECTIVES

Joining with others who share your enthusiasm for gifted education can be exciting; however, don't let that tempt you to take on too many things at once. At the outset, ask these important questions:

» What is the primary purpose of your group?

» Who are you trying to reach?

» How will you find members?

» How will you work with other organizations (schools, groups, etc.)?

» Where will you meet?

Start small. Find one, two, or a handful of individuals who share your vision. Set up clear expectations and common goals to ensure success of the group.

ESTABLISH THE STRUCTURE

Your new group can be formal or informal, depending on your members' needs and wants:

» **Informal.** Most local groups are formed to address a short-term need or because a small group of like-minded families shares a common interest. Many informal groups support enrichment activities, create fact sheets and brochures about giftedness, raise funds for classroom and teacher scholarships, run online discussion boards, and have an officer/committee structure.

» **Formal.** Often more formal models (e.g., a legally recognized 501(c)(3) tax-exempt organization) can boost credibility with certain officials and the media. Formal organizations must have bylaws and articles of incorporation that establish an overarching purpose and leadership framework. Each state has regulations as to how groups incorporate; the NAGC website has more information about lobbying restrictions.

Be sure to choose the organizational structure most comfortable to you and your members, and hold yourselves accountable. At minimum, the group should set goals, assign responsibilities, and craft a to-do list or work plan.

TIPS FOR NEW PARENT GROUPS[1]

ORGANIZATIONAL TIPS

» Start small; think big. Set realistic goals and prioritize activities.

» Look for holes, weaknesses, or inconsistencies in services and curricula—a great way to focus your group's activities.

» Help dispel the myths about gifted learners.

» Include parents of able learners who may not have been identified as gifted; they are also looking for high-end curriculum and enrichment activities for their children.

» Invite teachers or teacher representatives to join the group.

» Learn as much as you can about the nature and needs of gifted students and what the research says about them.

» Divide tasks into small, manageable parts so no one is carrying too big of a load.

» Send your newsletter to school board members, legislators, media, and other influential people.

» Develop and distribute a brochure about your organization; place at preschools, psychologists' offices, children's museums, libraries, public and private school events, chess competitions, and other places gifted parents might congregate.

» Make meetings meaningful—not personal storytelling time.

» Keep bylaws simple and flexible.

» Celebrate successes!

---

1   This section is adapted from *Starting and Sustaining a Parent Group to Support Gifted Children* (pp. 32–33), by the National Association for Gifted Children, 2011, Waco, TX: Prufrock Press.

IMPLEMENTATION TIPS

» Determine your non-negotiables for educational programming in the district and choose your battles carefully. Stay polite and persistent, but understand that compromise sometimes is the only way forward.

» Remember that gifted students have varying abilities and needs; what is right for your child may not be in the best interest of another student.

» Consider asking the superintendent to form a task force with parents, teachers, administrators, and community leaders.

» Learn consensus building.

» Piggyback speakers and programs with chambers of commerce, school systems, and state gifted organizations.

» Learn your district's and school's chain of command.

» Learn to practice "quiet lobbying." Much is decided outside of formal meetings, and a lot of positive change can be created over a few cups of coffee.

» Know the school district calendar and process for decision making (e.g., budget hearings, public hearings on program changes).

» Serve on relevant school district committees.

» Only have the president or designee speak publicly on behalf of the group.

» Seek common ground with those who appear opposed to gifted education services.

» Be sensitive to the pressures school district personnel are dealing with; gifted education is only one piece of the educational pie.

» Remember that schools and school districts are unique—find your niche!

ORGANIZE FOR ACTION

What is right for your group depends on many variables, including the geographic location of your members, time constraints, and your group's purpose. Meetings can be conducted in person, online, or using a hybrid of the two.

Consider topics of interest to your members. It's helpful to create a meeting committee of two to four members who can scout out possibilities and suggest a list of topics for the year ahead. Consider how different topics can be approached in a variety of formats: debates, panels, conversations, expert presenters, discussions of readings, webinars, and field trips.

KEEP THE SCHOOL INFORMED

Finding the right balance of involvement at a school can be a delicate issue because teachers can easily misinterpret the "one-two" forceful combination of strong interest and solid information coming from parents. Aim to establish a team approach with your school or district. It helps if the group is organized and functioning before reacting to any school problems, such as a proposed cut in programming.

Keep to a prepared program or agenda, no matter how simple. Parent groups need to encourage positive attitudes and discourage adversarial interactions. The most successful groups recognize what school districts are facing today and work in cooperation with their school and/or district.

TRANSFORM SUPPORT TO ADVOCACY

Advocacy from the perspective of a parent group simply means speaking or writing (or creating a website, video, or social media page) to promote improved education for gifted and talented students at the local, state, or national levels. Although the concept of advocacy is simple, being an effective advocate is not. NAGC has articles and resources available to help parent groups craft appropriate messages, communicate effectively, build bridges to administrators, and network appropriately when they are ready to extend their reach (see https://nagc.org).

Regardless of the size, format, or the goals of your parent support group, one thing is for certain: You, as the parent of a gifted child, will feel less isolated and enjoy the company of others who support you, understand your family, and are walking the gifted journey with you. Most likely, you will also experience a sense of gratification and accomplishment in knowing that you are channeling your energy in a positive way, taking care of yourself and your family, and helping raise awareness for not only your child, but the millions of gifted children in the country who deserve an education that meets their potential.

REFLECTION QUESTIONS

1. Do I have a support system that I can turn to for brainstorming solutions, sharing information, and providing support for me as I navigate the world of giftedness?
2. Have I looked for parent groups in my school district, community, or online that I could turn to for support?
3. What type of parent group is most needed within my community (informational, social, advocacy)? How might I start finding others with similar interests?
4. What would the benefits be to my family or me from joining and/or starting a parent support group?

REFERENCES

National Association for Gifted Children. (2011). *Starting and sustaining a parent group to support gifted children*. Waco, TX: Prufrock Press.

Smutny, J. (2003, March). Taking a larger stand for gifted education: Your district, your state . . . and beyond! *Parenting for High Potential*, 18–22.

CHAPTER 47

HOW TO START AN ACADEMIC COMPETITION IN YOUR CHILD'S SCHOOL

by Pamela M. Peters

Research suggests that academic competitions provide opportunities for content differentiation as well as emotional growth. Participating students learn how to cope with subjectivity, engage in friendly competition with their peers, get exposed to role models in their field of interest, and build resilience (Ozturk & Debelak, 2008). With limited resources, school districts often do not prioritize these types of programs. Starting a competition program at your child's school is a great way for parents to share their talents and support their child's school by providing challenging programming. I took the initiative and successfully started a Math Olympiads program at my child's school and want to encourage other parents to do the same. Following are the questions I am most often asked by parents on how to get started.

HOW DID YOU DECIDE WHICH PROGRAM OR COMPETITION TO BRING TO YOUR SCHOOL?

When my son skipped from second to fourth grade, I knew that fourth-grade math would still not be enough to challenge him. I'd heard that Mathematical Olympiads for Elementary and Middle Schools (MOEMS) was offered at other schools in our district, and I thought a program like that would challenge him and make him struggle a bit. I thought this would benefit my son and other students who did not know how to handle difficult academics because they were never forced to work outside of their comfort zones. And I knew it would help provide differentiated learning materials in a subject for which it is often difficult for teachers to develop curriculum.

WHAT TYPE OF RESEARCH DID YOU DO BEFORE PROPOSING THE IDEA TO THE SCHOOL?

I reached out to the assistant superintendent with a few district-specific questions. Were parents allowed to run afterschool programs? Yes. How many of the other schools in our district had MOEMS? Two out of five schools. How were those funded? The principal provided funding or parents paid related fees. Answers to my questions about the program requirements, fees, and time commitment were readily available on the website.

HOW DID YOU APPROACH THE SCHOOL?

That was super easy. I made an appointment with the principal, went in prepared with all of the information I had gathered, and got it approved that day. The teachers and the principal were very supportive and excited to have MOEMS on campus.

DID YOU COORDINATE WITH THE DEPARTMENT HEAD/SUBJECT HEAD OF THE SCHOOL?

No, because that position didn't exist at our school. If there had been a math subject leader, I would have consulted with her about my son's needs, and she would have been involved in my initial information-gathering process.

DID YOU ASK OTHER PARENTS OR TEACHERS TO HELP RUN THE PROGRAM?

Yes! Once MOEMS was approved, I was approved to send a note home to all fourth- and fifth-grade parents with information on the program and an invitation to all parents to get involved. Two parents immediately contacted me, excited to help. Having collaborators meant I was able to give students more individual and small-group attention. Due to other commitments, many parents may not be able to run the program, but may be interested in getting involved for short periods of time. For special events like Pi Day (March 14), I asked for additional parent volunteers, who helped us create a successful celebration of good pie and pi.

WHAT WAS THE TIME COMMITMENT?

We met for one hour a week after school. My time outside of that averaged about an hour a week, which I used for lesson prep (using the MOEMS curriculum) and grading or inputting scores from the monthly exams.

HOW DID YOU COMMUNICATE WITH ADMINISTRATORS, TEACHERS, PARENTS, AND STUDENTS?

I communicated with everyone directly. I sent an initial e-mail to fourth- and fifth-grade teachers, asking them to encourage students to participate. I also sent newsletters via e-mail and/or paper to the kids in the program. (For those in Title I schools, it's important to remember that not all families have Internet access.)

WHAT ABOUT FEES, TRANSPORTATION, AND SUPPLIES? HOW WERE THEY PAID?

MOEMS is inexpensive, but it's not free. To ensure the program was accessible to everyone, I decided against having parents contribute. Instead, I sought out a sponsor: Our local Mathnasium tutoring center sponsored the team every year I coached. They covered fees and supplies, and the Home and School Club paid for any copies I needed to make.

WHAT BENEFITS DID THE STUDENTS RECEIVE FROM THIS PROGRAM?

We called ourselves "mathletes," and all of us—parent, coaches, and kid mathletes alike—had a blast at our practices. The students were exposed to new math concepts and problem-solving skills that carried over to other areas. They had to work through challenges: No student got every problem correct, so it was tough for everyone.

I believed MOEMS at my child's school should be open to anyone, not just kids who were the top scorers on math achievement tests. This paid off tremendously. I saw students who were not known for being the strongest math students excel and surpass the kids who did better in the classroom. I saw one student work all year, never getting any questions correct. On the last exam he got 4 out of 5 correct, and was so incredibly proud of himself!

WHAT TYPE OF BENEFITS DID YOU GAIN FROM LAUNCHING THIS PROGRAM?

There are so many personal benefits to starting a program like this. First of all, I enjoyed it tremendously. I got to know the other coaches, the teachers, the principal, and the district administration much better. I also saw how much the kids enjoyed the program.

Also, the staff, teachers, and administration knew that I was willing to support them and help solve a problem they faced but lacked resources to solve: providing additional opportunities for advanced learning. Demonstrating my willingness to collaborate meant that when I brought an issue to their attention they saw me as more than a complaining parent. I became a founding member of our district parent advisory council, and I was asked to provide feedback as the district tried to address some issues with math education at the middle school level. I was also able to successfully advocate for my daughter to start kindergarten early.

WHAT IF I DON'T HAVE THE TIME TO RUN THE PROGRAM BY MYSELF?

When I started this project, I worried that I would have to do it all on my own. In the end, I found collaborative parents and a sponsoring organization. Based on that experience, my biggest piece of advice is: Ask everyone. It's much easier to reach out to people you know, but that may limit your circle and possibly make other parents feel unwelcome. In fact, none of the other coaches are people I would have thought to ask. All, with one exception, worked full-time jobs, but were able to get some flexibility one afternoon a week to volunteer. MOEMS would not have been possible without engaged, flexible collaborators like I was able to find.

HOW DO YOU GET STUDENTS INTERESTED?

It's like the movie *Field of Dreams*: If you build it, they will come. To be honest, I was worried that very few kids would want to stay after school every week to do math. I sent notes to the teachers and talked to them personally, asking them to encourage students. I had my son talk it up to the other kids, and he reported that kids seemed excited. MOEMS limits a team to 35 students, which made me laugh. At the outset, I imagined a handful of kids who would want to participate in this regularly. I got 30 students to enroll the first year, and every other year we had to start a waiting list. I built it—with help from a team of collaborators—and they definitely came.

HOW DO I GET STARTED?

Start by thinking about what your child or school needs. Talk to teachers and other parents. There are a number of national and international academic competitions that are easy to coordinate at your school. They typically have training materials, curriculum, and competition rules available online and have relatively low registration fees. See if one of them can help meet that need. Examples include:

» Destination Imagination (https://www.destinationimagination.org), in which students work in teams to research, design, and build a solution to a specific challenge;

» Future City (https://futurecity.org), a project-based learning program in which students in sixth, seventh, and eighth grades imagine, research, design, and build cities of the future; and

» Kids Philosophy Slam (http://philosophyslam.org), in which kids answer a philosophical question such as "What is the meaning of life?" in words, artwork, poetry, or song.

My focus was mathematics, so I use Math Olympiads for Elementary and Middle Schools (https://moems.org). There are also programs that focus on other subjects, such as National History Day (https://www.nhd.org) and Science Olympiad (https://www.soinc.org).

If one of these formal programs will not meet the need you have identified, think about an informal option. You could start a book club or teach students to play chess. Teach kids to converse in your home language. Celebrate Pi Day and explore the wonder of Fibonacci numbers in nature with a math club. Students who are interested in space might enjoy watching live feeds from the space station and thinking about how humans might live on Mars. The possibilities are endless.

The next step is to create a proposal and present it to the school or district administration. Be sure to include how this program will help the school community, what you are able to do, and what you would like from the school or district (space, transportation, communication, funding, supplies). Find out how other schools in your district manage this or similar programs. Think about how much time you can devote to this project so you can be clear about your needs. Bring your proposal and any additional information you have when you meet with the administration. It is much easier for you to make a case and for the administrator to make a decision if the relevant information is available. Remember to be flexible: Schools often have needs or conditions you don't know about.

Once you have approval, build enthusiasm. Talk to teachers, students, and parents about the program. Share your excitement. Ask your child and her friends to do the same. Remember, if you build it, they will come.

REFLECTION QUESTIONS

1. In what area do students at my child's school need more challenge? What is "missing" from the curriculum?
2. What skills and passions do I have that could help fill this gap?
3. Who could I ask for assistance or support? Who might want to help me?
4. What are some potential roadblocks? How can I work around them?

REFERENCE

Ozturk, M. A., & Debelak, C. (2008). Affective benefits from academic competitions for middle school gifted students. *Gifted Child Today, 31*(2), 48–58.

CHAPTER 48

THE IMPORTANCE OF TEACHING CHILDREN SELF-ADVOCACY

by Nancy Arey Cohen

Each of us is an *advocate* every time we stand up for our beliefs, hold our ground in a discussion, or express a point of view in defense of an issue. Given the complexity and nuances with respect to serving gifted and talented learners, it's important that parents develop necessary skills to advocate for their high-ability children—and, even more important, that parents teach their children how to advocate for themselves.

With the absence of a federal mandate to serve all gifted and talented learners, there is significant disparity among the states and local districts in identification, support, programming, and funding for gifted. There is little public accountability for delivery of gifted education services. Given these facts, gifted children are not guaranteed an educational environment in which they can flourish. Both parents and children must speak up so gifted and high-ability children receive an education commensurate with their abilities in a safe and nurturing environment.

When it comes to advocating for gifted education, parents may advocate for programs and services for their gifted child. However, children also need to learn to self-advocate rather than relying solely on their parents to solve every problem that arises. Rescuing your child repeatedly causes anxiety because it sends the message to your child that he is fragile and cannot manage for himself (Marano, 2004). Children do not learn life skills like self-reliance, sharing, and conflict resolution when parents hover (Strauss, 2006). If the child learns to rely on a parent to rush in every time he is unhappy, he will not learn the skills necessary to develop a sense of self-efficacy and independence.

Because parents cannot always be around when an issue arises, students need to solve problems in real time. Knowing the appropriate way to request a different book, for example, and to explain what they know and understand will likely make them more successful.

These skills can be employed in myriad situations throughout their lives. How many adults are unable to approach an employer to discuss a promotion? How many adults are hesitant to tell a friend that something he or she is doing is hurtful? How many young adults frequently call mom and dad asking for advice on issues they should be able to handle themselves? Teaching children while they are young to know what is important to them and to respectfully fight for it is critical.

Teaching gifted children to distinguish what is worth fighting for is not always easy. Their sense of justice, their propensity toward overexcitability, and their ability to synthesize facts, analyze a situation, and arrive at a logical solution (often before the decision maker) can be stumbling blocks. Additionally, all successful advocacy depends, in part, on relationships built on trust created over time. Sometimes built-in credibility speeds the process, but generally it takes time to develop a trusting relationship between advocates and decision makers. If children are to advocate for themselves, then, in academic or social situations, they first need to establish a trusting relationship with those involved. They can do this by:

» knowing their facts,
» knowing their audience,
» knowing their preferred outcome, and
» maintaining a respectful attitude.

If we are going to teach our young children to advocate for themselves, we need to first teach them what that means. It does not mean whining about homework because they already know how to do the work, or complaining about an assigned project being too simplistic. This means knowing what they want, assessing the situation to ascertain whether or not the desired outcome is feasible, thinking about the best way to approach the person who can make the decision, and arming themselves with evidence to support their position. It means being careful not to let extraneous issues become a distraction. It means choosing issues wisely rather than railing against every perceived injustice.

TIPS FOR STUDENT SELF-ADVOCACY[2]

Adolescents and teens must develop the skills and confidence to self-advocate with teachers and administrators. Share these suggestions with your child to help make the experience easier and more productive:

1. **Make an appointment.** This shows the teacher you are serious and understanding of his or her busy schedule. Tell the teacher how much time you'll need, be flexible, and be on time.

2. **If you know other students who feel the same way, consider approaching the teacher together.** There's strength in numbers. If the teacher hears the same thing from four or five people, there's a chance he or she will do something about it.

3. **Think through what you want to say before going into your meeting.** Write down your questions or concerns. Make a list of the topics you want to cover; copy it for the teacher so you both have something to refer to during the meeting.

4. **Choose your words carefully.** Instead of saying, "I hate doing reports; they're boring and a waste of time," try, "Is there some other way I could satisfy this requirement?" Use a different word other than *boring*. It's a meaningless buzzword to teachers.

5. **Don't expect the teacher to do all of the work or propose the answers.** Be prepared to make suggestions. The teacher will appreciate your initiative.

6. **Be diplomatic, tactful, and respectful.** Teachers have feelings, too. Be conversational, not confrontational.

7. **Focus on what you need, not what you think the teacher is doing wrong.** The more the teacher knows about you, the more he or she will be able to help. If the teacher feels criticized, he or she will want to help less.

8. **Don't forget to listen.** Many students need to practice this skill. Remember, the purpose of your meeting is not to just hear yourself talk.

---

2   *Note.* Adapted from Galbraith & Delisle, 2011, p. 133.

9. **Bring your sense of humor.** Don't tell jokes, but rather have a sense of humor that allows you to laugh at yourself and your own misunderstandings or mistakes.

10. **If your meeting isn't successful, get help from another adult.** Even if the teacher denies your request, the meeting can still be considered successful. If you had a real conversation—communicated openly, listened carefully, and respected each other's point of view—it was a great meeting! If the meeting was tense or you felt disrespected (or acted disrespectful), then it's time to bring in a guidance counselor, the gifted program coordinator, or another teacher you know and trust. Then, approach your teacher and try again.

COMPLAIN OR SELF-ADVOCATE?

As a parent, it is important to practice role-playing situations in which a child would have a choice whether to simply complain or to self-advocate for a desired outcome. These situations can include both academic and social settings. The following four examples show various situations that children may encounter.

SCENARIO 1

The class is studying pilgrims and the first Thanksgiving. The teacher has assigned *The First Thanksgiving* by Jean Craighead George. Johnny has a real interest in pilgrims and has already read that book.

Complaint: "I've already read that book."

Self-Advocacy: "I've already read that book. May I please go to the library and find another book to read on the pilgrims?"

SCENARIO 2

The teacher begins a lesson on the basic needs of farm animals, including shelter and living spaces. Susie has visited her uncle's farm every summer since she was born.

Complaint: "I know all about this already."

Self-Advocacy: "I know all about this already from visiting my uncle's farm. Would you like me to bring in some pictures and video to share with the class? I could interview my uncle and ask him for some fun facts that aren't in our textbook."

SCENARIO 3

David played baseball last season but wasn't very good. Wanting to get better, he attended a summer camp and practiced. The next season, disappointed to have him on the team, his new coach decided to bench him for the first game.

Complaint: "I hate baseball and never want to play again."

Self-Advocacy: "Coach, I know that I didn't play very well last season, but I went to summer baseball camp and I've been practicing really hard. Can I show you what I can do now? I want to help the team to win, not sit on the bench."

SCENARIO 4

Julie's younger sister is playing with a fragile toy, and Julie doesn't want her to damage it.

Complaint: "Give it to me!" yells Julie as she grabs the toy, making her sister cry.

Self-Advocacy: "You don't want to play with that old toy. Here's another one that is way more fun. Let's play with it together." Julie then gently replaces the fragile toy with something more robust and plays for a few minutes with her sister.

These examples are just a handful of ways to help gifted children self-advocate. If we diligently model behaviors for our children that show them how to respectfully and politely express their needs, we will be leading them down the path to independence with the ability to achieve their goals and fulfill their potential—academically, socially, and emotionally.

REFLECTION QUESTIONS

1. Does your child frequently complain or seem angry about being unchallenged at school? If so, when he or she does this, what is your initial reaction?

2. What is your parenting style in helping your child work through issues or problems? Do you tend to hover and quickly jump in, or are you more hands-off?

3. What have you done (or could you do) to help teach your gifted child how to self-advocate?

4. Are there specific instances right now—either at home, school, extracurricular activities, or community experiences—where your child could use his self-advocacy skills?

5. What do you notice (or what might you expect to notice) in your child's demeanor when she takes the initiative to self-advocate?

REFERENCES

Galbraith, J., & Delisle, J. (2011). *The gifted teen survival guide: Smart, sharp, and ready for (almost) anything* (4th ed.). Minneapolis, MN: Free Spirit.

Marano, H. E. (2004). The pressure from parents. *Psychology Today*. Retrieved from https://www.psychologytoday.com/us/articles/200403/the-pressure-parents

Strauss, V. (2006). Putting parents in their place: Outside class. *The Washington Post*. Retrieved from http://www.washingtonpost.com/wp-dyn/content/article/2006/03/20/AR2006032001167.html

IT'S TIME TO REVAMP THE PARENT-TEACHER CONFERENCE PROCESS: LET'S INCLUDE THE CHILD

by Janette Boazman

Take a moment to reflect on the parent-teacher conferences you've attended or what parent-teacher conferences were like when you were in school. In many instances, the parent-teacher conference has not changed a great deal over the years. The typical routine often goes something like this:

>> The school sets aside a date for parent-teacher conferences.
>> Parents sign up for a time to meet with their child's teacher.
>> On conference day, during their timeslot, the parents and teachers meet for a short time.
>> There is discussion of the child's academic progress and behavior.
>> The child, for whom the conference is being held, waits outside of the classroom or at home to get a report from the parents.
>> Post conference, parents report what they feel is best for the child to hear and in a way they want their child to hear the news. They may or may not discuss all of what was said in the conference.

What's missing from this process? The child is missing from this process. The child, the most important stakeholder, is visibly absent and a passive participant in the process. Other problems occur with this model:

>> Gifted children who participate in curriculum enrichment or gifted pullout programs often have a special teacher for those classes. Because conferencing frequently takes place

with only the general education teacher, the development and the progress of the gifted learner in the gifted setting is not always discussed when the parents and the general education teacher meet.

»   When gifted children are accelerated, they often have multiple teachers. This can lead to multiple parent-teacher conferences in which the gifted student is left outside of the conversation.

»   Parents often choose to conference with the one teacher who is perceived to be accountable for the largest portion of their child's academic profile and expect that teacher to share reports from their child's other teachers.

Now, clear the traditional image of parent-teacher conferences from your mind and contemplate a conference process and setting that has the potential to bring together multiple teachers to collaborate on the growth and development of your child. Picture a process that allows for active student participation, positive psychological growth, planning for academic achievement, self-evaluation, and the development of a strong and trusting team of the child, parents, and teachers.

One conferencing process that allows for such learner growth, development, and connection is the *student-led conference*. The student-led conference really is what it implies: It's a parent conference where the student takes the lead role in preparing and presenting personal achievements, areas for improvement, and goals for the future (Hubert, 1989).

WHAT IS A STUDENT-LED CONFERENCE?

In the educational setting, students are led by the classroom teacher or an advisor on the preparation for leading the conference. The preparation begins at the start of the school year and continues, at least, through the last formal parent conference day held by the school. Throughout the school year, students, with teachers or advisors, build a performance portfolio of work and assignments they are working on or have completed. By using their performance portfolio at the parent conference, the student explains progress toward mastery of academic, character, and behavioral objectives and goals (Guyton & Fielstein, 1989; for more details on the process, refer to the references listed at the end of this chapter).

In general, the process usually includes the following:

» Preconference preparations are made by the student with the guidance of the teacher or advisor. This includes practice in speaking and leading the discussion for the conference.

» At the time of the conference, the parents are invited into the classroom. Their student greets them and introduces them to all members present at the conference. They include parents, the teacher(s), and other involved individuals whom the student wants present.

» The student thanks the family and all parties for assembling for the meeting and gives an overview of the format and objectives for the conference.

» The student explains work samples from all content areas and discusses academic grades, goals, and the action plan for positive development. If the conference is held at the time report cards are issued, the student usually addresses the grades presented on the report card.

» Discussion of behavior and character development is led by the student.

» The student leads a discussion on how the parents can help at home.

» The conference ends, and the student thanks all participants for being present.

» Participants in the conference complete post-conference paperwork.

The student-led conference is not new. Written work about this concept began to emerge in professional journals in the late 1980s (Little & Allan, 1989). The student-led conferencing style is not exclusive to one educational population: It can be used in general education or special education settings. It's not just for middle and high school age students, and can be used as early as third grade—and possibly earlier in gifted learner circumstances. And, the student-led conference process can be implemented schoolwide or in select environments, such as those settings where we see gifted learners.

HOW PARENTS CAN INSPIRE CHANGE

Implementation of student-led conferences is gaining momentum. However, empowering the student through the use of student-led conferences assigns a nontraditional purpose to the parent conference. Parents can help schools make the shift to student-led conferences.

If you value this process and your child's school has not put student-led conferences in place yet, ask your child's teacher(s) or school administrators to consider implementing the student-led conference with the gifted student population. Present your vision and hopes for your child and the other gifted children that will come with use of this process. Volunteer to help with the preparations and getting the program started. Your advocacy for this program and your help could spark a schoolwide change that could make an important difference in the lives of many students in gifted education and general education settings.

WHY ARE STUDENT-LED CONFERENCES VALUABLE FOR GIFTED LEARNERS?

Studies as far back as 1931 indicate that gifted students demonstrate different learning characteristics and traits (Hollingworth, 1931). Gifted learners:

» grasp concepts more quickly and tend to show competency in basic skills at an early age,
» think creatively,
» tend to have a positive self-image and leadership qualities,
» examine topics more deeply than those around them,
» are curious,
» read more than that the average student, and
» may demonstrate a high and sustained devotion to self-directed projects.

When gifted students are allowed to progress and achieve personal goals, they display independence, self-initiative, and metacognitive ability. These characteristics indicate that student-led conferences are a natural fit for gifted students. Students can become more reflective learners who develop self-regulation.

In the student-led conference, the student has the opportunity to show academic knowledge, behavioral practice, and personal achievements. It also allows for reflection, recognition, and discussion of academic and behavioral weakness. The learner can discuss a plan for mastering regular education objectives, along with a plan for what he or she would like to learn beyond the regular education curriculum. Learners have the chance to set goals and ask for the support they need to achieve those goals.

Student-led conferences—and the growth that comes with regularly occurring student-led conferencing—have the potential to positively impact the emotional and academic development of students and move students closer to talent development, happiness, and thriving throughout their formative years and beyond. Isn't it time for a change?

REFLECTION QUESTIONS

1. What is the desired outcome or end result for student progress conferences?
2. How does the student-led conference process help parents, teachers, and students?
3. What are the benefits and the burdens of the student-led conference process? Do the benefits outweigh the burdens?
4. How can parents, teachers, and administrators work as a team to implement the student-led conference process at your school?

REFERENCES

Guyton, J. M., & Fielstein, L. L. (1989). Student-led parent conferences: A model for teaching responsibility. *Elementary School and Guidance Counseling, 23,* 169–172.

Hollingworth, L. S. (1931). The child of very superior intelligence as a special problem in social adjustment. *Mental Hygiene, 15*(1), 1–16.

Hubert, B. D. (1989). Students belong in the parent-teacher conference, too. *Educational Leadership, 47*(2), 30.

Little, A. W., & Allan, J. (1989). Student-led parent teacher conferences. *Elementary School Guidance and Counseling, 23*, 210–218.

PART VIII

DIVERSITY OF SPECIAL
POPULATIONS

Often gifted and talented children are approached as a homogenous group with a central focus on their intellectual characteristics. Recognizing and understanding the range of diverse backgrounds and experiences these children possess, parents and caretakers can become better advocates for their children at school or seek out a range of opportunities or interventions that are appropriate to their needs. This section includes pieces that address students who are twice-exceptional and those who remain underserved in gifted and talented programs.

Luckey Goudelock provides parents of African American gifted and talented children essential information that addresses identification procedures, types of gifted programming, and potential obstacles that their children may encounter at school. This information can then be used to advocate for a child's needs at school, which she also outlines at the end of the section.

Drawing on her experiences as a classroom teacher, Ritchotte (and her coauthor, Matthews) discuss realities of having a twice-exceptional (2e) student in a class. This included acknowledging the disparate abilities of her student who was both exceptional in English but struggled due to his dyslexia. Ritchotte educated herself on what it meant to have a 2e student and joined forces with the student's parents to advocate for services at school. The piece also includes an interview conducted with the child's mother.

Mullet and Rinn introduce the complexities of giftedness and Attention Deficit/Hyperactivity Disorder (ADHD). Included are practical strategies to support a child who is gifted with ADHD. Parents are also provided ways to improve their children's self-awareness about their behavior, which is not intentional but rather a result of neurobiological differences.

Mohammed also addresses the issues that can arise from the misconceptions and misunderstandings that come with having a 2e child. Discussed are parental and professional interventions for developing and maintaining a child's emotional and social understandings.

The authors in this section skillfully illustrate that gifted and talented children are not a monolithic group and, due to a variety of factors, need differentiated approaches to their affective and academic needs.

—Jennifer L. Jolly

CHAPTER 50

PARENTING GIFTED AFRICAN AMERICAN CHILDREN

by Jessa D. Luckey Goudelock

Gifted African American students express characteristics of giftedness in significantly diverse ways when compared to their White counterparts. However, parents are not often aware how to recognize giftedness in their children, and teachers are unaware of the nuances in identifying and supporting gifted African American students. For parents of African American students, being aware of identification procedures, types of gifted programming, and potential obstacles their children may face is important. Although this can seem daunting at times, parents and caregivers of gifted African American students should feel empowered in their role as advocates and collaborators in their child's educational journey (Ford, Dickson, Davis, Scott, & Grantham, 2018) and find strength in knowing they play an essential role in their child's success (Ford, Moore, & Trotman Scott, 2011).

OBSERVING GIFTED TRAITS IN YOUR CHILD

As primary caregivers, parents are in a key position to notice traits of giftedness in their child (Zhbanova, Rule, & Stichter, 2015). Teachers often overlook potential gifted behaviors in African American students (Henfield, Washington, & Byrd, 2014), so as a parent, being aware of these is especially important. Often the typical identification methods used by schools systems for identifying gifted children are sometimes not the best methods to identify African American gifted children.

Researchers Dr. Mary Frasier and Dr. E. Paul Torrance examined giftedness through a *cultural lens* and found ways to identify culturally diverse gifted children using observable behaviors, such as motivation, problem solving, inquisitiveness, humor, and creativity. Dr. Mary Frasier and her associates (1995) from the University of Georgia focused on 10 key traits, aptitudes, and behaviors of giftedness. As a more formal way for teachers to observe and report on traits, aptitudes, and behaviors that are present in potentially gifted persons of all cultures, the Traits, Aptitudes, and Behaviors Scale (TABS) was developed (Besnoy, Dantzler, Besnoy, & Byrne, 2016; Frasier et al., 1995).

The 10 traits parents and teachers should look for are the following (Frasier et al., 1995):

» **Communication.** Is the child highly expressive and effective in use of words, numbers, and/or symbols?

» **Motivation.** Does the child express an interest or enthusiasm for learning?

» **Interests.** Does the child have an intentness, passion, concern, or curiosity about something?

» **Problem-solving abilities.** Does the child use effective and inventive strategies to recognize and solve problems?

» **Memory.** Does the child retain and retrieve information?

» **Humor.** Does the child bring unrelated ideas together in a recognizable relationship?

» **Inquiry.** Does the child question, experiment, and explore?

» **Insight.** Does the child grasp new concepts, make connections, and sense deeper meanings?

» **Reasoning.** Does the child use controlled, active, intentional, and goal-oriented thought?

» **Imagination/creativity.** Does the child produce many and/or highly original ideas?

These traits can manifest in both positive and negative ways, either of which can indicate advanced academic abilities. By observing their children, parents can begin to note concrete examples of their child's areas of giftedness.

Another way to identify giftedness is to leverage the work of Dr. E. Paul Torrance. Torrance was a creativity and education researcher at the University of Georgia who spent his career refining a series of creativity assessments, among other significant accomplishments. In addition to TABS, Torrance's signs of creative talent can be used as an additional indicator in identifying African American students.

Eighteen signs of creative talent developed by Torrance (1973) use "creative positives" to identify gifted characteristics in African American children. Many of these creative characteristics are often noted in racially and culturally diverse children (Grantham, 2013):

» ability to express feelings and emotions;
» ability to improvise with common materials;
» articulateness in role-playing and storytelling;
» enjoyment of and ability in visual art;
» enjoyment of and ability in creative movement, dance, dramatics;
» enjoyment of and ability in music and with rhythm;
» expressive speech;
» fluency and flexibility in nonverbal media;
» enjoyment of and skills in small-group activities;
» responsiveness to the concrete;
» responsiveness to the kinesthetic;
» expressive body language;
» humor;
» richness of imagery in informal language;
» originality of ideas in problem solving;
» problem-centeredness;
» emotional responsiveness; and
» quickness of warm-up.

Both of these strategies examine children's behaviors in a positive light and observe negative or disruptive behaviors as possible indicators of giftedness. By using the work of Frasier and Torrance as guides, parents and educators can begin to develop a more comprehensive understanding of gifted African American children.

IDENTIFYING GIFTED AFRICAN AMERICAN STUDENTS

Identification procedures for gifted education vary widely among states and districts. However, common elements of the identification process include teacher referrals, intelligence testing, rating scales, and portfolios. Many districts require a referral to begin the process of gifted identification, and most often these recommendations come from teachers.

Unfortunately, research has shown that teachers are more likely to recommend Asian and White students than African American and Hispanic students for gifted identification (Ecker-Lyster & Niileksela, 2017; Jordan, Bain, McCallum, & Bell, 2012). Teachers may not be aware of the ways in which giftedness manifests in culturally diverse children and may, therefore, overlook children who demonstrate their giftedness in nontraditional ways (Henfield et al., 2014). However, teachers who are aware of measures such as the TABS and creative positives can be invaluable allies and advocates for gifted African American children. As a matter of policy, schools may wish to consider incorporating the TABS and Torrance Tests of Creative Thinking as part of their formal identification strategies.

Intelligence testing is another aspect of gifted identification that can be a barrier for African American students. Intelligence tests have been criticized for their tendency to result in lower scores for racially and culturally diverse students (Ecker-Lyster & Niileksela, 2017). Many districts rely on verbal ability tests and high cutoff scores, which can unfairly discriminate against African American students (Naglieri & Ford, 2015). One way to mitigate this issue is to use one or more of these strategies for identifying African American gifted students:

» **Nonverbal tests.** Nonverbal tests focus on reasoning ability instead of language and other academic knowledge (Ecker-Lyster & Niileksela, 2017; Ford, Wright, Washington, & Henfield, 2016; Naglieri & Ford, 2015).

» **Screen all students using local norms.** Universal screening gives all children the opportunity to show their strengths. Local norms allow children's scores to be compared to other students in their school or district, rather than at the national or state level (Plucker & Peters, 2018).

» **Rating scales.** Rating scales provide information about a child that extends beyond just a test score. These scales often assess characteristics of giftedness such as creativity, leadership, and academic abilities (Jordan et al., 2012).

» **Portfolios.** Portfolios provide an opportunity for educators to judge a product or collection of work that represents a student's knowledge or problem-solving ability. Portfolios can also help educators understand the best ways to support students in gifted education programming (Schroth & Helfer, 2008).

All of these methods can aid schools in identifying African American students who would benefit from gifted education services. Equipped with information about various identification methods, parents can work to advocate for their child's school or district to adopt equitable procedures for identifying gifted students.

ADDRESSING GIFTED AFRICAN AMERICAN STUDENTS' NEEDS

Schools choose to address the needs of gifted students in a variety of ways based on available resources. Parents of gifted African American students should pay attention to the types of programs that are offered, as each may impact students differently. Enrichment-focused programs likely involve a classroom teacher or gifted teacher providing services within the regular classroom setting. Pull-out programs or special schools involve students being placed in a separate classroom or facility for a portion or all of their school day (Rimm, Siegle, & Davis, 2018). Practices such as whole-grade or single-subject acceleration may be used to help students access content that matches their ability level (Assouline, Colangelo, & VanTassel-Baska, 2015).

For gifted African American students, the type of gifted program matters. In districts that experience underrepresentation, pull-out programs or special schools may cause African American students to be one of only a few minority students in their class. Enrichment programs or acceleration may allow students to remain in a more diverse environment but can make their advanced abilities more noticeable to their classmates, which may be ostracizing. Being aware of the differences in programming options can help parents remain on alert to notice if students are facing any of the common difficulties that can result from the intersection of race and giftedness.

COMMON RACIAL ISSUES ENCOUNTERED BY GIFTED BLACK STUDENTS

Although each student's schooling experience is unique, there are several common race-related issues that gifted African American students may encounter at school that parents need to understand. These include deficit thinking, microaggressions, stereotype threat, and the "acting White" phenomenon.

Deficit Thinking. In education, deficit thinking is the notion that when students fail to achieve, the blame lies solely with the student and his or her family circumstances (Ford et al., 2011). Gifted African American students can be negatively impacted when educators or other professionals have a deficit thinking perspective. Obtaining appropriate programming can be difficult if students are blamed for underachievement or behavioral issues that stem from not having their academic or affective needs met. Tools such as the TABs and Torrance's "creative positives" (see pp. 352–353) can help parents and educators to combat deficit thinking and see that all students have potential and their unique abilities should be nurtured.

Microaggressions. Gifted students, including African American students, are susceptible to microaggressions (inappropriate comments, attitudes, actions, or gestures based on a person's history or characteristics) from educators and peers (Stambaugh & Ford, 2015). Gifted African American students often experience microaggressions in the form of having their academic performance second-guessed. Students who consistently experience microaggressions can begin to exhibit academic problems such as underachievement, social and emotional issues, and additional stress in school (Ford, Trotman Scott, Moore, & Amos, 2013).

Stereotype Threat. When microaggressions become a constant part of one's education environment, students can easily begin to buy into stereotype. Stereotype threat is a situation where a gifted Black student fears that her performance is being judged based on existing stereotypes someone has about her (Wasserberg, 2017). This fear can impact performance in situations such as high stakes testing and lead to underperformance. Because gifted Black students are likely to have the potential for high achievement, the effects of stereotype threat can lead to a larger than average gap between potential and actual achievement. Because identification for gifted programs is often based on test performance, if students are unable to perform at their potential, they may not qualify for gifted education programming (Ford et al., 2011).

"Acting White". The "acting White" phenomenon is a form of race-based bullying (Grantham & Biddle, 2014). Positive school behaviors such as following rules in class, getting high grades, and speaking standard English can be perceived as "acting White" (Ford et al., 2011; Grantham & Biddle, 2014). Gifted African American students who are concerned about accusations of "acting White" are less likely to take advantage of educational opportunities such as Advanced Placement classes. These decisions have significant, long-term consequences; however, as they may decrease students' chances for higher education opportunities (Ford, Grantham, & Whiting, 2008).

The impact that being accused of "acting White" can have on gifted African American students is important to understand. Bullying in any way is harmful to any student. However, for gifted African American students, the ability to develop positive racial and academic identities is important in combating the effects of discrimination and microaggressions.

All of these issues can contribute to the academic success of gifted African American students. When parents and educators have the knowledge to recognize these issues and the tools to effectively advocate for students, issues can be quickly addressed to reduce the negative impact of race-related issues.

ADVOCATING FOR YOUR GIFTED CHILD

Parent advocacy is essential to the identification and appropriate programming for gifted African American students (Grantham, 2011). Advocating for gifted identification or gifted programming requires that parents know the school or district gifted education policies (Luckey & Grantham, 2017) and work with teachers and administrators. In order to be an effective advocate for a gifted African American student, parents must understand their child's needs, have developed ideas for meeting those needs, and be willing to communicate and collaborate with the school (Grantham, Frasier, Roberts, & Bridges, 2005). Being an advocate requires motivation and a consistent presence in the school setting, even outside of advocacy work. Parent involvement, in general, helps parents to gain familiarity with the school staff and the daily operations of the school. This can be useful when thinking about appropriate ways to meet a child's educational needs.

CONCLUSION

Parents of gifted African American students have an important role in their child's education. Taking the time to understand characteristics of giftedness, identification procedures, and programming options is essential to being able to interact effectively with the school system. Knowing the hurdles gifted African American children may face is the best way for parents to ensure positive academic and social experiences for their children in school.

REFLECTION QUESTIONS

1. Where can you access your district's gifted education policy? What does it include? What may be missing?
2. Consider the characteristics of your school or district. What types of gifted services would be most useful for African American students (e.g., pull-out classes, enrichment programs, acceleration)?
3. What resources does your district have to support the academic, social, and emotional needs of gifted African American students? What resources may be needed?

REFERENCES

Assouline, S., Colangelo, N., & VanTassel-Baska, J. (2015). *A nation empowered: Evidence trumps the excuses holding back America's brightest students* (Vol. 1). Iowa City: University of Iowa, The Connie Belin & Jacqueline N. Blank International Center for Gifted Education and Talent Development.

Besnoy, K. D., Dantzler, J., Besnoy, L. R., & Byrne, C. (2016). Using exploratory and confirmatory factor analysis to measure construct validity of the Traits, Aptitudes, and Behaviors Scale (TABS). *Journal for the Education of the Gifted, 39,* 3–22.

Ecker-Lyster, M., & Niileksela, C. (2017). Enhancing gifted education for underrepresented students: Promising recruitment and programming strategies. *Journal for the Education of the Gifted, 40,* 79–95.

Ford, D. Y., Dickson, K. T., Davis, J. L., Scott, M. T., & Grantham, T. C. (2018). A culturally responsive equity-based bill of rights for gifted students of color. *Gifted Child Today, 41,* 125–129.

Ford, D. Y., Grantham, T. C., & Whiting, G. W. (2008). Another look at the achievement gap. *Urban Education, 43,* 216–239.

Ford, D. Y., Moore, J. L., & Trotman Scott, M. (2011). Key theories and frameworks for improving the recruitment and retention of African American students in gifted education. *The Journal of Negro Education, 80,* 239–253.

Ford, D. Y., Trotman Scott, M., Moore, J. L., & Amos, S. O. (2013). Gifted education and culturally different students: Examining prejudice and discrimination via microaggressions. *Gifted Child Today, 36,* 205–208.

Ford, D. Y., Wright, B. L., Washington, A., & Henfield, M. S. (2016). Access and equity denied: Key theories for school psychologists to consider when assessing black and Hispanic students for gifted education. *School Psychology Forum, 10,* 265–277.

Frasier, M. M., Hunsaker, S. L., Lee, J., Mitchell, S., Cramond, B., Krisel, S., . . . Finley, V. S. (1995). *Core attributes of giftedness: A foundation for recognizing the gifted potential of minority and disadvantaged students.* Storrs: University of Connecticut, The National Research Center on the Gifted and Talented.

Grantham, T. C. (2011). New directions for gifted black males suffering from bystander effects: A call for upstanders. *Roeper Review, 33,* 263–272.

Grantham, T. C. (2013). Creativity and equity: The Legacy of E. Paul Torrance as an upstander for gifted Black males. *Urban Review, 45,* 518–538.

Grantham, T. C., & Biddle, W. H. (2014). From bystander to upstander teacher for gifted black students accused of acting white. *Gifted Child Today, 37,* 178–187.

Grantham, T. C., Frasier, M. M., Roberts, A. C., & Bridges, E. M. (2005). Parent advocacy for culturally diverse gifted students. *Theory into Practice, 44,* 138–147.

Henfield, M. S., Washington, A. R., & Byrd, J. A. (2014). Addressing academic and opportunity gaps impacting gifted Black males: Implications for school counselors. *Gifted Child Today, 37,* 147–154.

Luckey, J. D., & Grantham, T. C. (2017). Upstander parents for academic acceleration of gifted black students. *Parenting for High Potential, 6,* 2–5, 22.

Jordan, K. R., Bain, S. K., McCallum, R. S., & Bell, S. M. (2012). Comparing gifted and nongifted African American and Euro-American students on cognitive and academic variables using local norms. *Journal for the Education of the Gifted, 35,* 241–258.

Naglieri, J. A., & Ford, D. Y. (2015). Misconceptions about the Naglieri Nonverbal Ability Test: A commentary of concerns and disagreements. *Roeper Review, 37,* 234–240.

Plucker, J. A., & Peters, S. J. (2018). Closing poverty-based excellence gaps: Conceptual, measurement, and educational issues. *Gifted Child Quarterly, 62,* 56–67.

Rimm, S. B., Siegle, D. B., & Davis, G. A. (2018). *Education of the gifted and talented* (7th ed.). New York, NY: Pearson.

Schroth, S. T., & Helfer, J. A. (2008). Identifying gifted students: Educator beliefs regarding various policies, processes, and procedures. *Journal for the Education of the Gifted, 32,* 155–179.

Stambaugh, T., & Ford, D. Y. (2015). Microaggressions, multiculturalism, and gifted individuals who are black, Hispanic, or low income. *Journal of Counseling and Development, 93,* 192–201.

Torrance, E. P. (1973). Non-test indicators of creative talent among disadvantaged children. *Gifted Child Quarterly, 17,* 3–9.

Wasserberg, M. J. (2017). High-achieving African American elementary students' perspectives on standardized testing and stereotypes. *The Journal of Negro Education, 86,* 40–51.

Zhbanova, K. S., Rule, A. C., & Stichter, M. K. (2015). Identification of gifted African American primary grade students through leadership, creativity, and academic performance in curriculum material making and peerteaching: A case study. *Early Childhood Education Journal, 43,* 143–156.

CHAPTER 51

GIFTED AND LEARNING DISABLED: ADVOCATING FOR THE NEEDS OF YOUR 2E CHILD

by Jennifer A. Ritchotte and Michael S. Matthews

At first glance, the twice-exceptional (2e) student seems like a paradoxical idea. After all, a student who is bright should be able to outperform his same-age peers effortlessly with little adult help. Yet, these students do exist and often their needs go unmet (Foley-Nicpon, Allmon, Sieck, & Stinson, 2011; Foley-Nicpon, Assouline, & Colangelo, 2013). One common scenario is the 2e student who remains unidentified for gifted services because his disability masks his giftedness. Another frequent example is the 2e student who struggles all year in an advanced class because special education services are not believed to be appropriate for gifted students.

As a classroom teacher, I (Jennifer Ritchotte) was fortunate to have a student identified as both gifted and having a learning disability. Christian (pseudonym) helped me demystify what it meant to be 2e and strengthened my advocacy for these unique students. Advocacy by parents and other stakeholders is an important step toward achieving new, expanded, or improved educational services for gifted students (Matthews, Georgiades, & Smith, 2011; Rubenstein, Schelling, Wilczynski, & Hooks, 2015). Such efforts also should include the student in the decision-making process (Baum, Schader, & Hébert, 2014); this inclusion in the process is especially appropriate in the case of the student who is 2e.

At the beginning of the school year, Christian was a quiet presence in my seventh-grade Academically and Intellectually Gifted (AIG) language arts classroom; I often worried I was not engaging him. Then in late September this quiet presence came to life. After a class discussion of the short story "The Scarlet Ibis," Christian approached me with a beautiful drawing of a scarlet ibis sketched on a scrap piece of lined paper. His love of language arts was apparent from that point on. By October, Christian was one of the youngest editors of the literary magazine I advised. Had it not been for the telltale signs of dyslexia I noticed in Christian's writing, I may never have known he had a learning disability.

Like many students with disabilities, Christian had become adept at compensating for his dyslexia. It was only through communication with his parents that I learned how much he still struggled with reading and writing. One afternoon in the spring, I witnessed this firsthand. Christian came to my classroom to receive extra help with Latin roots and grammar after failing an exam. With his face pressed firmly in the palms of his hands, he broke down and cried. I was unaware how many hours he had spent making flashcards, paying painful attention to ensuring each letter in the word, sentence, and definition was written correctly. Unfortunately, rather than actually learning the material, completing this task had become his focus. I also discovered he was extremely aware of the time it took his peers to finish the exam. He refused to take extra time because that might place unwanted attention on him. It was that afternoon that I began to comprehend fully what it means to be gifted and have a learning disability.

My frequent interactions with Christian's parents also provided me with insights into what it means to be the parent of a 2e child. As Christian's teacher, I often observed his parents' frustration as they tirelessly advocated for his needs to uninformed members of the school community. At the end of the academic year, the school convened a team to discuss whether Christian should continue to receive 504 accommodations[3]. As a member of the team, I was surprised when I was the lone voice, aside from Christian's parents, who spoke in favor of his accommodations continuing into eighth grade. Persistently, I fought alongside his parents to ensure services were not denied simply because he masked his learning difficulties so well in class. The next day I received a card from Christian's parents thank-

---

3   Section 504 refers to a part of the federal Rehabilitation Act of 1973 that prohibits discrimination on the basis of disability. In schools, accommodations offered to students in response to Section 504 generally are developed by a team of teachers, parents, and other school staff. These plans must be documented to monitor schools' compliance with the provisions of this act.

ing me for my advocacy. Enclosed in the envelope were several pages of typed records documenting Christian's progress, successes, and hurdles, maintained by his parents from the time he was born. My eyes filled with tears as I read their struggles and triumphs in raising a 2e child. Their story is one of perseverance. To capture this story, I interviewed Christian's mother. Any parent who has tried or is currently trying to advocate for a 2e child should read this interview:

INTERVIEW WITH CHRISTIAN'S MOTHER

Q: Can you give some basic background information about your son's giftedness and disability?

A: Christian is the youngest of three children. He was extremely late in talking and didn't even say his own name until he was almost 4. Even though others could not understand him, it was obvious he understood a lot and also followed multiple-step directions at a very young age. We have a family history of speech issues and dyslexia, so we were able to notice a lot of "red flags" at an early age with Christian. I think we knew ourselves that he was dyslexic in about first or second grade. He disliked writing but loved dictating stories. He struggled with letter recognition in kindergarten and reading. He received additional one-on-one help in the classroom and tutoring after school for his reading and writing issues even though his teachers also told us how incredibly smart he was. Most of his elementary report cards would comment on how well his oral answers were expressed but said that they wished he would put those thoughts down in writing in the same manner, or that he struggled to apply phonological rules.

Because Christian was bright, he was not a priority for the school system in terms of testing. Having fought similar issues with the school with his older sister (also 2e), we opted to have Christian privately tested in fourth grade. Although we were well aware of the laws and what he was entitled to, rather than spending time battling the school and the high costs of fighting to receive services in the school system, we chose to take a different route. Because we had dealt with the Exceptional Children (EC) department previously with our daughter, we already knew that although they wanted to be helpful, they lacked the awareness and understanding that were key to providing appropriate services for 2e students. The AIG department, however, seemed to be more knowledgeable and more passionate about helping Christian to achieve his potential. Therefore, we chose to pursue a 504 plan and advocacy through the district's AIG department, rather than an Individualized Education Plan (IEP) through the EC department

Q: What struggles have you encountered as the parent of a 2e child?

A: The biggest problem is the lack of awareness by many employees in the school system. Early on, we had to fight with an assistant principal for a 504 plan. Although we provided overwhelming testing data and years of information on his struggles, and both his classroom teacher and his gifted teacher gave numerous examples of his learning disability and classroom struggles, the assistant principal had the mindset that a bright kid, especially one in the gifted program, could not have a learning disability, even though Christian would have easily qualified for an IEP. Sadly, this is something we have encountered many times over the years. In middle school, he had a teacher who wanted to sit him closer to the board so he could "read better" even though dyslexia has nothing to do with his vision. Day-to-day frustrations for Christian typically centered on busywork assignments that tended to emphasize his weakness and prevented him from showing his knowledge on a subject or prevented him from learning the material in a way that was best for him. Luckily, he also had some great teachers who understood that he needed to learn things in his own way, and they allowed him to do things outside of the box.

Q: How have you triumphed over obstacles you have encountered?

A: We have always tried to focus on his strengths and helped to build his confidence outside of the classroom. His art teacher at school encouraged his art at an early age and became a great mentor and teacher to him over the years. Art became a way for Christian to express his thoughts and record memories that other people may express in writing. He also started volunteering with a science museum when he turned 12 years old, and his passion for science grew exponentially. He sought out volunteer opportunities with reptiles/ herpetology at a local college. He was able to tag along on field research on turtles. When he is involved in activities that he enjoys, he forgets how much he dislikes writing. In all of his outside activities, he shines with his strengths. This in turn has given him extra confidence in the classroom and awareness that the classroom is not the only measure of "academic" success.

Q: How have you educated yourself about 2e children?

A: As an attorney, my background is in the law so I am quite comfortable with the legal ramifications of twice-exceptionality, which of course also frustrates me when the school system is not. But laws and school systems can only help so much. The biggest thing I had to do was to educate myself on how to deal with dyslexia, teachers and school administrators, etc. In addition to educating yourself about the ins and outs of twice-exceptionality, find advocates within the school system for your child. We were lucky to have several over the years who truly understood our child, and that can make a huge difference in a child's attitude toward school and his or her ability to succeed. I would also recommend you spend time nurturing your child's passions outside the classroom.

Q: What advice would you offer parents who are struggling to advocate for their 2e child?

A: Document, document, document! Keep a record of struggles, difficulties, and accomplishments. Often the giftedness masks the weaknesses, and the struggles are not evident to a teacher on first glance. With a record of difficulties, issues, and history, it is easier to educate and help a teacher to understand your child. Sometimes it may also take a little time to help educate a teacher on twice-exceptionality, but a good teacher will understand and will be willing and able to help your child in more ways than you can imagine. Determine what works best for your own child and do not be afraid to pursue it. We personally opted not to pursue an IEP because we had better success with advocacy within the AIG department, working directly with teachers and with tutoring and outside activities. Each child is different, and no solution is the same.

FINAL THOUGHTS

Christian's case highlights the importance of awareness and close collaboration between parents, school staff, and the 2e learner (Ritchotte & Zaghlawan, 2019). By sharing Christian's story, we hope that other parents and teachers with children who are 2e will be better equipped to support these unique learners.

REFLECTION QUESTIONS

1. What does advocacy mean to you? What steps will you take to become a stronger advocate for the twice-exceptional learners in your life?
2. Christian's mother describes many activities that allowed her son to cultivate his strengths outside of school. What are your child's strengths and interests, and how might they be developed through outside learning opportunities?
3. Choose an area of exceptionality. What specific accommodations would be appropriate in helping someone with this diagnosis become more able to focus on developing his or her talents?

REFERENCES

Baum, S. M., Schader, R. M., & Hébert, T. P. (2014). Through a different lens: Reflecting on a strengths-based, talent-focused approach for twice-exceptional learners. *Gifted Child Quarterly, 58,* 311–327.

Foley-Nicpon, M., Allmon, A., Sieck, B., & Stinson, R. D. (2011). Empirical investigation of twice-exceptionality: Where have we been and where are we going? *Gifted Child Quarterly, 55,* 3–17.

Foley-Nicpon, M., Assouline, S. G., & Colangelo, N. (2013). Twice-exceptional learners: Who needs to know what? *Gifted Child Quarterly, 57,* 169–180.

Matthews, M. S., Georgiades, S. D., & Smith, L. E. (2011). How we formed a parent advocacy group and what we've learned in the process. *Gifted Child Today, 34*(3), 28–34.

Ritchotte, J. A., & Zaghlawan, H. Y. (2019). Coaching parents to use higher level questioning with their twice-exceptional children. *Gifted Child Quarterly, 63*, 86–101.

Rubenstein, L. D., Schelling, N., Wilczynski, S. M., & Hooks, E. N. (2015). Lived experiences of parents of gifted students with autism spectrum disorder: The struggle to find appropriate educational experiences. *Gifted Child Quarterly, 59*, 283–298.

CHAPTER 52

WHAT PARENTS SHOULD KNOW ABOUT ADHD

by Dianna R. Mullet and Anne N. Rinn

Does your gifted child challenge authority, show inattention, wander off-task, and demonstrate unusual amounts of high energy? These traits and characteristics are often signs of giftedness, but are also symptoms of Attention Deficit/Hyperactivity Disorder (ADHD). Gifted traits and ADHD can look similar, so it's important for parents to be aware that both misdiagnosis and dual diagnosis are possible in gifted children.

DOES MY GIFTED CHILD HAVE ADHD?

Some gifted children suffer from ADHD, a neurodevelopmental disorder that impairs a child's functioning. For a diagnosis of ADHD, children under the age of 17 must display at least six symptoms of inattention or hyperactivity/impulsivity in at least two different settings (school and home, for example), and those symptoms must interfere with the child's normal functioning (American Psychiatric Association, 2013).

The severity of ADHD varies among children (Webb et al., 2016):

» Some children display primarily inattention, which can appear as an inability to remember verbal instructions or to focus on routine tasks.

» Other children display hyperactive or impulsive behaviors, such as trouble staying seated or talking out of turn.

» Some children display both types of symptoms.

» Symptoms may appear different in different children.

» Some children are mildly affected, while others have severe symptoms.

» Although gifted children without ADHD can also demonstrate high levels of activity or inattention, their problems tend to be specific to certain situations (for example, a particular subject or class that lacks stimulation or challenge).

In school, teachers are often the first point of referral for special programming, yet the overlapping characteristics of giftedness and ADHD can make it difficult to correctly refer a child. Research suggests that when a child presents characteristics that span both giftedness and ADHD, teachers and counselors are more likely to identify a disability than giftedness (Hartnett, Nelson, & Rinn, 2004).

Therefore, in order to avoid a misdiagnosis or missed diagnosis, it is important to seek a comprehensive evaluation by a professional experienced in working with gifted children (Webb et al., 2016). The evaluation includes tests of intelligence, achievement, and cognitive processing; interviews with teachers, parents, and the child; observation; and developmental history.

HOW TO AVOID A MISDIAGNOSIS

Research indicates that 25% to 50% of gifted children diagnosed with ADHD are actually misdiagnosed and fail to meet the diagnostic criteria for ADHD (Webb et al., 2006). Gifted children who do not have ADHD but who display behaviors similar to symptoms of ADHD typically display only one or two ADHD-like symptoms and not the full set of six symptoms required for diagnosis.

Gifted children may exhibit ADHD-like behaviors due to lack of challenge or stimulation in the classroom (Webb et al., 2016). Willard-Holt (1999) suggested asking the following questions when you suspect your gifted child may have ADHD:

» Could the behaviors be responses to inappropriate placement, insufficient challenge, or lack of intellectual peers?

» Is the child able to concentrate when interested in the activity?

» Have any curricular modifications been made in an attempt to change inappropriate behaviors?

>> Has the child been interviewed? What are the child's feelings about the behaviors?

>> Does the child feel out of control? Do the parents perceive the child as being out of control?

>> Do the behaviors occur at certain times of the day, during certain activities, with certain teachers, or in certain environments? (pp. 11–12)

An accurate diagnosis of ADHD requires a comprehensive evaluation by a trained professional experienced in working with gifted children (Webb et al., 2016). The evaluation includes tests of intelligence, achievement, and cognitive processing; interviews with teachers, parents, and the child; observation; and developmental history.

SUPPORTING YOUR GIFTED CHILD WITH ADHD

If your gifted child is diagnosed with ADHD, it is important to provide the appropriate supports necessary for him or her to succeed. In addition to ensuring appropriate medical treatment, parents play an important role in helping their gifted children with ADHD succeed with educational accommodations, behavioral strategies, and opportunities to apply their strengths.

KNOW STRENGTHS AND STRUGGLES

To help set expectations for self, school, and other pursuits, children must become aware of their strengths, weaknesses, and learning styles. Armed with that information, parents can set expectations and help advocate for younger children, and encourage older children to be self-accepting and, ultimately, to self-advocate.

STRENGTHS

>> **Superior general intelligence.** General intelligence is unaffected by ADHD. A gifted child with ADHD is still a gifted child. Many children learn to use intellectual strengths to partially compensate for impairments caused by ADHD (Antshel et al., 2007).

» **Exceptional creativity.** Research suggests that the combination of impaired short-term memory and high intelligence actually enhances creativity (Fugate, Zentall, & Gentry, 2013).

» **A desire for complexity and abstract thinking.** Gifted children with ADHD excel at analyzing big problems and understanding the way that ideas are connected to each other.

» **Self-awareness of how they learn.** Gifted children with ADHD need to understand their strengths and weaknesses and recognize which learning strategies work best for them.

STRUGGLES

» **Deficits in short-term memory and speed of processing information.** Your child may have trouble quickly recalling facts and details.

» **Mood, anxiety, and behavior disorders.** Research shows that gifted children with ADHD are more likely to experience mood, anxiety, and behavior disorders (Antshel et al., 2007). Your child is aware of his or her high potential and may feel frustrated and anxious at being unable to tap into it.

» **Difficulty organizing and managing time.** Most gifted children with ADHD need to be explicitly taught how to organize their time and tasks.

» **Difficulty with transitions.** Gifted children with ADHD have difficulty shifting their frame of mind from one task to another (Webb et al., 2016). Your child may be capable of sustained attention on an interesting task, but shifting attention requires a great deal of effort—often more effort than your child can expend without support.

» **Uneven performance across academic areas.** Gifted children with ADHD are often unable to perform equally well in all academic areas (Brown, 2014). Your child may display extremes in strengths and weaknesses—he or she may earn A's in some classes yet fail others.

» **Academic underachievement.** Your child may experience academic struggles when the demands of school increase beyond his or her ability to compensate with intelligence alone.

HELP MANAGE SYMPTOMS

Gifted children with ADHD thrive when they learn strategies, tools, and skills that help them tap into their intellectual potential. Although children may need help learning to use the strategies, the ultimate goal is for them to become self-directed and request help as needed.

HOMEWORK AND OTHER TASKS

» **Chunking.** Demonstrate how to break a task into smaller, more manageable parts.

» **Checklists.** Have your child create and follow a checklist for evening activities.

» **Self-monitoring.** Help your child use a timer to monitor progress on tasks. Set timers as reminders to take breaks and again to resume work. After some practice using a timer, your child will be able to track time without using a timer.

» **Positive reinforcement.** Reward the use of strategies. Always describe the behavior being rewarded and explain why that behavior is important. Reward your child with motivators that she finds meaningful.

ORGANIZATION

» **Organizer systems.** A Simple Organization System (SOS) is a helpful way to stay organized at school. The SOS is a 2-inch binder organized by subject with sections for agendas, essential supplies (e.g., pencil, pen, and ruler), and important papers such as permission slips. Each subject section begins with a two-sided pocket divider: one side for homework due, the other for returned work. Class notes on loose leaf paper are added to the end of the section.

» **Visual systems.** Gifted children with ADHD often find time and tasks easier to organize visually. Kanban (see Figure 52.1) is a visual tool for tracking tasks. Kanban consists of a whiteboard or poster board divided into three columns:

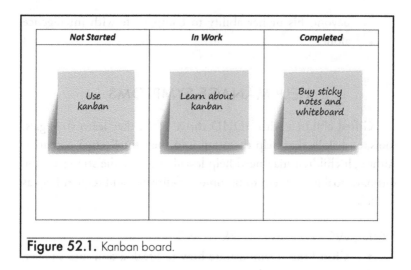

Figure 52.1. Kanban board.

"Not Started," "In Work," and "Complete." New tasks are written on sticky notes and placed in the "Not Started" section. After beginning a task, the task is moved to "In Work" and eventually to the "Complete" section. Kanban allows immediate awareness of all tasks past, present, and future, giving the child a sense of control and accomplishment.

» **Graphic organizers.** Many children with ADHD struggle with writing and prefer to convey ideas visually. Graphic organizers, such as concept maps, timelines, and Frayer diagrams, help children collect and organize their thoughts, making it easier to initiate writing. The Frayer diagram (see Figure 52.2) is a useful way for students to collect and organize thoughts visually and can serve as a precursor to a writing assignment.

TECHNOLOGY

» **Reminders, calendars, and smartphone apps.** Your child can set reminders or use calendar events to alert him or her about a task at a particular time or GPS location (e.g., home or school). Some students keep track of assignment instructions and written information on the classroom whiteboard using the camera in their smartphone.

» **Manage notes.** Google Keep is a free, user-friendly note-taking app that allows notes in text, image, or audio for-

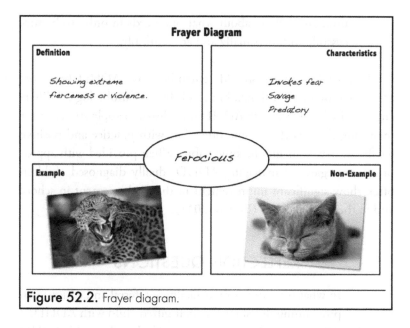

Figure 52.2. Frayer diagram.

mats. After adding notes, your child can sort them into online notebooks and sync them across devices.

DEVELOP SELF-AWARENESS

The greatest gift parents can give their child with ADHD is to nurture self-awareness, self-confidence, and self-advocacy:

» **Show your child that he or she is not alone.** Share stories of famous gifted people who overcame the problems associated with ADHD.

» **Encourage independence.** Gifted children often disengage from activities they find uninteresting. For gifted children with ADHD, however, it's not a matter of choice—these children lack the ability to focus and sustain effort on less desirable activities (Reis, Baum, & Burke, 2014). When allowed to choose personally meaningful activities, the child is better able to focus and complete activities successfully.

» **Promote self-advocacy.** Self-advocacy requires clearly communicating one's needs and desires to others. Use role-play to practice dialogs that include introducing oneself, talking about one's interests and strengths, asking for an explanation, and talking about what one needs in order to be successful, both personally and academically.

Ultimately, parents should remember that ADHD behaviors are not willful or intentional, but result from neurobiological differences. Gifted children with ADHD must learn to apply strategies for managing their work and emotions, but with practice and positive feedback, new strategies become habit. When provided with appropriate strategies for managing ADHD, dually diagnosed children often show significant improvement in their achievement in school and in their self-concept (Brown, 2011).

REFLECTION QUESTIONS

1. In what ways can parents facilitate referral and educational programing decisions for their gifted child with ADHD?
2. What issues might arise when a gifted student with ADHD is referred for accommodations? For gifted programming?
3. Do gifted children with ADHD face extra challenges when it comes to emotion and motivation?

REFERENCES

American Psychiatric Association. (2013). *Diagnostic and statistical manual of mental disorders* (5th ed.). Washington, DC: Author.

Antshel, K. M., Faraone, S. V., Stallone, K., Nave, A., Kaufmann, F. A., Doyle, A., & Biederman, J. (2007). Is attention deficit hyperactivity disorder a valid diagnosis in the presence of high IQ? Results from the MGH Longitudinal Family Studies of ADHD. *Journal of Child Psychology and Psychiatry, 48,* 687–694.

Brown, T. E. (2011). Executive function impairments in high IQ children and adolescents with ADHD. *Open Journal of Psychiatry, 1,* 56–65.

Brown, T. E. (2014). *Smart but stuck: Emotions in teens and adults with ADHD.* San Francisco, CA: Josey-Bass.

Fugate, C. M., Zentall, S. S., & Gentry, M. (2013). Creativity and working memory in gifted students with and without characteristics of attention deficit hyperactive disorder: Lifting the mask. *Gifted Child Quarterly, 57*, 234–246.

Hartnett, D. N., Nelson, J. M., & Rinn, A. N. (2004). Gifted or ADHD? The possibilities of misdiagnosis. *Roeper Review, 26*, 73–76.

Reis, S. M., Baum, S. M., & Burke, E. (2014). An operational definition of twice-exceptional learners: Implications and applications. *Gifted Child Quarterly, 58*, 217–230.

Webb, J. T., Amend, E. R., Beljan, P., Webb, N. E., Kuzujanakis, M., Olenchak, F. R., & Goerss, J. (2016). *Misdiagnosis of gifted children and adults: ADHD, Bipolar, OCD, Asperger's, Depression, and other disorders.* Scottsdale, AZ: Great Potential Press.

Webb, J. T., Goerss, J., Amend, E. R., Webb, N. E., Beljan, P., & Olenchak, F. (2006). Diagnosis or misdiagnosis. *Understanding Our Gifted, 18*, 15–17.

Willard-Holt, C. (1999). *Dual exceptionalities.* Retrieved from ERIC database. (ED430344)

CHAPTER 53

BULLY PROOFING YOUR TWICE-EXCEPTIONAL CHILD

by Amra Mohammed

Casey was diagnosed with Attention Deficit/Hyperactivity Disorder (ADHD) at approximately 3 years old. His mother noticed that Casey was an outcast at school, and he often felt angry and frustrated. However, as a 1-year-old, Casey's speech was fluent. He could recite some nursery rhymes, sing the national anthem, and have conversations with adults. He was a creative child who invented his own games and stories.

School assessments identified Casey as having an IQ in the gifted range, but he often had difficulty with social skills, self-esteem, and self-control. He did not get along with other children, who viewed him as strange and often teased him. Casey seemed to live in his own world, playing by himself.

Unable to manage peers' teasing, Casey acted out. He talked out of turn and too much, left his seat, and fought with peers during group work. Teachers punished him for those behaviors, which only made him act out more. Punishment after punishment and failure after failure diminished his sense of self. His mother reported that he often said, "I don't know why I was born; I'm worthless." Because of this, he hurt himself. When she went to get Casey from school one day during third grade, Casey's mother found him sitting on the floor at the door of the classroom, hitting his head with a sandal, upset with himself for being punished. Each day, on the way back home from school, he would complain about how peers and teachers didn't understand him, how they treated him unfairly, and how he felt low and worthless.

Twice-exceptional (2e) students are those who demonstrate a gift or talent in one or more areas and have a disability in another area

(Neumeister, Yssel, & Burney, 2013). One identifying characteristic of 2e children is asynchronous development, or the display of unusual talent or maturity in one or more areas alongside a struggle to develop in other areas. Asynchronous development may exhibit internally or externally. Internally, asynchronous development indicates different rates of physical, intellectual, emotional, and social skills development. In contrast, external traits may include a lack of inclusion with both same-age peers and age-related expectations of society. These external traits illustrate the importance of special efforts to facilitate healthy social and emotional development in 2e children (Boothe, 2010).

The social and emotional issues that 2e children demonstrate can be as debilitating as their other challenges. Parents see a frustrated, angry, and depressed child; however, parents of a 2e child may also experience similar emotional and psychological issues.

Challenges that 2e students encounter may include:

» **Hidden issues.** The child's psychological or emotional issues are often hidden behind negative behavior. For example, antisocial behavior may mean a lack of social skills in general or a disability that affects social skills, such as autism. Inappropriate behaviors, such as teasing, clowning, anger, withdrawal, apathy, and denial of problems, may signal poor self-esteem.

» **Frustration.** The twice-exceptional student's lack of initiative may indicate frustration when directly associated with a low level of academic performance (Nielsen, 2002).

» **Discrepancy in expectations.** In addition, the discrepancy between the 2e child's own high expectations and performance in gifted areas in contrast to areas of disability can also be an underlying cause of social and emotional difficulties for 2e children (King, 2005).

» **Social impact.** Twice-exceptional students often struggle with developing healthy social relationships and frequently suffer from isolation, teasing, or aggressive bullying. Negative social experiences leave these children wounded and alienated from peers, in many cases well into adulthood.

» **Lack of school support.** Furthermore, it is often difficult for schools to provide the specialized attention and learning environment that these children require.

STRATEGIES TO HELP

Parents can play a vital role in helping their 2e child build resiliency—or the ability to bounce back—in the face of difficulties by intervening and advocating on several levels (Wood & Estrada-Hernández, 2012). Early identification and support in problem areas is the most effective way to support positive social and emotional development, and parents have the earliest opportunities to provide vital input and guidance to their children. Furthermore, students who know, understand, and accept their strengths and weaknesses are more likely to achieve desired outcomes. One activity that enhances deeper understanding and self-esteem is for 2e children to learn about famous people who are also twice-exceptional. Through studying such people and how they have overcome their learning or behavioral challenges, 2e children can see that they, too, can excel (Bradunas, 2014).

Even with a tailored learning program, 2e children will experience negative emotions and setbacks. During these times, children need to talk openly about their feelings and problem solve to resolve negative emotions. This support can take place during informal discussions with teachers, parents, or peers, but in some cases, a more formal intervention may be appropriate, such as individual counseling for mild issues or therapy for more severe issues (Olenchak, 2009). See Table 53.1 for examples of interventions. With practice, your child can become bully-proof.

Positive parental—and sometimes professional—involvement is critical to the social and emotional well-being of 2e children because they frequently face significant difficulty in these areas. Self-awareness, self-acceptance, empathy, and the ability to adapt to different social situations are key factors in developing social and emotional resilience. See Table 53.2 for parental and professional support scenarios.

TABLE 53.1
INTERVENTIONS FOR SOCIAL AND EMOTIONAL HEALTH (TRAIL, 2011)

Emotional Understanding	Social Understanding
» Facilitate your child's understanding of personal strengths, interests, and weaknesses. » Encourage and teach empathy for others. » Facilitate the development of self-esteem. » Nurture your child's personal awareness, understanding, and acceptance. » Help your child learn to set realistic expectations and engage in structured goal setting. » Celebrate attaining individual goals and self-actualization. » Help your child develop a healthy locus of control and the ability to self-regulate. » Seek specialized counseling for any child exhibiting signs of anxiety, dysfunctional perfectionism, depression, stress, or suicidal tendencies.	» Model a respectful environment that values individual differences. » Provide opportunities for your child to work with intellectual peers and those with similar interests and abilities. » Encourage your child's involvement in school clubs, interest groups, or other extracurricular activities. » Attend social groups to aid your child in developing social skills and building peer relationships. » Teach self-advocacy skills. » Learn to empower, versus enable, your child. » Provide explicit instruction to help students improve relationships with peers, teachers, and family. » Facilitate mentorships or apprenticeships. » Seek specialized counseling for any child dealing with intensities, sensitivities, and extreme feelings.

REFLECTION QUESTIONS

1. Each twice-exceptional child is a unique child in his or her individuality, specialty, and exceptionality. From your experiences with your child, what strategies work best for him or her?

2. What are some academic, social, and emotional challenges that your 2e child has faced? How did you overcome these challenges?

TABLE 53.2
PARENTAL AND PROFESSIONAL SUPPORT SCENARIOS

Scenario 1: Parent Support	Scenario 2: Professional Support
Problem: My son did not know how to think and respond when there were unpleasant situations, like being teased.	**Problem:** Socially she's . . . very empathetic, and she doesn't ever want to hurt her friends' feelings even if it's to say, "No, that's my snack. You can't have my snack." She sees it as, "I'm sharing," but sometimes the way that they do it is more . . . aggressive. She really does need to stand up for herself and say, "No, this is my snack. You need to ask."
Strategy: I told him that we can't control others' behaviors; we can only control ours. People that tease you want to see you angry and react, so you must not serve them. If they call you names, give them unexpected responses, such as telling them, "Thank you for teasing me," or telling them you take that as a compliment. They will soon learn that their teasing can't affect you.	**Strategy:** The school psychologist is working with her and she participates in a social group to practice skills in advocating and standing up for herself to her friends.
Result: It was hard for him, but he practiced for years. We also tried to help him understand other kids. Among those that bullied him verbally, most of them also had ADHD like my son. So, I explained to him they shared ADHD in common, and that instead of being angry, he could be empathetic. When he was in high school, bullying did not affect him.	**Result:** She has one really good friend, but she is very aggressive [who] tells her what to do [more] than asks. When [my daughter] does eventually stand up to her, she gets really nasty. I say, "You're doing what you're supposed to do. I know this person is not being kind about it because you're actually telling her you're not okay with being told to do everything."

Note. Quoted material gathered from personal interviews.

3. From reading this chapter and your knowledge about 2e children, how can you improve your child's development in both areas: giftedness and disability?
4. Do you have any resources that you find helpful to share with other parents who have a 2e child?

REFERENCES

Boothe, D. (2010). *Twice-exceptional: Students with both gifts and challenges or disabilities.* Boise, ID: Idaho Department of Education.

Bradunas, G. (2014). *Understanding and helping twice-exceptional students* [Web log post]. Retrieved from https://blog.connections academy.com/understanding-and-helping-twice-exceptional-students

King, E. W. (2005). Addressing the social and emotional needs of twice-exceptional students. *Teaching Exceptional Children, 38*(1), 16–20.

Neumeister, K. S., Yssel, N., & Burney, V. H. (2013). The influence of primary caregivers in fostering success in twice-exceptional children. *Gifted Child Quarterly, 57,* 263–274.

Nielsen, M. E. (2002). Gifted students with learning disabilities: Recommendations for identification and programming. *Exceptionality: A Special Education Journal, 10,* 93–111.

Olenchak, F. R. (2009). Effects of talents unlimited counseling on gifted/learning disabled students. *Gifted Educational International, 25,* 144–164.

Trail, B. A. (2011). *Twice-exceptional gifted children: Understanding, teaching, and counseling gifted students.* Waco, TX: Prufrock Press.

Wood, S. M., & Estrada-Hernández, N. (2012). Rehabilitation counselors' awareness, knowledge, and skills regarding twice-exceptional consumers. *Journal of Applied Rehabilitation Counseling, 43*(1), 11–18.

CHAPTER 54

WHY IS THERE A GAY PRIDE FLAG ON MY 9-YEAR-OLD'S BACKPACK?

by Paul James "PJ" Sedillo

Gifted children are often empathetic, morally sensitive, and feel a responsibility toward others. As they become aware of the injustices in their surrounding communities, they may embark on a quest for justice for individuals who are oppressed, marginalized, or misunderstood (Silverman, 1994). Each June, as Gay Pride Month brings increased visibility and awareness to the issues affecting the GLBTQ (gay, lesbian, bisexual, transgender, queer, questioning, and others) community, justice-focused gifted child or adolescents may gravitate to events and groups that support gay rights.

So, how can parents empower and educate gifted children who now have a Pride flag on their backpack or who plan to attend the Annual Gay Pride Festival? How can you support your child when she signs up for a lesbian poetry reading at a local bookstore, or when he helps design a float for a local Alternative Sexual Expressions group for the annual Gay Pride Parade?

START BY EDUCATING YOURSELF

Parents must educate themselves on the issue their child is passionate about. With respect to GLBTQ, a foundational understanding of what GLBTQ children face in schools is important regardless of whether your child identifies as GLBTQ. Educating yourself about the issues GLBTQ children face is a vital step, and it can spark thoughtful, action-oriented conversations with a gifted child. The Gay, Lesbian and Straight Education Network (Greytak, Kosciw, Villenas, & Giga, 2016) reported staggering statistics for GLBTQ students, faculty, and staff. The school environment can pose numerous threats and obstacles: Hateful language, verbal harassment, and the threat of physical violence are a reality (see Figures 54.1–54.4).

In a groundbreaking survey of more than 10,000 GLBTQ-identified youth ages 13–17, the Human Rights Campaign (2017) found high incident rates of both verbal and physical harassment in school. The survey revealed the following:

» GLBTQ students are more than twice as likely to have skipped school in the past month because of safety concerns.
» Ninety-seven percent of GLBTQ students hear derogatory phrases used in school, and half of teachers fail to respond to homophobic language when they hear it.
» Ninety percent of 15–24-year-olds have been called names because of their sexuality.
» The majority of respondents who are out or perceived as transgender while in school (K–12) experience some form of mistreatment, including verbal or physical harassment (54%) or sexual assault (24%).

TALK TO YOUR CHILD ABOUT GLBTQ CULTURE AND HISTORY

The GLBTQ community in American history is marked by many inequities and discriminating obstacles; however, there are numerous milestones of moral courage and victories that are not typically included in mainstream history. School libraries rarely have GLBTQ book titles for students to read and check out—an upsetting fact for many children.

Examples of books to help introduce children to GLBTQ history and culture include:

» *Gay and Lesbian History for Kids: The Century-Long Struggle for LGBT Rights* by Jerome Pohlen: This book looks at the positive gains and struggles with the GLBTQ movement with the intent to provide information for the perspective of our adolescents.
» *Pride: Celebrating Diversity and Community* by Robin Stevenson: This book goes into detail about Pride events not being just a party but an event for social justice that began

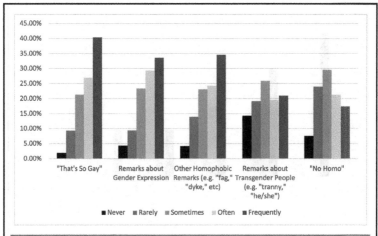

Figure 54.1. Frequency that GLBTQ students hear anti-GLBTQ remarks at school (Greytak et al., 2016).

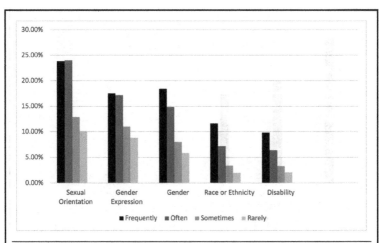

Figure 54.2. Frequency of verbal harassment experienced by GLBTQ students in the past school year (Greytak et al., 2016).

with a riot. The book showcases stories about fighting for freedom and equality by protesting and celebrating around the world with an event known as Pride.

» *This Day in June* by Gayle E. Pitman: This book welcomes readers to experience a Pride celebration and share in a day when we are all united. The book also includes facts about GLBTQ history and culture.

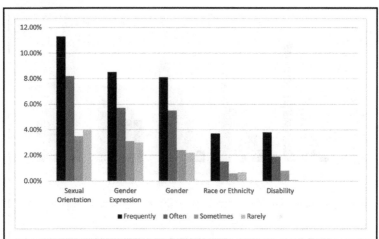

Figure 54.3. Frequency of physical harassment experienced by GLBTQ students in the past school year (Greytak et al., 2016).

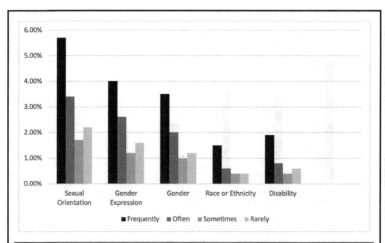

Figure 54.4. Frequency of physical assault experienced by GLBTQ students in the past school year (Greytak et al., 2016).

Important historical milestones that defined the Gay Rights Movement are presented here for you and your child to explore:

» **The Stonewall Riots.** The catalyst behind the many Pride celebrations held throughout the world, the Stonewall Riots have become the defining event that marked the start of the Gay Rights Movement in the U.S. and around the world.

> » **Harvey Milk.** The first openly gay man in 1977 to win a seat on the San Francisco Board of Supervisors, Milk was an advocate for many marginalized groups of people on the fringes of society, including gay people and senior citizens. (Notably, José Sarria, "The Widow Norton," was the first person to run for public office in the U.S. in 1961.)
>
> » **The Briggs Initiative of 1978.** Requiring the termination of any teacher or school employee who publicly supported gay rights, this proposed California legislation faced a huge backlash and was defeated.
>
> » **Legalization of same-sex marriage.** On February 8, 2014, the U.S. Supreme Court legalized same-sex marriage.

Acknowledge that your gifted child may challenge authority and question rules. Remind your child of the many famous individuals—such as Mahatma Gandhi, Harvey Milk, and Martin Luther King, Jr.—who were rule breakers and change agents. Encourage letter-writing to challenge unfair laws, and help your child use her intelligence, critical thinking, and creative skills to identify alternative solutions to the unjust practices she sees in the world around her.

Locate role models and mentors. If possible, locate a GLBTQ role model and go-to person who can inspire, provide knowledge, motivate your child, and provide the wider perspective that you may lack. A good mentor can offer resources and connections for new ideas, which can in turn further sharpen your gifted child's intellectual and emotional skills.

Direct their passions. Allow your child to participate in community service or volunteer activities with GLBTQ organizations. Contact your local GLBTQ Pride organization and volunteer through InterPride (https://interpride.org); attend Parents and Friends of Lesbians and Gays (PFLAG) events to support confidential peer support, education, and advocacy in communities in nearly all states; and/or identify if there is a Gay-Straight Alliance at your child's school.

Become an ally. As an ally, you honor the efforts of all activists. Celebrate the historic events of the past by honoring GLBTQ Pride Month. Attend a local Pride parade or find out what other GLBTQ events are occurring in your city during Pride Month and throughout the year. Demonstrate pride, love, and acceptance.

Start or support a Safe Zone Program at your child's school. Safe Zone Programs are common in schools and are usually designated by a placard outside a teacher's classroom, the principal's office, the school cafeteria, or other school entryway. A Safe Zone is a place for a person who needs help, advice, or just a safe space to talk. For more information, contact The Safe Zone Project (https://thesafezone project.com).

Start or support an anti-bullying policy at your child's school. A strong policy protects all students, but many schools need explicit guidance on safeguarding GLBTQ students. If starting an anti-bullying policy at your child's school, be sure to include language specifically prohibiting harassment based on nonconformity to gender norms, gender identity, and gender expression, as well as give examples of harassment based on actual or perceived sexual orientation. Once in place, evaluate the effectiveness of your school's anti-bullying program annually using student and staff surveys.

Staff and faculty members specifically trained to prevent and respond to bullying incidents play a pivotal role in developing and maintaining a school's anti-bullying program and are essential if a bullying incident occurs. Also important is the designation of an anti-bullying coordinator and an anti-bullying task force. Communicate effectively and often with students, parents or guardians, and the community about issues such as bullying. Post the name and contact information for the school's anti-bullying coordinator in the office, on the school website, and in the student handbook. Ensure that reactions to reports of harassment do not further stigmatize students who were targeted for their real or perceived GLBTQ identities.

By becoming educated and involved, we can unlearn or dispel negative perceptions and attitudes of others by replacing malice and hostility with positivity and love. The catalyst for your child's interest in GLBTQ issues could be the seemingly unfair reprimand a classmate receives for an infraction he did not commit, a rebuff from an unrequited love because of an imperfect body type or same-sex attraction, questions about one's own emerging sexual identity, or the developing awareness of poverty, racism, gender discrimination, homophobia, and other forms of social injustice. We must remember that although many gifted children have a desire and intense passion to change unjust individuals and unfair situations, they are still children.

As a parent, you can help your gifted child become more educated and feel more comfortable to manage situations that may arise. Honor your child's questions, concerns, and anxieties—not only about GLBTQ issues, but also all injustices in our lives—with understanding and respect.

REFERENCES

Greytak, E. A., Kosciw, J. G., Villenas, C., & Giga, N. (2016). *From teasing to torment: School climate revisited: A survey of U.S. secondary school students and teachers.* New York, NY: GLSEN.

Human Rights Campaign. (2017). *Growing up LGBT in America.* Retrieved from https://www.hrc.org/youth-report

Silverman, L. K. (1994). The moral sensitivity of gifted children and the evolution of society. *Roeper Review, 17,* 110–116.

ABOUT THE EDITORS

Kathleen Nilles, a parent and passionate advocate, has served as the National Association for Gifted Children (NAGC) parent services and communications manager and editor of *Parenting for High Potential* magazine since 2013. In this role, Kathleen serves as the outreach liaison contact for parents, grandparents, and caregivers of gifted and talented children to help families connect with the resources they need. She is a frequent speaker and workshop facilitator for parents and educators at the national, state, and local level, and codirector of the film *Through Gifted Eyes*.

Jennifer L. Jolly, Ph.D., is a professor of gifted education at the University of Alabama. She is coeditor of the *Journal for the Education of the Gifted*. Her work has been published in *Gifted Child Quarterly*, *Journal for the Education for the Gifted*, *Roeper Review*, and *Gifted Child Today*. Jennifer has written and edited several books, including *A Century of Contributions to Gifted Education: Illuminating Lives* with Ann Robinson and *Parenting Gifted Children*. She also served as editor of *Parenting for High Potential* from 2007 to 2012.

Tracy Ford Inman, Ed.D., associate director of The Center for Gifted Studies at Western Kentucky University, has coauthored and coedited six books, with four winning the Texas Association for the Gifted and Talented's Legacy Book Award in parent, educator, and scholar categories. She is active on the state (past-president and chair of foundation), national (current board member of both NAGC and The Association for the Gifted, Council for Exceptional Children), and international (presenter/member of World Council for Gifted and Talented Children and European Council for High Ability) levels in gifted education. Tracy has provided professional learning opportunities for tens of thousands of educators as well as challenging instruction in summer programs for gifted and talented youth.

Joan Franklin Smutny is founder and director of the Center for Gifted and the Midwest Torrance Center for Creativity. Winner of the NAGC Distinguished Service Award in 1996 and the Illinois Association for Gifted Children's Sally Walker Distinguished Service Award in 2019, she directs programs for thousands of talented students in the Chicago area each year. She has authored, coauthored, and edited 22 books on gifted education.

ABOUT THE AUTHORS

Jill L. Adelson, Ph.D., research scientist at Duke University's Talent Identification Program, graduated with a joint Ph.D. in gifted education and measurement, evaluation, and statistics at the University of Connecticut. The coeditor of *Gifted Child Quarterly*, she has earned awards from NAGC, including the Early Leader Award, Early Scholar Award, GCQ Paper of the Year Award, and A. Harry Passow Classroom Teacher Scholarship Award.

Patti Ensel Bailie, Ph.D., is an assistant professor of early childhood education at the University of Maine at Farmington. She has worked in the field of early childhood environmental education for more than 25 years, with previous positions including assistant director of the Nature-Based Early Childhood Education Certificate program at Antioch University and various leadership and educator roles at three different nature centers in the Midwest.

Jennifer G. Beasley, Ed.D., has more than 25 years of experience in education as an elementary school teacher, gifted facilitator, and university professor. She is currently the Director of Teacher Education and a professor in curriculum and instruction at the University of Arkansas. She specializes in gifted education and differentiation.

George Betts, Ed.D. (1944–2019), was a professor at the University of Northern Colorado, founder and director of Center for the Education and Study of the Gifted, Talented, and Creative, and the founder and director of Summer Enrichment Program. Developer of the Autonomous Learner Model, he served on NAGC's Board for 21 years, including as president.

Janette Boazman, Ph.D., is an associate professor of education at University of Dallas. She holds a Ph.D. in curriculum and instruction, and an M.S. in educational psychology. Her research centers on positive psychological attributes in the educational setting and the personal and psychological well-being of gifted individuals and their success.

Elissa F. Brown, Ph.D., is a distinguished lecturer and director of the Hunter College Gifted Center. She coordinates and teaches the Advanced Certificate Program in Gifted and Talented at Hunter College. She has served as an adjunct professor at several universities, including Rutgers University and Duke University, and has served as a state director of gifted education, a federal grant manager, a district gifted program coordinator, principal of a specialized high school, and a teacher of gifted students. She is a published author in the field of gifted education and presents widely.

Karen L. Brown is the director of gifted and accelerated programs for the Scottsdale Unified School District. A National Board Certified Educator, she works extensively with teachers in grades K–12. Karen is the 2018 NAGC Master's and Specialist Award winner.

Dina Brulles, Ph.D., is the gifted education director at Paradise Valley Unified School District in Arizona and the gifted program coordinator at Arizona State University. Dina serves on the NAGC Board of Directors. She has coauthored several books and is a recognized expert in the Schoolwide Cluster Grouping Model.

Micah N. Bruce-Davis, Ph.D., received her doctorate in educational psychology from the University of Connecticut in 2013. Currently, she is a fourth-grade teacher for Fulton County Schools in Atlanta, GA. She has also served as the director of children's programs for the Universtiy of Louisiana at Lafayette Center for Gifted Education.

Ashley Y. Carpenter, Ph.D., is an associate professor and the director of professional development and publications at William & Mary's Center for Gifted Education. She previously worked as the research site director for the National Center for Research on Gifted Education at the University of Connecticut and as a middle school teacher. She is also the proud parent of a twice-exceptional child.

Tutita M. Casa, Ph.D., is an associate professor of elementary mathematics education in the Neag School of Education at the University of Connecticut. She was codirector and coauthor on Project M^2 and a staff member for Project M^3. Her work supports elementary students engaging in mathematical reasoning through talk and writing.

Nancy Arey Cohen is a lifelong advocate for gifted children. As the proud (but not hovering) parent of two adult gifted sons, she spent many years advocating in schools in Massachusetts, Texas, and Minnesota for the needs of gifted children, providing hundreds of hours of enrichment opportunities, and counseling parents on ways to work collaboratively with teachers.

Lori Comallie-Caplan is a private practice therapist, consultant, and evaluator for the gifted and president elect of the New Mexico Association for the Gifted. She is a member of NAGC, past president of SENG, gifted education coordinator, and adjunct professor for the New Mexico gifted endorsement classes.

Bonnie Cramond, Ph.D., professor of educational psychology at the University of Georgia, has been a member of the Board of Directors of NAGC, director of the Torrance Center for Creativity and Talent Development, a journal editor and reviewer, an international and national speaker, researcher, school teacher, and parent.

Joy Lawson Davis, Ed.D., has held multiple roles in gifted education for the past three decades. She is author of numerous publications and is recognized as one of the nation's foremost experts on addressing the access and equity needs of culturally diverse gifted students.

James R. Delisle, Ph.D., teaches gifted teenagers part-time after being a professor at Kent State University for 25 years. With more than 275 articles and 23 books, Jim's work focuses on the social and emotional needs of gifted individuals. He consults nationally and internationally advocating for gifted children, their parents, and their teachers.

Deb Douglas is the president of GT Carpe Diem, a consultancy specializing in teaching self-advocacy skills to gifted children. She worked with gifted children for more than 34 years in the Manitowoc Pubic School District and served as board member of Wisconsin Association for Talented and Gifted, including 2 years as president from 2011–2013.

J. Denise Drain retired as a director of gifted education in 2014. During her career she taught gifted students in inclusion settings, pull-out programs, and self-contained classrooms as well as at the university level. She raised two gifted daughters and now enjoys four gifted grandchildren. She consults on gifted programming, professional development, and program review.

Janine M. Firmender, Ph.D., is an associate professor in the teacher education department at Saint Joseph's University, Philadelphia, PA. She worked with the authors on developing and field-testing Project M² units. She is pursuing research interests in the areas of engaging students in mathematical writing and meeting the needs of mathematically talented students.

Leigh Ann Fish, Ph.D., is an assistant professor of early childhood education at the University of Maine at Farmington where she also teaches graduate courses in gifted education. Leigh Ann is a primary grades National Board Certified Teacher, serves on the board of the Maine Association for the Education of Young Children, and has worked as a K–12 coordinator and teacher of gifted education. Professional interests include gifted girls, the importance of play, Reggio-inspired practices, and nature-based education.

Carol Fisher has been involved with gifted children for more than 40 years, teaching, coordinating, and creating curriculum in mathematics for the Chicago Public Schools. She has worked with the Center for the Gifted in Glenview, IL, for more than 30 years, creating math and integrated curricula for summer and weekend programs. A recipient of the Golden Apple Award for Excellence in Teaching, she is looking forward to new adventures.

Joanne Foster, Ed.D., has been a gifted education consultant for more than 30 years. She wrote *Bust Your BUTS: Tips for Teens Who Procrastinate* (silver 2018 Benjamin Franklin Award) and *Not Now, Maybe Later: Helping Children Overcome Procrastination*. She is coauthor of *Beyond Intelligence: Secrets for Raising Happily Productive Kids* and the award-winning *Being Smart About Gifted Education*. She focuses on children's intelligence, creativity, productivity, and well-being.

John P. Gaa, Ph.D., is professor emeritus in Educational Psychology from the University of Houston. He graduated with a Ph.D. in educational psychology from the University of Wisconsin. He has served as the chair of the Arts Network of NAGC and is currently chair of the Awards Committee of NAGC. During his career, his areas of research have included motivation, goal setting, sex role identity, and ego and moral identity, most recently focusing on artistically talented adolescents.

M. Katherine Gavin, Ph.D., is an associate professor at the Renzulli Center for Creativity, Gifted Education, and Talent

Development at the University of Connecticut. Her research focuses on development of advanced math curriculum for talented elementary students. She is the director and senior author on the Projects M³ and M² units.

Jessa D. Luckey Goudelock is a graduate assistant and doctoral candidate in the University of Georgia Department of Educational Psychology, specializing in gifted and creative education. Her research focuses on academic acceleration of underrepresented students, military-connected gifted students, and gifted education law and policy. Jessa previously worked as an early childhood educator and received her bachelor's and master's degrees from Howard University.

Keri M. Guilbault, Ed.D., parent of a profoundly gifted learner who was accelerated, is an assistant professor at Johns Hopkins University. She served on the NAGC Board of Directors from 2014–2018 and is a trustee of the Mensa Education and Research Foundation.

Melissa R. Hasan graduated from the Indiana Academy of Science, Mathematics, and Humanities and holds a B.A. in creative writing and an M.A. in Near Eastern Languages and Cultures. She lives with her husband and two children in California, and currently teaches elementary school.

Stacy M. Hayden is a doctoral student at the University of Connecticut in the Giftedness, Creativity, and Talent Development Program. Prior to pursuing her Ph.D., she taught gifted elementary students and worked with the Young Scholars Program in Alexandria City Public Schools, VA.

Kathryn P. Haydon works with teachers to integrate rigorous creative thinking throughout academic content. An award-winning educator, she writes and speaks widely on creative learning and the secret strengths of outlier learners. She is the author of four books and has written extensively for educational journals and publications, including *Psychology Today, The Washington Post,* and *The Creativity Post.*

Ellen Honeck, Ph.D., is an academic program manager for the gifted and talented department of Denver Public Schools and has been involved in gifted education as a classroom teacher, administrator, gifted specialist, curriculum developer, consultant, and adjunct professor. She is currently serving on the NAGC Board of Directors.

Angela M. Housand, Ph.D., is an associate dean for academic affairs and associate professor at the University of North Carolina Wilmington (UNCW), and a national consultant. As a former teacher, she brings an applied focus to her instructional programs for teachers, as well as her research testing the effectiveness of the FutureCasting digital life skills program.

Michele Joerg completed her certification in gifted and talented education at Hunter College after 10 years as a stay-at-home mother. She is a founding board member of DREAM Charter School in East Harlem and serves on the board of DREAM, an afterschool and summer program that uses team-based methods to provide a comprehensive, enriching experience for more than 2,200 inner-city youth. Michele is a former New York City classroom teacher and teacher trainer with degrees in education and administration.

Anne Johnson has been involved in gifted education as a parent, teacher, and administrator for a private school utilizing the Schoolwide Enrichment Model in Lafayette, LA. She is an active member of NAGC and served as chair of the NAGC Special Schools and Programs Network. She serves as president of the Association for Gifted and Talented Students Louisiana.

Alessa Giampaolo Keener lives and works in Maryland as an educational consultant specializing in special student populations and holistic learning needs. In addition to providing testing and educational planning services, she works with civil and criminal defense attorneys as an expert witness in cases that involve an educational component.

Kenneth A. Kiewra, Ph.D., is a professor of educational psychology at the University of Nebraska, Lincoln. Kiewra's research pertains to the SOAR teaching and learning method he developed and to talent development, particularly the roles parents play. He has published four books, and his latest is *Nurturing Children's Talents: A Guide for Parents.* He is a frequent presenter.

Scott Lutostanski is the director of academic consulting for Galin Education in Madison, WI. A former special education teacher and licensed professional counselor, he works as an academic coach and consultant assisting students and families with executive function issues throughout the country.

Dona Matthews, Ph.D., has been writing about children's development since 1985. Books include *Beyond Intelligence, Being Smart About Gifted Education, The Development of Giftedness and Talent Across the Life Span,* and *The International Companion to Gifted Education.* She was founding director of the Hunter College Center for Gifted Studies and Education, City University of New York. She writes a blog for *Psychology Today*: "Going Beyond Intelligence."

Michael S. Matthews, Ph.D., is a professor of gifted education at the University of North Carolina at Charlotte.

Margaret Maxwell, Ph.D., is a professor at Western Kentucky University in the Libraries, Informatics, and Technology in Education program. Her research interests include effectiveness of online instruction, integrating critical thinking, authentic learning, and technology to produce deeper student learning, and connecting reform with standards.

D. Betsy McCoach, Ph.D., is a professor in the Research Methods, Measurement and Evaluation program at the University of Connecticut. She is the founder of the Modern Modeling Methods conference. She is past editor of *Gifted Child Quarterly* and is research director for the National Center for Research on Gifted Education.

Christy D. McGee, Ed.D., became interested in gifted education in the 1980s with her gifted daughter. She has been a classroom teacher and is a professor at Bellarmine University, Louisville, KY. An active member of NAGC, she has served as chair of the Curriculum Division and Parent and Community Network.

Sal Mendaglio, Ph.D., is a licensed psychologist, professor, and chair of the counseling program in the Werklund School of Education, University of Calgary. His primary research interest is the psychology of giftedness, which underlies his area of passion: counseling gifted individuals.

Amra Mohammed is a faculty member at the University of Jeddah, Saudi Arabia. She also is a doctoral candidate at the University of Northern Colorado (UNC). Amra served as program coordinator and teacher for the Summer Enrichment Program at the UNC. Her areas of specialization are gifted education and twice-exceptionality.

Dianna R. Mullet, Ph.D., is an assistant professor of psychology and program advisor for the counseling education program at Navajo Technical University. Her research focuses on culturally relevant approaches to talent development in higher education, particularly in science and technology.

Gwen Olmstead, Ph.D., is a former assistant professor at Western Connecticut State University in the instructional leadership doctoral program. Prior, she worked as a research associate at the University of Arkansas in the National Office of Research, Measurement, and Evaluation Systems; as the director of the Cincinnati Children's Museum; and as an English teacher in an inner-city high school. Olmstead advocates for and conducts research on homeschooling, gifted, and creativity education.

Paula Olszewski-Kubilius, Ph.D., is the director of the Center for Talent Development at Northwestern University and a professor in the School of Education and Social Policy. Over the past 35 years, she has created programs for all kinds of gifted learners and written extensively about talent development.

Megan O'Reilly Palevich, M.Ed., is the Head of School at Laurel Springs School, an accredited private online K–12 school. She has experience in Pre-K–grade 12 curriculum design, signature innovative program development, technology integration, and personalized professional development for educators.

Pamela M. Peters, the mother of two gifted children ages 14 and 8, is currently pursuing a doctoral degree in educational psychology focusing on both gifted education and research methods, measurement, and evaluation at the University of Connecticut. Pam also consults with parents as they advocate for gifted services.

Jean Sunde Peterson, Ph.D., Professor Emerita from Purdue University, has focused most of her clinical work and research on the social and emotional development of gifted youth. She has received 10 national awards for her scholarship and 12 at Purdue for teaching, research, or service. Her first career was in K–12 education.

Linda E. Pfeiffer, Ed.D., is a special education generalist and former middle school gifted education specialist. As a parent of gifted adult children, she understands firsthand the struggles of parents of gifted learners and has advocated for gifted learners and their needs for more than two decades.

Diana Reeves is a mother, parent group facilitator, university instructor, former elementary teacher, and education consultant. Diana collaborated in the development of NAGC's *Mile Marker Series* and received the NAGC 2009 Community Service Award.

Diana now works inside prison walls with those who have seriously failed, fostering habits of success as they prepare for release.

Sylvia B. Rimm, Ph.D., psychologist, directs Family Achievement Clinic and specializes in gifted children. She speaks and publishes internationally on parenting, giftedness, creativity, and under-achievement. She was a longtime contributor to NBC's *Today Show*, hosted *Family Talk* on public radio nationally, and received national awards for lifetime contributions to gifted children.

Anne N. Rinn, Ph.D., is a professor of educational psychology and director of the Office for Giftedness, Talent Development, and Creativity in the College of Education at the University of North Texas. Her research focuses on the social, emotional, and psychoso-cial development of gifted adolescents.

Jennifer A. Ritchotte, Ph.D., is an associate professor of gifted education at the University of Northern Colorado.

Karen B. Rogers, Ph.D., Professor Emerita from University of St. Thomas in Minnesota, has taught and researched in the U.S. and abroad for the past 40 years. She served on the NAGC Board of Directors, as American Educational Research Association Special Interest Groups Gifted Chair, and as president of CEC-TAG. She has written five books and too many journal and professional articles to count.

Amy S. Rushneck, Ph.D., is the executive director of the Center for Bright Kids Academic Talent Development in Denver, CO. She has been involved with talent development programs for more than 25 years across regions in multiple roles and has been a professor and director of graduate programs in teacher education.

Robin M. Schader, Ph.D., former Parent Resource Advisor for NAGC, continues to write and speak about talent development. She is coauthor of *To Be Gifted and Learning Disabled: Strength-Based Strategies for Helping Twice-Exceptional Students*, which received the 2018 NAGC Book of the Year Award. Robin is a trustee at Bridges Academy, a school for twice-exceptional students.

Susan Scheibel, Ed.D., gifted and talented parent and advo-cate, completed her graduate studies at the University of Northern Colorado. She actively supports the Colorado Association for Gifted and Talented, Colorado Coalition for Gifted, Colorado Educational Success Task Force, State Advisory Committee for Gifted Student

Education, and Colorado Academy of Educators for the Gifted, Talented, and Creative.

Paul James "PJ" Sedillo, Ph.D., is an assistant professor at New Mexico Highlands University, where he teaches courses in special education and gifted. His work has been published in *Gifted Child Today*, and his recent book, *Solidarity Through Pride*, a historical account of the GLBTQ Albuquerque Pride movement from 1976 to 2016, is winner of the 2018 New Mexico-Arizona Book Award in the Gay/Lesbian (GLBT) category. He is past president of the New Mexico Association for the Gifted, chair of NAGC's GLBTQ Network, and local arrangements cochair of the 2019 NAGC 66th Annual Conference in Albuquerque, NM.

Patti Garrett Shade, as Indiana Gifted/Talented Program Director, authored legislation to include creativity gifted identification. As an educator, she developed one of the first nationally recognized elementary science lab programs. She served on the World Creativity Center Development Team with Dr. Edward de Bono. She is an international presenter and author.

Richard Shade, Ed.D., received outstanding educator awards from two universities for innovative teaching practices. Oxford University recruited him to lead a national creativity/gifted training program. He authored seven books including *The Creativity Crusade: Nurturing and Protecting Your Child's Creativity*, which received the Texas Association for the Gifted and Talented Legacy Book Award.

Del Siegle, Ph.D., is the associate dean for research and faculty affairs in the Neag School of Education at the University of Connecticut and past president of the National Association for Gifted Children. He serves as director of the National Center for Research on Gifted Education and is a professor in gifted and talented education.

Sheri Nowak Stewart, Ed.D., is the past president of the Kansas Association for the Gifted, and past SENG board member and parent group leader, as well as a member of several NAGC committees. In addition, she has been a classroom teacher, professor, program coordinator, state director for gifted, and consultant.

Rebecca Stobaugh, Ph.D., is an associate professor at Western Kentucky University, teaching assessment and unit-planning courses in the teacher education program. She is the author of six books, including *Fifty Strategies for Cognitive Engagement* (2019). She consults with school districts on critical thinking, assessment, and other topics.

Sarah E. Sumners, Ph.D., is a faculty member and interim director of the Torrance Center for Creativity and Talent Development at the University of Georgia. She has led creativity trainings at national and international levels; coauthored publications on creativity; taught courses in teacher education, giftedness, and creativity; and served as a board member for the Future Problem Solving Program International. She holds an M.Ed. in gifted studies and a Ph.D. in curriculum and instruction.

Janet Tassell, Ph.D., is an associate professor at Western Kentucky University and teaches gifted masters/specialist and elementary mathematics methods courses. She is currently the codirector of DuPont-funded Bowling Green Scholars of Promise (Math for High Potential Underserved Students). Her latest coedited book is from Springer Publishing: *Creativity and Technology in Mathematics Education* (2018).

Alicia M. Welch is a Ph.D. candidate in educational psychology at the University of Georgia. Her research focuses on factors that may influence the development of attention skills. She is also an analyst and adjunct instructor at the University of West Georgia, and an accomplished musician, former music educator, and academic counselor.

Hope (Bess) E. Wilson, Ph.D., associate professor of education at the University of North Florida, teaches graduate and undergraduate courses in assessment, educational psychology, and statistics. This 2017 NAGC Early Leader Award recipient was associate editor for the *Journal of Advanced Academics* and is a published author in *Gifted Child Quarterly*, *Journal for the Education of the Gifted*, and *Roeper Review*.

LIST OF ARTICLE
PUBLICATION DATES

"Discovering Creative Thinking Process Skills: A Win-Win for Children" originally appeared in the March 2015 issue of *Parenting for High Potential.* Copyright ©2015 by National Association for Gifted Children.

"May the Creative Forces Be With You: Uncovering Creative Genius" originally appeared in the February 2015 issue of *Parenting for High Potential.* Copyright ©2015 by National Association for Gifted Children.

"Creative Thinking Skills for All Seasons: A Reflection" originally appeared in the March 2015 issue of *Parenting for High Potential.* Copyright ©2015 by National Association for Gifted Children.

"Creative Underachievers: Children Who Are Too Out of the Box" originally appeared in the March 2015 issue of *Parenting for High Potential.* Copyright ©2015 by National Association for Gifted Children.

"Advocating For Your Child's Creativity in Schools: Your Right, Your Responsibility" originally appeared in the Summer 2016 issue of *Parenting for High Potential.* Copyright ©2016 by National Association for Gifted Children.

"Full STEAM Ahead!" originally appeared in the June 2017 issue of *Parenting for High Potential.* Copyright ©2017 by National Association for Gifted Children.

"How Parents Can Nurture a Lifelong Love of the Arts" originally appeared in the June 2017 issue of *Parenting for High Potential.* Copyright ©2017 by National Association for Gifted Children.

"Parenting Artistically Gifted Children: Advice From the NAGC Arts Network" originally appeared in the March 2013 issue of *Parenting for High Potential.* Copyright ©2013 by National Association for Gifted Children.

"Academic Acceleration: Is It Right for My Child?" originally appeared in the June 2012 issue of *Parenting for High Potential.* Copyright ©2012 by National Association for Gifted Children.

"Advocating for Grade-Based Acceleration" originally appeared in the December 2014 issue of *Parenting for High Potential.* Copyright ©2014 by National Association for Gifted Children.

"Supporting Social and Emotional Learning for Gifted Learners With the Common Core State Standards" originally appeared

"CReaTE Excellence: Using a Teacher Framework to Maximize STEM Learning With Your Child" originally appeared in the October 2013 issue of *Parenting for High Potential*. Copyright ©2013 by National Association for Gifted Children.

"How to Discuss Books With Your Kids (Even When You Haven't Read Them!)" originally appeared in the March 2018 issue of *Parenting for High Potential*. Copyright ©2018 by National Association for Gifted Children.

"Centennials: The World Is Waiting!" originally appeared in the February 2016 issue of *Parenting for High Potential*. Copyright ©2016 by National Association for Gifted Children.

"Roles in Gifted Education: A Parent's Guide" originally appeared in the September 2018 issue of *Parenting for High Potential*. Copyright ©2018 by National Association for Gifted Children.

"Communicating Effectively With Your Gifted Child's School" originally appeared in the August 2015 issue of *Parenting for High Potential*. Copyright ©2015 by National Association for Gifted Children.

"How to Start the School Year on a Positive Note With Your Gifted Child's Teacher" originally appeared in the Summer 2016 issue of *Parenting for High Potential*. Copyright ©2016 by National Association for Gifted Children.

"Parents Need Support, Too! How to Start and Sustain a Parent Group" originally appeared in the January 2014 issue of *Parenting for High Potential*. Copyright ©2014 by National Association for Gifted Children.

"How to Start an Academic Competition in Your Child's School" originally appeared in the September 2018 issue of *Parenting for High Potential*. Copyright ©2018 by National Association for Gifted Children.

"The Importance of Teaching Children Self-Advocacy" originally appeared in the January 2014 issue of *Parenting for High Potential*. Copyright ©2014 by National Association for Gifted Children.

"It's Time to Revamp the Parent-Teacher Conference Process: Let's Include the Child" originally appeared in the September 2014